COMPOSING
A NARRATIVE
EXPERIENCES OF EARLY SCHOOL LEAVERS

COMPOSING LIVES IN TRANSITION:
A NARRATIVE INQUIRY INTO THE
EXPERIENCES OF EARLY SCHOOL
LEAVERS

COMPOSING LIVES IN TRANSITION: A NARRATIVE INQUIRY INTO THE EXPERIENCES OF EARLY SCHOOL LEAVERS

EDITED BY

D. JEAN CLANDININ
PAM STEEVES
VERA CAINE
University of Alberta, Canada

United Kingdom – North America – Japan
India – Malaysia – China

Emerald Group Publishing Limited
Howard House, Wagon Lane, Bingley BD16 1WA, UK

First edition 2013

Copyright © 2013 Emerald Group Publishing Limited

Reprints and permission service
Contact: permissions@emeraldinsight.com

No part of this book may be reproduced, stored in a retrieval system, transmitted in any form or by any means electronic, mechanical, photocopying, recording or otherwise without either the prior written permission of the publisher or a licence permitting restricted copying issued in the UK by The Copyright Licensing Agency and in the USA by The Copyright Clearance Center. Any opinions expressed in the chapters are those of the authors. Whilst Emerald makes every effort to ensure the quality and accuracy of its content, Emerald makes no representation implied or otherwise, as to the chapters' suitability and application and disclaims any warranties, express or implied, to their use.

British Library Cataloguing in Publication Data
A catalogue record for this book is available from the British Library

ISBN: 978-1-78052-974-5

ISOQAR certified
Management System,
awarded to Emerald
for adherence to
Environmental
standard
ISO 14001:2004.

Certificate Number 1985
ISO 14001

INVESTOR IN PEOPLE

Contents

List of Contributors	xi
Acknowledgement	xiii
Foreword	xv

Chapter 1. Introduction	1
D. Jean Clandinin, Pam Steeves and Vera Caine	
Situating Our Work	3
Composing Diverse Identities	4
Narrative Beginnings	6
Jean's Narrative Beginnings	7
I. Early landscapes	7
II. High school graduation	8
III. Becoming a teacher	9
IV. Becoming a narrative inquirer	9
Pam's Narrative Beginnings	10
Vera's Narrative Beginnings	11
Revisiting Our Research Puzzle	12
Chapter 2. Literature Review	15
Vera Caine	
Methodology for the Literature Review	15
Coming to Terms: Shifts over Time	16
Statistical Overview	20
Canada	20
Provincial dropout rate	21
Framing Early School Leavers	22
Individual Deficit Model (Risk Factors)	22
Trends with dropouts	22
Risk factors — clusters	24
Critique of risk factors	25
Process theories of disengagement	27

School Context	28
Rhythms in and out of school — continuous moving	29
Voices in and outside of school	30
Unquestioned assumptions	31
Mismatch between education and schooling	31
Positions of power	32
Relational being	33
Being different in schools/continuous rubbing up	34
Social-Cultural Contexts	35
Policies	35
Consumer culture	35
Social issues	35
Community	36
Identity formation	36
Youth in Flux	38
Issues and Directions for Future Research	38
Primary Focus on Individual (Risk/Deficit Perspective)	39
School Leaving as a Point in Time Rather than a Process	39
No Coherent Framework for Early School Leaving Exists	39
Missing Perspectives	40
No Consideration of Early School Leavers in Context and over Time	41
Methodological Considerations	41
Chapter 3. Methodology	**43**
D. Jean Clandinin, Vera Caine and Pam Steeves	
The Three-Dimensional Narrative Inquiry Space	44
Finding Our Participants	45
Challenges in Recruiting Participants	47
The Research Team	47
Narrative Inquiry with Participants	48
Ethics	49
From Field Texts to Interim Research Texts	50
One Version of a Final Research Text	50
Three Years Later: Another Research Text	50
Chapter 4. A Narrative Account of Robert	**53**
Marilyn Huber	
Chapter 5. A Narrative Account of Scott	**73**
Marni Pearce	

Chapter 6. A Narrative Account of Jasmine *Yi Li*	85
Chapter 7. A Narrative Account of Andrew *D. Jean Clandinin*	103
Chapter 8. A Narrative Account of Billie Bob *Claire Desrochers*	115
Chapter 9. A Narrative Account of Kevlar *Pam Steeves*	129
Chapter 10. A Narrative Account of Ben *Vera Caine*	145
Chapter 11. A Narrative Account of Truong *D. Jean Clandinin*	153
Chapter 12. A Narrative Account of Lynn *Joy-Ruth Mickelson*	167
Chapter 13. A Narrative Account of Christian *Vera Caine*	177
Chapter 14. A Narrative Account of Skye *Sean Lessard*	191
Chapter 15. Exploring Transitions within Lives *D. Jean Clandinin, Vera Caine and Pam Steeves*	207
Thread 1: Composing Transitions with Attention to What is "Normal"	208
Thread 2: Composing Transitions while Situated in Webs of Relationships	212
Thread 3: Conflicting Responsibilities in Composing Transitions	214
Thread 4: Composing Forward-Looking Stories Amidst Transitions	215
Thread 5: Intertwining Transitions and Identities	217
Narrative Understandings of Transitions	219

Qualities of a Narrative Understanding of Transitions   219
   Quality 1: Shifting over time and place   219
   Quality 2: Composing lives as a process of change   220
   Quality 3: Transitions as liminal spaces   221
   Quality 4: Improvisation as part of transition   221
   Feature 5: Imagination and relationship as part of transitions   222
Summary   223

Chapter 16. Stories to Live By: Composing Identities   225
Pam Steeves, D. Jean Clandinin and Vera Caine

Lives Shaped by Landscapes Threaded by Multiple Narratives   226
   Lives Shaped by Landscapes Threaded with Familial Narratives   228
   Lives Shaped by Landscapes Threaded by Cultural Narratives   230
   Lives Shaped by Landscapes Threaded by Institutional Narratives   231
   Lives Shaped by Landscapes Threaded by Linguistic Narratives   233
   Lives Shaped by Landscapes Threaded by Geographic Narratives   234
Experiencing Landscapes as Filled with Competing and Conflicting Plotlines   234
Resisting the Shaping of Storied Landscapes   235
Representing Their Stories to Live By   237
Shifting Their Stories to Live By   238
Conclusion   239

Chapter 17. A Reflective Turn: Looking Backward, Looking Forward   241
Vera Caine, Sean Lessard, Pam Steeves and D. Jean Clandinin

Shifting Personal Justifications   241
Shifting Practical Justifications   244
   Red Worn Runners   244
   Fox Den Berries   248
Pow-Wow School   249
Thinking about Layers ...   251
Going Back to Place   253
Shifting Social Justifications   255

Evolving Wonders	257
Contemplating Old Wonders	258
References	261
About the Authors	271
About the Editors	273
Index	275

List of Contributors

Vera Caine   University of Alberta, Canada
D. Jean Clandinin   University of Alberta, Canada
Cheryl Craig   University of Houston, USA
Claire Desrochers   University of Alberta, Canada
Marilyn Huber   Government of Alberta, Canada
Sean Lessard   University of Regina, Canada
Yi Li   University of Manitoba, Canada
Joy-Ruth Mickelson   University of Alberta, Canada
Marni Pearce   Ministry of Education, Alberta, Canada
Pam Steeves   University of Alberta, Canada

Acknowledgement

Many people have been a part of this book. We first acknowledge the youth who allowed us to come alongside and who shared their lives with us. We know that it is not easy to share hard to tell stories with others and we are indebted to them for inviting us into their lives to hear their stories.

This work grows out of a project funded by the Alberta Centre for Child, Family and Community Research. We appreciate their financial support. There were 11 members in the original research team. George Buck and Marion Stewart were both members of the original team alongside the authors of the chapters in this book. Lindsay Krawchuk and Geoffrey Maina assisted us with the literature review at different stages of this project.

Kirstie Blackmore provided ongoing support throughout the project and provided valuable support as we prepared this manuscript. Lauren Starko transcribed many hours of conversations. We are grateful to both of them.

D. Jean Clandinin
Pam Steeves
Vera Caine

Foreword

This narrative inquiry of school leaving will linger with you long after you read this work. The stories you encounter will continue to stir you in the days/weeks/months ahead. They will shape chapters in your and others' lives that you have long considered closed. There are terms that you may want to purge from your vocabulary (i.e., student dropout). There are moments that appear innocuous, but pack a wallop of meaning. There are words once released to the world that cannot be withdrawn. There are feelings so raw that it took extreme acts of courage to name them and even greater fortitude to share them. There is human vulnerability that seeps through the warp and weft of this volume, a vulnerability experienced by research participants and researchers alike.

In *Composing Lives in Transition: A Narrative Inquiry into the Experiences of Early School Leavers*, you will learn first-hand the flesh-and-blood experiences of early school leavers: Robert, Scott, Jasmine, Andrew, Billie Bob, Kevlar, Ben, Truong, Lynn, Christian, and Skye (pseudonyms). Through the living and telling, and reliving and retelling of their stories, you will also become acquainted with researchers, Marilyn, Marni, Yi, Jean, Claire, Pam, Vera, Joy Ruth, and Sean. These researchers worked alongside the youths while bringing their personal and collective sense of knowing to bear on the narratives that were formed. Through probing lives in motion, the profound shaping effects of landscapes and the bevy of stories influencing them bubble to the surface. Readers become immersed in multiperspectival views of school leaving. The carefully constructed accounts reflect the unique signatures and characters of those whose lives lived in relationship/in context form the focus of research attention. At the nexus of the stories lie three narrative truths common to all of the youths whose experiences were studied. The first is that remaining in school at the junctures of time featured in this work would not have supported the early school leavers' best-loved selves (Craig, in press; Schwab, 1954/1978). Those narratives were being ignored/down-graded/extinguished, and were no longer sustaining the young people's school staying stories. Second, because school was no longer central to the youths' plotlines, it did not mean that the young people's making of life compositions had ceased. Even amid the rubble, new seeds (for better or worse) were being planted. Concomitantly, a third narrative truth was at play. It is that the accounts are replete with moments which could have been otherwise — an understanding word instead of deafening silence; a hug instead of a stare; encouragement rather than rejection.

As this volume unfurls, readers will find the coeditors frequently adjusting the apertures of the experiential lens. One moves from the autobiographical sharing of the coeditors' high-school stories to an expansive literature review, then on to the heart of the book: the eleven plurivocal narratives. Next, overarching themes are presented, the researchers retrospectively reflect on the longitudinal investigation, and the coeditors bring the volume to a fitting conclusion. Throughout, the fluidity of narrative inquiry as a research method and the relationships so vital to its living are constants. Added to this winning combination is a highly ethical stance and the lacing of innumerable wonders and ponders throughout the text. The work ends in a state of inconclusivity as narrative inquiries are inclined to do. There is no doubt that the research team successfully demonstrates how "to move back and forth, to comprehend the domains of policy and long-term planning while also attending to particular children, situation-specific undertakings, the unmeasurable, and the unique" (Greene, 1995, p. 11). They painstakingly instantiate how individuals' small stories can be swallowed by any number of metanarratives (Olson & Craig, 2009) as readers shall soon see. The question that remains, however, is whether you and I – and the policymakers we choose to elect – become "provoked [enough] to heal and to transform" (Greene, 1994, p. 15). After reading *Composing Lives in Transition: A Narrative Inquiry into the Experiences of Early School Leavers*, I know that I, for one, would welcome long overdue changes.

Cheryl Craig

Chapter 1

Introduction

D. Jean Clandinin, Pam Steeves and Vera Caine

This research study emerged from an increasing concern about the experiences of youth who leave school early, that is, leave without a high school completion certificate. Early school leaving is, we believe, one of the most complex and persistent social and educational occurrences, and one of the least understood. Although early school leaving was first recognized as a concern in the mid-20th century, demand for better skill, and knowledge levels, in most areas of employment has increased the concern of educators and policy makers in the 21st century. The concern is often focused on the multiple costs of early school leaving and its complex social and health consequences.

While our concern about early school leaving is shared globally, our empirical research is situated in Alberta, a western Canadian province. Alberta is considered a wealthy province within the context of Canada and has a history of attracting large numbers of migrants from other countries as well as those from other provinces and territories in Canada. During the time we undertook this inquiry, stories of early school leaving were often framed within the context of youth taking up well-paying jobs in the oil and gas industry, jobs that did not require a high school diploma. At the same time, stories about early school leavers were also often racialized, and public discussions focused on the high number of Aboriginal, immigrant, and refugee students who left school early. Often their stories were placed alongside stories of criminal activities, substance use, gangs, and underachievement.

According to Alberta Education (2012), 74.1% of youth who began high school in 2008–2009 in Alberta schools graduated in 3 years, a further 4%

Composing Lives in Transition: A Narrative Inquiry into the Experiences of Early School Leavers
Copyright © 2013 by Emerald Group Publishing Limited
All rights of reproduction in any form reserved
ISBN: 978-1-78052-974-5

graduated in 4 years, and another 1% were expected to graduate in 5 years, by 2011, for a total of 79.6% graduating. Approximately one fifth (20%) of the students who began high school would not graduate. This high dropout rate concerns us as educators and researchers and we, and others, see it as an urgent problem in the province of Alberta. Our concerns were also about how early school leaving was framed in the public discourse, and about the impact these discourses had on the lives of youth who left school early. Alberta's Commission on Learning (2003) recommended a province-wide strategy be developed with a goal of ensuring 90% of students complete Grade 12 within 4 years of starting high school. Lack of high school education has lifelong consequences for the youth, including lower earning capacities, less job satisfaction, and lower levels of health (McCain & Mustard, 1999). The loss of a well-educated work force of Alberta's young people has significant consequences for Alberta's economy, and for the social fabric of our society.

A comprehensive and expansive perspective is needed to provide a better understanding of the phenomenon of early school leaving. While research undertaken from a quantitative perspective indicates rates and general patterns of early school leaving, there is little research that explores the life experiences of youth who leave school early. Without an in-depth look across the long-term experiences of youth who leave school early, it is difficult to plan appropriate policies and interventions to support them in their efforts toward school completion. This research contributes to the beginnings of such information and understandings.

The purposes of this research study are

- to describe the life stories of early school leavers, including their accounts of the part school played in their life stories as well as their accounts of the part leaving school early played in their life stories;
- to understand the impact early school leaving without a certificate had on early school leavers' lives.

There are also three subsidiary purposes for the study:

- to conceptualize early school leavers' experiences on their identity formation;
- to examine the shaping influences of personal, family, cultural, social, and institutional contexts on early school leavers;
- to identify influential people in early school leavers' stories.

This narrative inquiry into the experiences of youth who left school early begins with the stories youth told about their experiences and the ways they experienced early school leaving in their lives. Youth were drawn from a wide range of contexts in Alberta that included Aboriginal, immigrant, refugee, English as a second language, urban, suburban, and rural contexts. The study is timely given the high overall early school leaving rate, the differential rate for various groups of youth, and the need to inform educational policies and practices. This research seeks to include the youth's voices in order to inform policy debates and public understandings. George Buck, Vera Caine, Jean Clandinin, Claire Desrochers, Marilyn Huber, Sean Lessard, Yi Li, Joy Ruth Mickelson, Marni Pearce, Marion Stewart, and Pam Steeves were members of the research team. The original research on which this book is based was funded by the Alberta Centre for Community, Family, and Child Research.

Situating Our Work

Much of our previous work has been situated in schools. For many years now, we have engaged in narrative inquiries into the experiences of teachers as they composed their lives in and out of schools (Clandinin, 1983; Clandinin & Connelly, 1986; Connelly & Clandinin, 1988; Steeves, 2000), narrative inquiries into the experiences of families, children, youth and others (Clandinin et al., 2006; Huber, 2008; Huber, Murphy & Clandinin, 2011; Murphy, 2004; Pearce, 2005; Zhao, 2007), as well as narrative inquiries into the experiences of physicians, medical students and others both in and out of hospitals (Clandinin & Cave, 2008, 2010, 2011). Vera's work alongside youth and adults in (Caine, 2010) marginalized contexts are shaped by, and shape, questions of social justice, disparities, and the institutional narratives in which they are embedded. Through all of these studies we came to understand the links between embodied narrative knowledge, the contexts of schools and other institutions understood as professional knowledge landscapes, and identities understood narratively as stories to live by. We came to understand lives as always in the midst, as unfolding over time, as lived in diverse places, and as always in relation with events, other people, and as situated within larger social, cultural, familial, and institutional narratives.

This earlier work allowed us to develop a complex set of narrative terms and concepts to make sense of the complex negotiations that teachers live as they compose their lives on personal and professional landscapes, negotiations that shape their everyday practices in schools, that make visible the silences, tensions, and also possibilities teachers experience as they engage with students and families. Jean, Pam, and Vera worked alongside children in elementary classrooms and made visible the children's ongoing stories of composing their lives within and outside of school. This work is important to our current study; it raises multiple questions about the relationships of youth who left school early with teachers, and administrators, as well as with peers. It opens up questions about how the experiences youth have in school shape their lives, and their sense of who they are in relation to others. Pam and Jean have particular interests in understanding the experiences of teachers and principals, preservice teachers, and teachers beginning to teach, as they transition to school landscapes that are new to them. We share our interest in how transitions are an integral part of lives in the making. Understanding lives as always in the making, and as requiring imagination and improvisation responsive to relational contexts (Caine & Steeves, 2009), shape ways to consider how we compose our lives. These interests shaped our curiosity in this study of looking across time as youth compose, and continue to compose, their lives as they experience early school leaving. Vera, Jean, and Pam have also been interested in understanding diverse, and often marginalized lives.

Composing Diverse Identities

Prior to engaging in our current study, we were involved in narrative inquiries that inquired into the interwoven lives of children and teachers (Clandinin et al., 2006). While Vera was not an author of the book we wrote around that project, she was integrally involved in the ongoing work with teachers, children, and the school principal. This shared project provided a backdrop to our current study and helped us raise questions about who, and what, education is for. The work also raised questions about the silences and lives that drift in and out of school landscapes, some noticed, some unnoticed. It was our work together in this project where we attended to young children who were already drifting away from school that helped us frame this current study. We return often to our stories alongside participants.

Vera worked closely with boys who were seen as having learning difficulties or behavioral problems in a grade 2/3 split classroom. As Vera worked in the classroom, she co-composed a visual alphabet with the children that focused on their understandings of community (Caine, 2010). During the year-long inquiry and her weekly time in the classroom, Vera grew close to children and it became visible how different the children's understandings of community were from those embedded in mandated curriculum that their teacher was required to teach. In one of the visual images Allan composed, as a way to explore notions of community, he troubled the notion of his classroom as a space of community. He particularly wondered about the way the teacher was positioned in relation to him. Allan decided to stage a photograph that depicted him as king. The photograph was simple in its composition and, interestingly, he directed the photographer to a vantage point where the photograph was taken with an upward gaze toward Allan, as from a position of subservience. Visually, it was evident that Allan was playing with the notion of power and dominance in his image. When asked about the image of king, Alan recounted a classroom story. Allan's teacher was the only female within the classroom, as the students were all boys. On several occasions his teacher announced she was the *Queen* of the classroom and the children had to follow her orders. Allan stated, when asked about his photograph, that he composed it in response to the story of *Queen*. Vera was unsure of how to respond initially, as she too had been troubled by the teacher naming herself as queen. Following a brief period of silence, Allan looked at Vera and said "but I will never be king."

The story stayed with Vera and entered conversations when we first conceptualized our work with youth who leave school early. Vera wondered: what are the long-term impacts of teachers' relationships with students? How do students work across inequities marked by issues of gender, power, and agency? What role do school systems and school administrators play in these encounters? How do students re-story their experiences over time?

The questions Jean raised were also around how we can compose schools as safe places for children and youth, places where they can belong, and feel safe enough to ask hard questions about their lives. Knowing that children's and teachers' lives are deeply entwined in the professional knowledge landscapes of school, Jean wondered about the ways that teachers are shaped by their lives in different places on their professional knowledge landscapes, about the ways they shape classroom spaces, and about their stories of why students leave school early. As Jean wrote the last chapter in the book, *Composing Diverse Identities: The Interwoven Lives of Children and Teachers*, the stories of the children stayed with her. She wondered about Julie and what would happen as she sought to find belonging places in school. And what of Sadie who did not feel safe in the spaces between her familial stories and the stories of school? What also of Dylan's life-composing as he moved from school to school, home place to home place, always looking for places to belong? She thought of the principal and the teacher who worked to create places for Dylan, a boy of Aboriginal heritage, to continue to compose his life. Jean wondered about schools and teachers, and how they shaped, and were shaped by, the stories of the children and their families, about what happened to children who did not feel like school was a place for them to compose their lives.

Pam's wonders were around transitions. Pam was particularly caught up in stories that involved Jeanette, the principal Pam had come alongside for over two years in an earlier narrative inquiry (Steeves, 2000). Jeannette's move to the school had not been an easy one. She felt caught in the script of principal framed by the story of school, a script where she was expected to be "in charge," the one who made decisions, and the one who shaped the school by her vision, a new vision to replace the vision of the previous principal. Jeannette resisted that script and, with Pam alongside, began, through imagination and improvisation, to co-compose a different story of school, a story of a relational community, a counter story of school. From working alongside Jeanette, Pam knew it would take time for one story to fade and another to emerge. Pam returned to the school during the narrative inquiry that was shaped into *Composing Diverse Identities*. Pam, too, was taken up in the stories being lived and told by Dylan. Dylan had been storied in other school stories as transient, as causing trouble in school, and as having poor attendance. Jeanette, Dylan's teacher Lian, and Shaun Murphy who worked in Lian's classroom, co-composed a counter story for Dylan in which he expressed his agency in choosing to leave the classroom when he felt he might get into difficulty. At these moments he went to Jeanette's office where he was given opportunities to draw, something he was proud to do, and something that connected him with his family stories. Pam wondered about the places where students, teachers, administrators, and families could live out different stories in spaces that allow them to imagine, and improvise, in response to who they are and are becoming. She wondered about the narrowness of school spaces, and the lack of space to imagine being and becoming otherwise for children, for youth, for families, for teachers, for administrators.

As Jean wrote in the last chapter of *Composing Diverse Identities* as we completed our work at Ravine Elementary School:

> We realize that what we are imagining requires radical shifts in the story of school but we also realize that too many schools are not educative places for children, youth, and families nor for their teachers and administrators. We see this in the trends and patterns of school leaving, of truancy, of families seeking home schooling, and of families searching for alternative forms of education. (Clandinin et al., 2006, p. 174)

Narrative Beginnings

The wonders that evolved from our earlier work shaped our current study. Our wonders reminded us of the importance of inquiring into our own stories of school, stories that shaped our assumptions, understandings, and experiences in and out of schools. This was important to us, as it helped us recognize reasons to engage in this work that grew out of our experiences, in and out of schools. In what follows, we share three representations of our autobiographical narrative inquiries.

Jean's Narrative Beginnings

I. Early landscapes.

> School
> marked by memories of long bus rides
> of school bus yards
> of long rows of buses, waiting for some children
> knowing those who rode the buses
> belonged in other worlds.
>
> Leaving school each day
> leaving the small town
> returning to the unpainted farm house.
> Leaving one world and
> entering another.
>
> The school world
> marked by books, pencils, paper
> for reading
> for writing
> for stars and grades
> teacher praise
> marked by pavement for skipping rope
> fields for playing sports.
>
> The home world
> marked by fields of grains and grass,
> physical labour,
> animals.
> Just barely enough
> for responsibilities
> for worry
> for play
> for freedom
> for laughter
> for not worrying about

having the right clothes
having friends to be with at recess
for not having parents with money to buy
new cars
clothes
store bought bread
exotic fruit, not berries harvested in August.

The tensions and contradictions
lived each day, each week, each month.
Leaving one world
entering another world.
Each day
each week
each year.

II. High school graduation.

High school graduation
if you like
if it works
not the only path
whatever works for you.

No family stories of graduation.
Stories of composing a life as a farmer's wife
marriage, children
a life on a farm
hard work,
not enough things, too much work
the intergenerational patterns.

High school graduation
if you like
if it works
not the only path.

The school world
a belonging place
maybe
a place of ease

sometimes
always uncertain.
Do I fit in?

III. Becoming a teacher.

Becoming a teacher
teachers belong in schools.
Leaving one world
entering another.
Living always the embodied memories
of living in two worlds
each day, each week, each year.

Noticing
watching
attending to others' dis/ease.
Coming alongside
as teacher/counselor
as teacher/researcher
as teacher/teacher educator.

Not quite at ease
world travelling
knowing multiple worlds
children, teachers, families
live in.
Knowing each of us
lives in multiple worlds
some worlds of ease
other worlds of dis/ease.

IV. Becoming a narrative inquirer.

Complexities
lived over time
lived in multiple places
in multiple relationships
of what it means to know multiple worlds
of children and families
who are seen as other

whose stories don't fit
the dominant plotlines.
Recognizing
desires to tell and live stories of otherwise
of possibility.

Pam's Narrative Beginnings

We were always moving. My early landscapes were continually shifting. There was no putting down roots as we traveled from province to province and country to country. Everything was constantly new again and pretty exciting. School didn't matter much. It was something to go through as I composed my life around the relationship with my sister, having fun, trying out new stories to live by in different places. We were not bound by the stories we left behind and we paid no mind to stories of newcomer awaiting at each school we went. We seemed to live outside of that. We were merrily bopping along.

Life changed shortly after the birth of my second child, born with disabilities. For a while it was back and forth whether this was for sure or not. Mixed messages were circling around our baby boy, all dark curls and smiling eyes; the genetics doctor who pronounced he'd never come across a "case" like this and our family doctor who noted he was curious, grabbing the tissue paper on the examining table to play with when he was just an infant. I clung to that story.... But on the eve of his 4th birthday, when he was still unable to say even single words, I remember crying quietly into my pillow that night.

We packed up and moved across the country so that Matthew could attend a special school; one that had speech therapists, occupational therapists, and physiotherapists, as well as teachers. Matthew enjoyed watching the children play in kindergarten. I imagine he wanted to join in but he needed help. School started early in his life and ended late. So much needed to be done, we were told. The wholeness of Matthew's life was not considered in the rush to fix and serve him. There was not as much time for imaginative play as there was when I was a child.

But at school, "on the side," there were a few with whom he *could* imagine. One was his speech therapist, Megan. Matthew was released several times a week from his classroom to be with her. He would "drive" Megan on his imaginary bus down corridors of closed doors, winding round corners, pulling up to a screeching stop just outside her office door. Playing was Matthew's way of communicating and Megan came alongside. She became part of Matthew's life and still is.

And then there were the yellow school bus drivers. They would ask Matthew about his stuffed toy cat. For many years the ride to school and back was the main event of Matthew's school day. Matthew's stories to live by, like my own, were composed outside of school and "on the side." But there was a difference. As Matthew was composing other stories, the scripts composed for Matthew followed him relentlessly. They were always interfering; records saying what he *couldn't* do. No records followed me. No visible difference caught me out. I was never slotted, never defined, but rather free to imagine and re-imagine who I was and was becoming.

Vera's Narrative Beginnings

Standing at the bottom of the stairs, I can still feel the loud voice rising in my throat and being muted by the tears that were welling up. I had just come from the local hospital visiting a friend who had attempted suicide; a friend for whom I had called the ambulance, after finding her with multiple empty bottles of various medications just yesterday. That morning I could not come to school on time, that morning I was drawn to my responsibilities toward my friend.

When I arrived, an hour late at school, my school principal stood at the top of the stairs. He stopped me from entering the classroom with his deep and penetrating voice, demanding to know where I had come from. I still can feel that slight rush of panic as I scrambled for words. I knew I had to find words that would give no reason for him to ask further questions, or questions that would implicate my friend. I did not want to implicate her in my being late, as by that time in my school career, I knew well enough what the common plotlines were of someone who was seen as unable to cope with, and in, schools. Standing at the bottom of the stairs, I struggled to find words and my prolonged silence and avoidance to look at my principal, only fuelled his anger. He yelled at me, demanding explanations and answers to his question of what I thought he ought to do with me. I briefly wondered what he thought and I knew he didn't really want an answer. I do recall being torn between anger and dismay and most of all of being completely overwhelmed with what had just happened in the past two days.

I remember leaving the school ground in silence.

While I did not leave high school that day, I did eventually leave. When I left, my principal informed my mother that I cared too much for others, when school was more important, that I wasn't putting my intellectual abilities to the best use, and that missing school was not possible in his school. In many ways, he named the reasons for my leaving of school in far better ways then I ever could have at the time.

I turned that year away from school for a long while to work in a psychiatric hospital in a nearby city, primarily as a volunteer with paid room and board. I could not stay in school, or walk up the stairway that held the memories of the pointless conversation. My disappointment of, and in, schools was reaffirmed; but that moment was the first time I began so clearly to question whether schools were good and educative spaces.

After a year of working in the psychiatric hospital, and with a year short of graduating from high school, I returned to the same high school. I made an appointment with the principal and asked if he would support my return and completion of the last year of high school. I still do not know why I returned. His consent came with obligations: no missed school days; weekly reporting to him; reporting test results to him; and no show of opposition to his requests.

I remembered that I left school long ago, and that for now I just had to play the game, his game. I graduated and in my last year I saw my principal every week. I left school the day I wrote my last exam; I refused to come to the graduation ceremony. He told my brother, who graduated six years after me, that it was worth it to "save me." When my brother shared this with me, I recall bitter memories and anger surfacing. The school principal died that year of a heart attack.

I recall many school events that created a sense of dis/ease and discomfort in my life; school was not a place I loved, or a place that I felt shared my values. I recall in grade 10 refusing to write the social studies test. I came to the test, but was struck by the unimaginative and mundane questions and wrote poetry in response. When the test was returned, I was given back a blank page without my poetry. I, too, did not answer the math test, the music test, the English test, and I no longer shared my poetry with any teacher. To me these remain some of the outward signs of my struggles, but they, too, remain the stories that reinforced why schools are difficult places for me.

As we began to contemplate the work of this project, I knew that it would take me to uncomfortable places of resistance, tears, questions, and, most of all, hard stories of my life. At that time in my life, people composed identities in, and with, schools as predominant plotlines, as obedient and good students, and somehow these were not my stories to live by.

Revisiting Our Research Puzzle

Looking back across our earlier research and our narrative beginnings, we could see that "Plotlines convolute and spiral, lives intertwine, coincidences collide, seemingly random happenings are laced with knots, figure eights, and double loops, designs more intricate than the fringe of a silk rebozo" (Cisneros, 2002, p. 429). By revisiting our earlier research we realized that youths' lives were more than the lives we came to know in schools. We also came to see how our lives intersected, resisted, and confirmed that schools were not always educative places. There were times when turning away from school was the only possible story.

As we read and re-read our narrative beginnings and laid them alongside Allan's story of king, Dylan's stories of coming to Jeanette's office, and Sadie's story of silencing what happened at school, we wondered about the stories of youth who leave school early over time. We wondered about the places that shape our sense of belonging. We wondered about the social contexts and places that shape the relationships youth were, and are, living in their lives. Our autobiographical narrative inquiries reminded us that lives are always in the midst of turmoil, and are continuously composed in response to the landscapes we live within, composed with imagination, improvisation, and agency. But most of all we wondered about the experiences of early school leavers as they composed their lives.

Chapter 2

Literature Review

Vera Caine

Educators, policy makers, and politicians are increasingly concerned about the complex and multiple costs of early school leaving. These costs involve factors at a personal level (such as poorer quality of life, and compromised health and well-being), an economic level (such as higher levels of unemployment and lower income), and a societal level (such as increased demands for social services, increased crime, and reduced community participation). Estimates of past and current school leaving rates fluctuate and are often inconsistent due to varied definitions and measurements of early school leaving. Great variations are also found in the explanations for early school leaving, depending on the political, sociological, or philosophical framework chosen. Current understandings are shaped by assumptions that it is advantageous for adolescents to be in school rather than out of school, that any education is superior to no education, and that there are explicit social and personal costs to early school leaving.

Methodology for the Literature Review

In order to understand the process, and implications of early school leaving, an extensive literature search was conducted. A wide-ranging body of research exists on the subject of school leaving, reflecting perhaps the magnitude of the phenomenon. Intervention studies were excluded from the search, as was the phenomenon of school leavers returning to school, or attending alternative schools, after school leaving. In our search, we looked to studies published since the mid-1990s, published in English and focused on studies conducted in North America, Australia, and New Zealand. Studies from Europe, Asia, and South America were excluded mainly for reasons of different schooling systems and research published in languages other than English.

Coming to Terms: Shifts over Time

It is quickly evident when searching the literature in this area that various terms were used, often interchangeably, to describe children and youth who left school prior to obtaining a graduation certificate. Terms such as *school leaver, dropout, disengagement/engagement,* and *push out* carry clear labels or have connotations attached to them, yet these terms are rarely defined. Historically, the term *dropout* first surfaced in the early 1900s but was not used widely until much later in the 20th century (SickKids, 2005).

The phenomenon of early school leaving received attention starting in the 1950s. Prior to this time, early school leaving was considered normal, as children and youth often left school to contribute to the family income, or worked on farms and in family businesses. The term *dropout* carrying an at-risk label began to appear in the research literature in the early to mid-1960s. It was around this time that the phenomenon of early school leaving began to be seen as a problem. Initially, the term described a new kind of deviance on the part of the student, particularly in the context of juvenile delinquency and other adolescent issues (SickKids, 2005). However, during this time, it is important to note that students who had dropped out of school tended to be welcomed back to school. Until the present time, most prevention, retention, and recovery programs are targeted toward youth who are considered dropouts (SickKids, 2005). Around the mid-1960s the term *early school leaver* appeared. Remaining popular, it is a descriptive term that generally carries few labels and holds less of a negative valence than other terms.

Willis (1977) introduced the idea of *resistance* in the 1970s in the United Kingdom. He saw early school leaving as a quasi-political rebellion by working class youth in response to class inequalities in schooling (Davies, 1999). The conditions for resistance included the actuality of being powerless, the conscious feeling of being powerless, the realization that school is not working for the individual, and the clear rejection of an unequal education experience, one that is oppressive (Munns & McFadden, 2000; SickKids, 2005). Often, students who leave due to resistance have cultural support that provides both a community safety net, and a sense of solidarity. The term *resistance* has been criticized for its lack of emancipatory vision (Choi, 2005) in which youth are regarded as having more agency in their lives. The term continues to be used not only to reflect a class-based rebellion but also to highlight that young people exercise their power, and are actively engaged in forming their identities.

In the mid-1980s, there continued to be a philosophical shift in understandings of early school leavers, which brought with it recognition that early school leaving comes from a process of *disengagement*, in which early school leavers disengage themselves from schooling. Educationists generally agree that student engagement (e.g., time-on-task and participation) produces positive outcomes but note that there is disagreement about what counts as engagement (Appleton, Christenson, & Furlong, 2008; Harris, 2008). Finn's (1989) taxonomy of engagement and participatory behaviors identified three levels of engagement. In level 1, the student demonstrates adherence to the school and classroom rules; in level 2, the student shows initiative in his/her own learning; in level 3, the student is clearly involved in the social aspects of school life. Finn sees disengagement as presenting behaviors that are contrary to engagement (e.g., not completing homework) in both academic and nonacademic school activities, as well as to what degree the student identifies with, and values, school outcomes (Davison, 2003). Disengagement is seen as a nonlinear process or pathway with a transition to adulthood. This term also pays attention to the relational impact of early school leaving on others, and that early school leaving is contingent on promises (kept or broken) between people. Furthermore, student engagement or disengagement sees early school leaving as a complex and often emotional process (Harris, 2008; Langhout & Mitchell, 2008; SickKids, 2005). Current academic discussions view engagement or disengagement as a multidimensional construct.

In Britain, the focus was to develop policies that paid close attention to the *lost generation*, which included youth who had trouble completing school as a result of being truant and/or were expelled from school, and those beyond the age of schooling but not working, training, or otherwise being educated. These policies are linked with the term *disaffection* in the United Kingdom.

In the 1990s and onward, research in the United States on early school leavers identified *push out* and *pull out* factors as explanations for early school leaving. Youth or children are often pushed out because their presence in the school creates difficulty in meeting some school goals; this includes low-performing students as well as students with discipline and/or behavioral problems. Push outs tend to be students who have a history of suspensions; they do not easily fit into the school system, and are encouraged, or directly told, to leave. Hodgson (2007) described push out factors as poor relationships with teachers and perceptions about one's low academic ability; some of the factors creating push outs have led to "pervasive, highly personalized feelings of being unwelcome" (Tuck, 2011, p. 821), often foreshadowing the inflexible and indifference schools display toward students and ultimately lead to a sense of betrayal for the student (Tuck, 2011). Often, bureaucratic regulations governing schools pressure large number of students to drop out (SickKids, 2005). It is important to note that peers, teachers, and school systems are perceived by some students as "aggressive, unfair and condescending; [creating] a forceful political and relational dynamic where interactions are typically battles for control" (McGraw, 2011, p. 105).

Although students are able to stay in school until the age of 21, some students who are over the age of 18 get pushed out of school. Unlike dropouts, who are seen as having made bad decisions in their lives and may be welcomed back, push outs are rarely welcomed back to school. Frequently, schools see them as troublemakers who negatively impact other students. The term *push out* was developed, in part, because the term *dropout* has distorted, and misrepresented, the experience of students. Dropping out is not a clear choice of leaving school, yet a number of students are pushed out and simply fade away (Hattam & Smyth, 2003).

Pullout factors, an idea that indicates that students engage in a cost-benefit analysis, construct school as only one part of youths' complex lives. Within this conceptualization, leaving school becomes a conscious and rational choice. The cost-benefit analysis includes factors such as attraction of employment, start of a family, as well as a student's lack of ability, troubles with peer groups, boredom/irritation with school, cultural/social isolation, as well as feelings of discrimination. For example, in Hodgson's (2007) study, one participant's pullout factor was a clear sense of future employment which no longer required school. Interestingly, many school leavers, with stable feelings of regret over having left school, left due to push out factors, not pullout factors (Dekkers & Claassen, 2001; T. Lee & Breen, 2007; Smyth & Hattam, 2004). The concepts of push out and pull out in understanding the complexities of early school leaving remain significant; race/gender differences also play an important role in these factors (Bradley & Renzulli, 2011).

Around the 1990s, the term *opting out* also appeared in the literature, reflecting that some students simply do not want to be bothered with education. Within this conceptualization, schools do not always serve a meaningful or relevant purpose in students' lives. Students do not take the decision to leave school lightly and often leave school for good reasons. Some authors emphasis the importance to examine the decisions of students to stay in school; these authors argue that this context helps to later understand their subsequent decision to leave school (Abar, Abar, Lippold, Powers, & Manning, 2012). The term *opting out* recognizes that students have agency in their lives and are active participants in their identity formation.

The term *exclusion* also began to be used in the literature as researchers observed that disaffection and disengagement ultimately led to the exclusion of some students. More recently the term *facilitated out* has been introduced. The term stems from a broader framework, which has a social justice orientation toward the students and their community (Wotherspoon & Schissel, 2001). *Facilitated out* also reflects that, at times, school officials and teachers encourage students to leave school prior to school completion. Interestingly some students are labeled as *tune outs*. Tune outs are students who have disengaged from learning, but do not interrupt class or cause problems and are, therefore, tolerated or ignored (SickKids, 2005).

There is still no universally accepted definition of *early school leaving*. School leaving is seen as a complex, contradictory, and multilayered phenomenon (Olafson & Field, 2003).

Leavers are typically defined as students who leave school (not including transfers) before they graduate from high school with a diploma. Some students leave school before entering ninth grade (SickKids, 2005). There is also a general consensus that early school leaving is the result of a long process of disengagement (Archambault, Janosz, Fallu, & Pagani, 2009), and alienation, that may be preceded by less severe types of disengagement such as truancy and grade retention (SickKids, 2005).

Although it is appealing to use the terms *early school leaver* and *dropout* interchangeably, this would not reflect the findings of the literature accurately. Many researchers and policy makers use the terms without paying close attention to their individual philosophical, and logistical, underpinnings. Researchers conducting qualitative studies most often use the term *early school leaver*, whereas researchers conducting quantitative studies use the term *dropout*.

Quantitative researchers struggle with the determination of the extent of the dropout rate, as there are various ways in which it can be calculated and reported. Before a dropout rate can even be calculated, researchers must agree on what constitutes a dropout. Like calculating the dropout rate, the definition of *dropout* is not always consistent. Fortunately, most researchers provide a definition of the term and the way in the dropout rate is calculated in each research report or article. Therefore, it is usually of benefit to discuss the definitions of high school *dropout* in conjunction with the rates calculated. In the strictest sense, high school dropouts are those students who have left high school without meeting the requirements to receive a high school diploma. An environmental scan of the public literature, for example, newspaper articles, teacher association newsletters, policy and position papers, showed that the term *early school leaver* is now predominately used.

Statistical Overview[1]

Canada[2]

The reasons for students not completing high school are complex and of great interest to educators, researchers, and government officials, as well as parents and students. Although across Canada the rate of dropping out seems to be decreasing overall (Gillmore, 2011), the phenomenon of dropping out of school still needs to be investigated. It is important to ensure certain groups are not neglected within the seemingly overall decrease in dropout rates. For instance, the dropout rate continues to decrease in urban schools but continues to remain relatively high in rural schools (G. Bowlby, 2005). Provincial dropout rates generally remain higher in rural areas and in small towns than in urban areas, especially in Quebec, Manitoba, and Alberta. The dropout rate also continues to be higher among males. Recent data showed the rate for men aged 20–24 was 12.2% in 2004–2005, compared with 7.2% for young women, although both rates have fallen since 1990–1991 (J. W. Bowlby & McMullen, 2002; Statistics Canada, 2005). Also, other groups, particularly those of lower social economic status or Aboriginal heritage, are facing a high rate of dropout. Despite efforts to change the dropout rate for marginalized populations over the last two decades, a significant gap in the percentage of Aboriginal students completing high school compared to percentage of non-Aboriginal students still exists in Canada (Gillmore, 2011). Hango and de Broucker (2007) noted that Aboriginal youths are more likely than non-Aboriginal youths to leave the education system with a much lower level of attainment. This has to be understood within the context that Aboriginal youth often experience racism throughout their schooling (Hare & Pidgeon, 2011). In 2006, the proportion of Aboriginal peoples aged 20–24 who had not completed high school was almost three times higher than that of non-Aboriginal Canadians (Canadian Council on Learning, 2009).

Similarly, Mendelson (2006) indicated that among the Aboriginal populations in Canada, those aged 15 years and older had a much higher proportion of people failing to complete high school than the Canadian population as a whole (54% to 35%, respectively). According to the latest available data from 2007/2010 Labor Force Survey (LFS) (Gillmore, 2011), there was a decline in both Aboriginal and the population as a whole

---

1. For an international comparison of the pathways to school completion see Lam (2011).
2. For a detailed discussion of the Canadian education systems and school dropout see Janosz, Bisset, Pagani, and Levin (2011).

(15 years or older) who had "less than high school" as their highest level of educational attainment. For Aboriginal peoples, the rate decreased to 48% and the population as a whole to 31% (Mendelson, 2006). A recent study by Hallet et al. (2008), which explored the role of consistent ethnic self-identification and school attrition in Canadian Aboriginal youths, found that students who consistently declared their Aboriginal heritage had the highest school dropout rate.

Using data from the 2001 Aboriginal peoples survey, Siggner and Costa (2005) analyzed the reasons Aboriginal youths gave for dropping out of high school. The most frequent response by Aboriginal males was "boredom" (25%), compared with 19% of non-Aboriginal Canadian males reporting the same. For female Aboriginal youth, 25% stated that the main reason they dropped out was due to "pregnancy or caring for their children," whereas only 16% of non-Aboriginal female Canadians listed this as a reason for leaving school without a diploma.

One of the most common places to receive estimates of dropout rates is from government reports or statistics bureaus. The LFS data is collected by Statistics Canada, with the main objective to produce estimates and information about employment and unemployment in Canada. However, the LFS provides information on the educational attainment of the population along with school attendance estimates. When these two figures are combined with the age of respondents, a dropout rate can be calculated (G. Bowlby, 2005). Usually, the dropout rate is calculated using the 20–24 year age group as it accounts for those students who graduate high school in more than 3 years, or who leave school and return. Individuals in the 20–24 age group who have not graduated, or are not enrolled, in high school can be considered dropouts. Using LFS data, the dropout rate in 2004–2005 was 9.8%, which is a significant decrease from the rate of 16.7% in the 1990–1991 school year (G. Bowlby, 2005) and it was 8.5% in 2010 (Gillmore, 2011). Although overall dropout rates have decreased in recent years, there remain subpopulations where dropping out remains relatively high (G. Bowlby, 2005).

Provincial dropout rate

In Alberta, the Canadian province in which we undertook our research, it is estimated that approximately one in four students, who starts high school, does not graduate (Alberta Education, 2008). Recent provincial statistics reveal that high school completion rates have remained relatively constant over the last 5 years. According to Alberta Education (2008), the high school completion rate (in 3 years) was 71.0% in 2007. The completion rate has remained relatively constant since 2003–2005, when the average was 69.1%

(Alberta Education, 2008). Students in Alberta were considered to be high school completers if they had met the requirement to receive a high school diploma or equivalent within the tracking period of 5 years after entering Grade 10. Those who were not enrolled in school, or a high school completer, were therefore considered to be early school leavers.

The Alberta government also calculates the rate of early school leaving and returning to school for Alberta students aged 14–18 for each academic year. The results are the annual dropout and returning rates. Dropouts are those students who are not registered in the education system (which includes K-12, postsecondary, or apprenticeship programs) and who have not completed the requirement for a high school diploma from the previous year (i.e., if 2005–2006 is the year of interest, the rate from that year would be those students who dropped out in the 2004–2005 school year). For the 2004–2005 school year, the dropout rate was 5%; of those who dropped out, 21.4% returned to school within one year (Alberta Education, 2008).

Framing Early School Leavers

No one framework has been developed that is able to capture the complexity of early school leaving. In general, students at risk of early school leaving are viewed from either an individual deficit perspective that elaborates risk factors, or from disengagement perspectives, which take into account wider social inequities (Cassidy & Bates, 2005).

Individual Deficit Model (Risk Factors)

The individual deficit model relies on simple, causal attribution of risk factors and sees both the individual and family as the primary cause of early school leaving. Early school leavers and their families are seen as a homogenous group, despite increasing evidence that school leaving is a complex and multivariate process. Schools are seen as unable to prevent early school leaving and, in general, both institutional and societal problems are ignored. Knesting (2008) noted that understanding the problem of early school leaving "requires going beyond the limited scope of individual student characteristics to include school factors in students' decisions to leave or stay in school" (p. 3). It is important to note that proponents of the individual deficit model often emphasize the costs of dropping out (Hankivsky, 2008).

Trends with dropouts The research suggests that there is no typical dropout. Many factors seem to interact in the decision to drop out, and dropping out can be seen as more of a process than an event. There is much research that illuminates trends in those who drop out of high school in Canada. J. W. Bowlby and McMullen (2002) use the Youth in Transition Survey (YITS)³ data to compare dropouts and graduates on various characteristics. For instance, those who graduated high school were twice as likely to have at least one parent who had completed postsecondary education (56.6% vs. 27.9%, respectively). Dropouts were also more likely than graduates to have parents who had not completed high school (26.9% vs. 8.7%). In terms of grades, high school dropouts were more likely to have lower overall grade averages and were more likely to have overall grades under 60% than were graduates. However, not all of the dropouts in the sample had low grades. Half of the dropouts had a B average or better and an additional third had a C average or better. It was indicated that only 3.6% of dropouts had academic averages that fell below 50% (J. W. Bowlby & McMullen, 2002).

Another factor that is indicative of future risk of dropping out is repetition of a grade. According to J. W. Bowlby and McMullen (2002), dropouts were five times more likely to have repeated a grade in high school and boys were more likely than girls to have repeated a grade. Jimerson, Anderson, and Whipple (2002) investigated the relationship between grade retention and dropping out of high school by doing a literature review of studies of high school dropouts. They located 17 studies that met the criteria for their study and addressed the issues of grade retention and dropping out of high school. The results indicate that grade retention can be one of the most powerful predictors of dropping out of high school. Early school leavers' experiences seem to resonate with this, as illustrated by the words of an early school leaver: "When you are eighteen years old and you're in a classroom of grade ten'ers you just can't handle the garbage that goes on in school. I couldn't handle being in a class with a bunch of immature people" (Participant, cited in Tanner, Krahn, & Hartnagel, 1995, p. 51).

Another factor often cited as being strongly related to dropping out of high school is that of working while in high school. J. W. Bowlby and McMullen (2002) indicated that, of the entire sample surveyed, 61.5% of students worked for pay while 38.5% did not. Dropout rates were lowest among youths who worked a moderate number of hours during the week. Bushnik (2003) used YITS data to investigate the relationship between working while in high school and leaving school without obtaining a high

---

3. The YITS is a Canadian longitudinal survey, with a primary objective to collect information about major transitions in young people's lives. A particularly focus is on transitions those between education, training and work. For more information see http://www.pisa.gc.ca/eng/yits.shtml.

school diploma. Bushnik indicated that the "highest proportion of students to drop out were those who worked greater than 30 hours per week followed by those students that did not work at all" (p. 11).

Dropouts tended to have more negative behaviors, such as skipping classes, than high school graduates. They were also more likely than graduates to have friends with few educational aspirations (J. W. Bowlby & McMullen, 2002).

Another factor related to dropping out of high school is that of engagement. Finn and Rock (1997) sampled minority students from low-income families. Students were classified as either successful school completers, school completers with poor academic performance, or non-completers. The groups were compared in terms of psychological characteristics as well as engagement behaviors. The study uses Finn's (1989) taxonomy of engagement or participatory behaviors. Finn argued that with participation comes identification with school and a sense of belonging, which promotes a feeling of self-worth. Finn and Rock found that disliking school was a strong predictor of skipping school or dropping out.

Norris, Pignal, and Lipps (2003) discussed the measurement of school engagement. Although their sample was elementary students, the findings have relevance to the issues of engagement. They defined school engagement as "children's behavioral involvement in and emotional identification with the social and academic realms of school" (p. 27). They also differentiated between academic engagement and social engagement. Academic engagement involves interaction with teachers, the curriculum, and school governance, whereas social engagement refers to the out-of-classroom aspects of school life such as relationships with peers and extracurricular activities. More engaged students are less alienated from school and have higher academic achievement.

Research from the YITS (18–20 year old group) indicates that dropouts tend to be less engaged than graduates. To measure school engagement among the 15-year-old cohort included in the YITS, researchers asked students various questions related to their level of identification with the school, the social aspect of school, and academic aspects of school life (Bushnik, Barr-Telford, & Bussiere, 2004). They found that students who had dropped out by age 17 were less engaged at age 15 than those who had not dropped out. Approximately 26% of dropouts reported not being very socially engaged, and 39% reported they were not very academically engaged. Only 49% of dropouts participated in extracurricular activities (at age 15) while in school, whereas 66% of those who continued and graduated were involved in extracurricular activities.

Risk factors — clusters Looking at the extensive risk factors gleaned from the literature makes apparent that dropping out of high school is far from a situation in which a student simply decides to leave school without a diploma. Generally, it appears that students who drop out are likely to be those who are unmotivated by their class work; who have problems with either the school authorities, the police, or both; who skip classes or are often absent; who are pregnant or married; who are poor and must work; who have family problems; or who have drug or alcohol problems (Fall & Roberts, 2012; F. W. Lee & Ip, 2003). Although these are likely salient contributing factors, the high school dropout phenomenon is extremely complex.

The at-risk factors for early school leaving can be loosely categorized into several strands such as social factors, socio-political-economic factors, school-related characteristics, and family characteristics. By far the largest category is that of personal characteristics of the student. Although there is some indication of who drops out, as discussed above, it is likely many of these factors contribute to leaving school without a diploma, a process that may vary depending on grade level (Stearns & Glennie, 2006).

Critique of risk factors Although some key factors have been identified that likely are related to, and assist in, predicting who is at risk of dropping out (Henry, Knight, & Thornberry, 2012), these lists may not be that helpful in predicting who will drop out (Bowers, 2010). The purpose of identifying risk factors in the first place is to give educators a way of identifying those who may need interventions in order to keep them in school. Research on risk factors that lead to early school leaving may represent a starting point for understanding the complexity of the dropout process (Lessard et al., 2008). However, an important question is: How beneficial are risk factors in actually predicting who will eventually drop out of school? Gleason and Dynarski (2002) investigated middle school students and looked at which risk factors were effective in predicting who would eventually drop out of high school. They investigated five types of commonly identified risk factor categories each with various commonly reported risk factors contained within. The risk factor categories are (a) demographic characteristics and family background, (b) past school performance, (c) personal/ psychological characteristics, (d) adult responsibilities, and (e) school or neighborhood characteristics. Their results indicated that the factors associated with the highest dropout rates were high absenteeism and being overage by two or more years. However, none of the single risk factors contained within the above categories effectively predicted future dropouts. Three fourths of the students identified as at risk of dropping out were not dropouts 2 to 3 years later. Therefore, although risk factors assist in identifying those who may drop out, they are not as effective as one would hope. Gleason and Dynarski concluded that when risk factors are ineffective in predicting who will drop out, intervention programs end up serving those who would not have dropped out, and missing those who eventually do drop out.

Some researchers have even tried to categorize certain characteristics into types of dropouts. For instance, Kronick and Hargis (1990) suggest three types of dropouts: the low-achiever pushouts, the quiet dropout, and the in-school dropouts. Each of these categories has specific characteristics. The low-achiever pushouts are those students who experience repeated academic failures and react to these failures through aggressiveness and misbehavior. The misbehavior often leads to reprimands and sanctions from school and only ends when the student eventually is expelled. The quiet dropout, listed as a frequent dropout type by Kronick and Hargis, may have a history of academic failure but does not act out in the manner in which low-achiever pushouts react. The quiet dropout does not externalize the frustration. Due to the lack of outward indicators that there is a difficulty, these individuals may go unnoticed until the time of drop out. The in-school dropouts are those students who remain in school until the graduation year but, before graduation, fail the final exams due to deficiencies in their knowledge. Although these categories may be useful for categorizing some of the students who have dropped out, they may not be useful as they do not account for certain characteristics known to be related to dropping out such as family experiences, school related factors, and socioeconomic status.

Janosz, LeBlanc, Boulerice, and Tremblay (2000) endeavored to empirically explore the value of using a typological approach to prevent and study school dropouts. The variables used to develop the typology were based on individual school experience characteristics, such as school grades, grade retention, commitment to schooling, attitude toward schooling, level of stress in school, disciplinary sanctions, involvement in school and extracurricular activities, and school misbehavior, to name a few. The results of the study led to four categories: quiet dropouts, disengaged dropouts, low achiever dropouts, and maladjusted dropouts. The quiet dropouts are those that do not misbehave in school, demonstrate moderate to high levels of commitment to school, are usually involved in school activities, do not require disciplinary sanctions, have positive views about school attendance, and can have somewhat low achievement. The quiet dropouts appear to be fairly good students overall except for lower achievement. The disengaged dropouts are those that display some school misbehavior, have a low commitment to school, feel they are less competent than their peers, do not like school, care little for grades and have few educational aspirations, and demonstrate average academic performance. The low achiever dropouts are those who have a weak commitment to education and have some school misbehavior, but their defining characteristic is that they have very low school performance. These students often have difficulties meeting the requirements to pass their courses. The maladjusted dropouts are those individuals with poor academic performance, weak commitment to school, and a high level of school misbehavior. This type of dropout obviously has the most negative profile of the four listed. The quiet dropouts and the maladjusted dropouts are said to be the two most common types of dropouts (Janosz et al., 2000).

The utility of classifying dropouts has some strength in terms of assisting researchers and educators in being aware of the etiology of the dropout. It also draws attention to the necessity of further inquiry into those classified as quiet dropouts, as these students are usually not identified as being at-risk. They seem like good students and thus go unnoticed until the point when they decide to drop out completely. Brown and Rodriguez (2009) found "that the sources of [students'] progressive disengagement from school did not lie in the accumulation of risk factors" (p. 221).

Process theories of disengagement Although individual deficit models continue to be explored, process theories of disengagement have become more common (Brown & Rodriguez, 2009). These theories take into account that disengagement from school is a nonlinear, partial, and fragmented process that is often contradictory, complex, filled with subversive forces and tensions, as well as a struggle for most students (Archambault et al., 2009; Janosz, Archambault, Morizot, & Pagani, 2008; SickKids, 2005). Hodgson (2007) described school leaving as "having complex historical antecedents that form and grow over time" (pp. 1–2). In more recent work Vaughn et al. (2011; 2010) correlate psychiatric diagnosis (psychiatric distress and conduct problems in particular) with disengagement. In recent work for Drewry, Burge, and Driscoll (2010) multiple risk factors at the family, school, and community level are framed from a social capital perspective; students with multiple risk factors have less social capital. Others have also described students as having protective factors, and, after leaving school early, they still see the possibility of negotiating their way back to school (SickKids, 2005; Tilleczek et al., 2011).

Dropping out is not an event but is a process (Bradshaw, O'Brennan, & McNeely, 2008). It is not just a matter of deciding not to come back to school one day. Interesting in this context are ongoing discussions in diverse global contexts of raising the compulsory education age (Cabus & Witte, 2011; Landis & Reschly, 2011). According to J. W. Bowlby and McMullen (2002), many youth drop out and return to school several times before leaving school completely. Of the youth surveyed in the YITS, 59.6% of dropouts reported having left school at least one time before actually dropping out, 18.9% had left twice, and 6.3% had left three or more times. Students also had a variety of reasons for leaving: most cited school-related reasons (41.7%); others reported work-related reasons (27.3%); others reported personal reasons (16.9%), and others reported other reasons (14.1%). One of the main reasons within school-related reasons for dropping out of school, was being bored or uninterested (19.9% of dropouts) (J. W. Bowlby & McMullen, 2002).

Men were more likely than women (33.7% to 16.8%) to indicate that the main reason they left school was work. Of the men in this group, 19.8% indicated that they "wanted to work," but 13.95% indicated that they "had to work due to money problems" (J. W. Bowlby & McMullen, 2002). To the contrary, females were more likely (29.1%) than males (16.9%) to report personal or family reasons for dropping out of high school. Out of all female dropouts in their survey, 15.9% indicated that the reason for leaving school was due to being pregnant or to caring for their own child (J. W. Bowlby & McMullen, 2002).

At times, dropping out can be related to the number of times a student has school-related sanctions coupled with low achievement (Arcia, 2006). Suspended students had substantially lower pre-suspension achievements than did students in the comparison group, gained considerably less academically throughout 3 years with suspensions, and had high dropout rates. All patterns were considerably more marked with increases in suspensions and with decreases in achievement (Arcia, 2006).

When students were asked to reflect on their decision to drop out of high school, "45.9% were 'sorry' they had, and 29.6% had 'mixed feelings' regarding their decision to drop out"; "females were more likely than their male counterparts to have regretted their decision to drop out" (J. W. Bowlby & McMullen, 2002, p. 42).

Recently, Lessard and colleagues (2008) described how some factors influence the process of dropping out. In their qualitative study of the lived experiences of dropouts, Lessard et al. outlined three elements of this process as *setting the stage, teetering,* and *ending the journey.* Dropout participants described strategies to *prolong their journey* and strategies to *sabotage it.* Apt metaphors such as *teetering* (Lessard et al., 2008) and *winnowing* (Hodgson, 2007) describe the gradual but continuous process of moving in and out of school. T. Lee and Breen (2007) identified three phases of the early school leaving process as encompassing *exclusion from school, transition to the work force,* and the *"now"* phase. Participants described negative experiences in school that led to explicit or implicit exclusion, which in turn led them to seek alternatives outside schooling and to finding full-time work. They then described their current satisfaction or contentment to live with their decisions.

School Context

A key historical shift occurred in the late 1980s when researchers recognized the potential impacts of the environment on early school leavers. They argued that in order to understand early school leavers it was important that their behavior was framed as a reaction to cultural needs and aspirations. Early school leavers are impacted by the school contexts, structures, and norms, and their decision is often the end result of a longstanding struggle and various decisive moments along the pathway (McGrath, 2009; Munns & McFadden, 2000). Often multiple influences and experiences ultimately lead to the tactical maneuver of a student to completely disengage from school. Early school leaving is situated within the school context, as well as in a social-cultural context, and is explored from a perspective of identity formation (Smyth & Hattam, 2004). Sefa Dei (2008) also draws our attention to schooling as community, where education must cultivate a sense of identity within community and culture.

Rhythms in and out of school — continuous moving

> I don't know, I always felt I was kind of trapped at school, you know, trapped in this one little stream where I had to go along and do it and I couldn't get out and live my life. (Participant, cited in Smyth & Hattam, 2004, p. 79)

Some early school leavers describe their experiences as a feeling of being trapped in a narrowly defined identity story. Others describe it as a dropout dance, a dance in which they both flex their muscles and perform, as a way to exert power over their own choices (Davis, 2006). Frequently, these students move in and out of school and their school stories are marked by repeated absences. The rhythms of moving in and out of school are filled with signifiers of rejection, even if the goals of school leavers, and those who eventually graduate, remain the same (Tanner et al., 1995).

Early school leavers often move in and out of school for school-related reasons, not necessarily because of cultural resistance. The themes of alienation and boredom are particularly strong, and some children and youth are able to endure this, while, for others, it leads to a continuous moving in and out of school, where the final decision to not return to school is most often ambiguous and tentative (Langhout & Mitchell, 2008; Tanner, 2001). Lee and Breen (2007) described exclusion from school as either explicit (isolated and ostracized) or implicit (bullying, gossip). Participants described themselves as being an "outcast" or "like prisoners" and that school was a barrier to achieving their goals rather than a way to achieve them as reasons why to leave school early.

On the other hand, many school policies and procedures encourage disciplinarians to use suspensions and transfers to "get rid of" students they deem troublemakers. Langhout and Mitchell (2008) described a *hidden curriculum* explained as the values, norms, and beliefs transmitted via the structure of schooling. Implicit messages are conveyed in school that are mired in race, ethnicity, social class, and gender issues. Academic disengagement can occur for all students but can be especially strong for disadvantaged youth when they learn a different message from the stated one. Implicit messages that their engagement was inappropriate and subsequently learning that school is not for them are heard. Similarly, Hodgson (2007) explained the unconscious school operation of separating, categorizing, and labeling students into various groupings can imply an exertion of power and control. The continuous moving of students in and out of school is seen as a mechanism through which schools help perpetuate racial and class stratification in the larger society (Bowditch, 1993). This is particularly so in the case of students with histories of criminal activity, and students who are expelled from school due to troublesome and troubled behavior (Cassidy & Bates, 2005).

Switching schools continuously is associated with dropout (Gasper, DeLuca, & Estacion, 2012). It is important to note that the turbulence in the lives of children caused by residential mobility, school staff and peer turnover, and other elements of instability contributes to early school leaving (Hanna, 2003; Terry, 2008).

Voices in and outside of school

> Some teachers were really nice and understanding and did their best to try and help me catch up, but one teacher held it [my suspension] against me and called me a "waste of space" and that I was taking up space in the classroom. (Participant, cited in Smyth & Hattam, 2002, p. 388)

Voices both in and outside of school contribute to students leaving school prior to graduation. Some students are exposed to continuous remarks that clearly indicate that they are not welcome at school. Peer rejection in school or negative influences of peers outside of school can play a large part in why students leave school (Lessard et al., 2008; Terry, 2008). On other occasions it is that people outside of school do not acknowledge the relevance of the school experience for students, which leads to a feeling of being misunderstood or not being recognized at all. Family and friends have profound influences over students' decisions to leave school. Lack of parental support and unsupportive attitudes actively encourage students to quit. In a study by Terry, examples of unsupportive behavior include repeatedly being uprooted and moved or having family turmoil due to divorce or drug and alcohol use. Porowski and Passa (2011) have shown that programs that link community resources with schools to help students beyond academic success have a decrease in dropout rates and an increase in attendance rates; other

Unquestioned assumptions

> We did not like to go to school. It was useless and boring. We just went to school because our parents wanted us to do so and we don't know the meaning. (Participant, cited in Lee & Ip, 2003, p. 103)

In the current socioeconomic and political climate, schools often operate from a one-size-fits-all approach. This is evident in standardized testing, as well as in school resources and the provision of career advice given in schools (Archer & Yamashita, 2003; Fine & Weis, 2003). Schools neither attend to, nor question, issues of inequality or unequal distribution of resources and needs; schools are breeding grounds for competition, where everyone competes against everyone, and students are often troubled by the assumption of sameness. Schools create a horizon of im/possibility and un/desirability (Archer & Yamashita, 2003).

Schools rarely question their own assumptions and learning environments and often children contemplate: "Like most kids at school are there because they just don't know what else to do. And the school just doesn't allow that independence" (Participant, cited in Smyth & Hattam, 2002, p. 391). These seem to be the inexorable pathologies of the current school and government bureaucracy (Smyth & Hattam, 2001). More recently, Smyth and Fasoli (2007) stated that it is no easy task to reform schools to be less punitive and thus reinvent themselves to show students that schooling is relevant and worthwhile. Developing respectful relationships with students, parents, and community was essential for positive outcomes to happen, otherwise a "spiraling culture of worthlessness and hopelessness would likely persist" (p. 280).

Mismatch between education and schooling

> They had me going a little bit. That's what made me go for a couple of months, but the teachers there never did hands on training. They'd always stick to the books, and the books just put me to sleep. I'd just get tired. I was there for three months, and we never worked on anything. We just sat there with our books. My father's a mechanic, so I know something about mechanics, and I like it. But, since we never did anything, it never caught my attention. I could stay home and work with

my dad on cars and learn more. (Participant, cited in Jeffries, Nix, & Singer, 2002, p. 42)

The mismatch between education and schooling is well expressed in students' accounts of their early school leaving experiences, many of them indicating that attending school is often not about education but about attaining a certificate. In many cases students felt they did not learn anything or, at least, anything that was relevant to, or would help them improve, their lives. Lessard et al. (2008) described situations where students felt like they were "walking in the dark." Participants described how going through the motions of school was confusing to them and failed to link the educational journey with their futures. Similarly, Harris (2008) noted that until teachers are aware that students see purpose in schooling and class work, they are unlikely to engage and fail to see the relevance of learning.

Positions of power

> The school favors students who perform well in examinations. It can help the school build up its reputation. We are bad students, since we perform badly academically. Teachers are willing to spend time with good students to drill their examination skills after class. They would never spend time with us to discuss things taught by them we don't understand. (Participant, cited in Lee & Ip, 2003, p. 101)

The issue of power within schools, particularly between teachers and students and between administrators and students, has received little attention in research around early school leaving. Schools can be understood from a notion of schools as spaces of regulated confrontation. From this stance, schools are seen as places where teacher and student (counter)scripts intersect in often less than authentic forms of interaction (Smyth & Hattam, 2001). Indeed, these often inauthentic relationships are filled with power struggles that reflect not only when teachers and students engage, but also when teachers and students do not engage. Langhout and Mitchell (2008) described how the power dynamic favors the schools and teachers in a system "where the teacher is the police, judge and jury" (p. 605).

Teachers sometimes reflect the notion that schools become sorting stations in children's lives, and that those who do well are both rewarded and helped to become somebody. The educational powerlessness and the social disadvantage that accompanies many students of cultural difference are used to push students out of school. This particularly holds true for Aboriginal students (Munns & McFadden, 2000). As Smyth and Hattam (2004) write, "but they [Aboriginal youth] get pushed away because they don't have what the other kids do" (p. 87). Smyth and Fasoli (2007) described relational power when referring to the inequalities of allocating resources, such as who gets provided the necessary resources to succeed in school. Related to the notion of social capital, disadvantaged children may not have a say or any power and thus become less trusting of the school system.

Other times students who feel that teachers are not interested in them and do not care much about them, find themselves in what Dei, Mazzuca, McIsaac, and Zine (1997) referred to as a "network of disinterest," with detrimental emotional and cognitive effects (Hay et al., 2004). Lowered teacher expectations combined with some encouragement to opt out of mainstream education also leads to a pushing out of students, or perhaps a facilitating out of students (Davison Aviles, 1999). Students often do not have a choice about the school they would like to attend, leading to a feeling of powerlessness and being stuck.

> You know, it's like going to the job where you work and you hate your job. Every chance you get to leave that job, you will leave. And there's nothing that we can do ... The difference between us going to school and having a job is you can quit and find another job. This school — we cannot go anywhere else ... then you get stuck going to a school like this and you're just not learning. (Participant, cited in Fallis & Opotow, 2003, p. 110)

In the current era of high-stakes testing, it has also been noted that educators and students are under great pressure to increase students' academic performance; failure on the students' part to perform well often leads to a feeling of deficit among "low" achieving groups (Archer & Yamashita, 2003). Students not only are then exposed to an uninspiring pedagogy but also are made responsible for their failure (Bickerstaff, 2011). These discourses, practices, and policies indicate an area of new authoritarianism (Hodgson, 2007; Smyth & Hattam, 2001, 2002). Early school leavers often cite this authoritarianism as a reason for leaving. As well, they resist schools that are seen as embodying the essence of capitalist society (Munns & McFadden, 2000). Hodgson (2007) states "the way power operates in schools to produce particular kinds of cultures and identities and how these are resisted, reconstructed and bypassed by some students can lead to increased pessimism and loss of faith in school as a legitimate place to be" (p. 13).

Relational being

> If you don't enjoy the people you hang around with, you can't, you don't want to learn so you just leave, you know.

> If you don't, you know, if you're going to school and getting hassled out and you've got no-one to talk to or ... then you won't have a good time so you won't stay there. (Participant, cited in Smyth & Hattam, 2004, p. 83)

School personnel often do not connect with the lives, and worlds, of students with whom they are meant to engage (Cassidy & Bates, 2005). Often there is little time, amidst the administration of tests and the attention to individual characteristics, to engage with students. A report by the Ministry of Learning in Alberta (cited in Hay et al., 2004) identified issues such as negative teacher-student interaction, and low teacher expectations, as strong factors contributing to students dropping out of school. Feeling valued by available, open-minded, and patient teachers helped prolong the educational journey for some students (Lessard et al., 2008). While outright school failure is not particularly significant in early school leaving, the relationships with teachers, feelings of boredom, and an irrelevant curriculum, matter deeply (Tanner et al., 1995). As described by one researcher, "Melanie described feeling like a number among thousands without faces and without connections. She expressed feeling lost in the large student body once her few close friends were no longer there" (Jeffries et al., 2002, p. 41). Similarly, others talked about living invisibly by not wanting to attract attention and not being counted (Lessard et al., 2008).

Being different in schools/continuous rubbing up School is not about being different or being given a voice, or expressing opposition, as schools often legitimatize and reproduce large structured inequalities and silence students (Fine & Weis, 2003). Students can be explicitly or implicitly excluded from an education, simply because they were made to feel that they did not deserve it, because they did not fit the perception of a "normal" or ideal student (Lessard et al., 2008).

> Clearly, the wider power of school relations has some measure in shaping identity and aspiration, but equally, young people also bring their own indigenous cultures and sensibilities to what they are prepared to accept, and this may not always be consistent with the school's agenda of making them "obedient and subordinate citizens." (Smyth & Hattam, 2001, p. 380)

Unfortunately, these often happen to be students who choose to leave school early (Choi, 2005). Schools can position students in terms of class and gender and limit the discussion of their aspirations based on these categories.

The issue of poverty is largely silenced in schools, so that students from less than middle-class backgrounds feel alienated (Hattam & Smyth, 2003). Expecting students to come from middle class backgrounds also leads to a narrowly constructed identity story of children (Fine & Weis, 2003).

Social-Cultural Contexts

Policies Current government policies often see young people as human capital rather than socially and culturally embedded characters. Policy makers, most often, treat education as a technical rational choice, ignoring the larger, complex life stories of youths. Trying to compose a story of school engagement has to be understood in light of these policies (Ball, Maguire, & Macrae, 2000; Wishart, 2009). It is only in more recent years that current and past government policies have been critically examined; there has been a call that policies need to go beyond addressing obstacles to school success, and rather focus on prevention of school dropouts (European Commission, 2012).

Consumer culture More than in any previous period of history, teenagers now spend more time among their peers than in any other relational situations, leading to an unprecedented aged-based social segregation. When examining the school leaving story of Korean youths, Choi (2005) found that it became clear that the Korean consumer culture

> evoked these youths' consumer desires and accelerated disengagement from school. The youths were vulnerable to an environment that solicited their money such as game rooms, Internet cafes, dance halls, bars and taverns. In this culture money became a yardstick to measure the worth of a person. (p. 309)

The combination of economic dependence and age segregation offers an unappealing combination of a subordinate status, and all its anxieties, with an intensified reliance on peer approval (Davies, 1999). Lee and Breen (2007) described social networking changes when students drop out, and described how ties to friends were broken by the decision to leave school early.

Social issues

> I miss a lot of school but it's not because I want to. I miss school when I'm needed at home. I try to help out as much as

> I can, especially now that my dad's been laid off. Last year, Mom was sick and she called the school and they came and told me. I ran to my locker and grabbed everything and I ran out. I just ran out. If my mom needs me I'll come running home. (Participant cited in Olafson, 2006, p. 32)

In general there is an underestimation of the demands of private life for students, especially for those living in poverty and those who have experienced family turmoil (Hattam & Smyth, 2003; Lessard et al., 2008; Terry, 2008). Many opportunities in life are classed (Ball et al., 2000) and reflect the existing social structures. Some researchers have drawn attention to the societal barriers to achievement and attainment, particularly as it is reinforced and reproduced within the school system (Tanner et al., 1995).

Furthermore, the focus on young peoples' transitions to adulthood has failed to take account of fundamental shifts in social and economic relations, which affect both young and old people (Ball et al., 2000). It is critical to note that current social conditions are rapidly changing for youths, which affects their decisions of early school leaving (Davies, 1999). While Davies wrote these words in 1999, they certainly still resonate in 2012. These issues have not been well addressed, and silences exist, particularly regarding the role of leisure and pleasure in the lives of young people (Ball et al., 2000).

Community

> I don't get with the program because then it's doing what they [teachers] want for my life. I see Mexicanos who follow the program so they can go to college, get rich, move out of the barrio, and never return to give back to their gente (people). Is that what this is all about? If I get with the program, I'm saying that's what it's all about and that teachers are right when they're not. (Participant, cited in Weis & Fine, 2005, p. 93)

Children and youth are strongly shaped by the communities they come from. At times, obtaining educational achievements rarely encountered in the community leads to the possible alienation of students in their own homes. At other times, community members disapprove of certain programs because they are not comfortable with the program, for example, being embarrassed that their children attend special classes (Davison Aviles, 1999).

Identity formation Many adolescents live a story of being disaffected by school and struggle to gain even a minimal education from their school experience, with the result that many leave school disillusioned (Smyth & Hattam, 2001). School, for some, also becomes an alienating and irrelevant experience, and some of these children develop an oppositional frame of reference for their identity (Choi, 2005; Smyth & Hattam, 2001).

> I quit school because I enjoy freedom and fun-seeking with my friends ... I can see my friends for the whole day, talking, smoking, and playing in the playground ... even if we don't do anything, I enjoy freedom and companionship I get being with them. (Participant, cited in Lee & Ip, 2003, p. 105)

Once identities are inscribed at school through school failure and reputation, it is difficult to participate at school in the future (Archer & Yamashita, 2003). The scripting of an individual's life was sometimes initiated at school and at other times developed within a student's community. "Man, I never thought like that — I just hope to make it to the next day" are words from a young African American male, who described a limited life expectancy (Davis, 2006, p. 294).

Youth have a heightened sense of agency and are often not prepared to have their identities ignored or subordinated within the dominant school and policy framework. School trouble often stems from the interactive trouble between trying to become somebody, and the narrowly defined identity that schools expect (Smyth & Hattam, 2004). School policies, teacher attitudes, teacher reactions, and peer rejection all provide the message that those who leave school early do not belong (Lessard et al., 2008). Researchers and policy makers need to rethink the importance of context and its impact on students. T. Lee and Breen (2007) suggested opportunities for students to voice their needs and experience power and control.

Issues of identity and inequality surface for many students. At times an escape from learning has been interpreted as suggesting that learning identities are limited. At other times early school leaving is an attempt to preserve already fragile and fragmented identities (Archer & Yamashita, 2003; Ball et al., 2000). In the struggle to become somebody, early school leaving is a temporary improvisation (Ball et al., 2000). Unfortunately, through increasing pressures at school, young people view themselves as not good enough and leave school (Archer & Yamashita, 2003). Leaving school, then, is a tactical maneuver amidst the complex process of identity formation (Hattam & Smyth, 2003).

Making the decision to leave school is part of the process of becoming someone. At other times employment or caring for others is seen as choosing more adult-like identities (Archer & Yamashita, 2003). "I felt like the world was spinning without me. A lot of the people I knew had jobs and they were going out and doing things and they had money"

(Participant, cited in Tanner et al., 1995, p. 105). The performance of identities, expressed by fashion style and body image, helped some students stay in school while, for others, this was part of being pushed out or excluded (Smyth & Hattam, 2004). For other students the process of success, or even staying at school, involved muting their voices (Smyth & Hattam, 2004); interestingly few researchers examine the factors of why students stay in school (Behnke, Gonzalez, & Cox, 2010). Particularly children from minority groups experienced the constructing of very limiting identities for them (Toohey, 2000).

> Most of the teachers keep bugging me to get my work done. You have to do it their way, a certain way, and if you don't then you're just going to get punished for it. And it has to be done by a certain time. It just turns me off. Sometimes, I refuse to do the work. When they challenge me, I feel like I have to challenge them right back. It's my life, it's my school work. It just bugs me how they think they have control over our lives. (Participant, cited in Olafson, 2006, p. 41)

Youth in Flux

In recent work, Tilleczek (2011) argued for a consideration of early school leaving from within a focus on youth studies. In this way she considers the complex cultural nests are part of youth's lives. When viewed from this perspective, we see the need to complexify the understanding of transitions, that is, we see the need to understand transitions beyond the simple, linear structure often imposed. As well, when viewed from this perspective, we no longer can understand staying in school as reaching a successful end point.

Issues and Directions for Future Research

Around the world, early school leaving is one of the most protracted educational problems, but also one of the least understood (Smyth & Fasoli, 2007; Smyth & Hattam, 2002). Throughout the literature review it was evident that a number of issues exist with the available statistical data as well as with the interpretation of the statistical data. Many areas remain unexamined or are largely unexplored in the current literature. In the following section, key issues are highlighted which point to directions for future research and which influenced how we framed our narrative inquiry.

Primary Focus on Individual (Risk/Deficit Perspective)

Limited quantitative data exists that emphasizes and explores the complexities, resiliencies, and contexts of early school leavers' lives. The data collected is primarily gathered from individual risk and deficit perspectives. The early school leavers' survey conducted within Canada tends to reinforce the notion of individual deficits, pathologies, or inadequacies. The United States has focused predominately on breaking down data by race or ethnicity. Furthermore, very few studies examine data from multiple perspectives (Orfield, 2004) or from theoretical perspectives. For the most part, quantitative research presents student groups as homogenous, neglecting the great diversity within these populations both in school attendance, achievement, and resources among other things (Feinstein & Peck, 2008).

School Leaving as a Point in Time Rather than a Process

Most statistical studies delineate school leaving from a single point in time rather than from a process of disengagement. Consequently, most studies have not examined early school leaving from a longitudinal perspective (SickKids, 2005). Few studies have looked at the lives of early school leavers through the process of leaving school to transitioning to adulthood (Hickman, Bartholomew, Mathwig, & Heinrich, 2008). Paying attention to this process over time could provide invaluable information into the connections between health and well-being and early school leaving. Increasingly researchers, with backgrounds in educational psychology, call for intervention programs that address the connection between childhood trauma and school dropout (Porche, Fortuna, Lin, & Alegria, 2011). As well, problems relating to dropping out appear in the most acute form in the ninth grade, a critical transition for many students, yet most research on school leavers focuses on students in Grades 10–12 (Orfield, 2004).

No Coherent Framework for Early School Leaving Exists

School leaving has no clear definition or boundary; in fact, researchers use various and often unstated methods of determining leaver rates (SickKids, 2005). Researchers and school personnel often focus on societal and student characteristics to account for why some students make decisions to stay in or drop out of school. There are clear gaps and omissions in terms of who is selected for existing early school leaving studies. Research often ignores youth who withdraw prior to Grade 9, immigrants who never attend school, youth who attend private schools, and other groups such as youth in foster care (SickKids, 2005), despite the fact that others have shown that disengagement can start in elementary school (Langhout & Mitchell, 2008). Schools may choose to push out students in order to do well on achievement testing, yet no statistics account for the various reasons for early school leaving. There is a need to develop a universal definition of early school leaving (SickKids, 2005) which reflects the impact of school structure, size, and curriculum in relation to early school leavers, and in relation to the phenomena of push out and being facilitated out.

Missing Perspectives

Almost entirely missing in the attempt to understand the phenomenon of early school leaving are the voices of school administrators, teachers, and parents. Only recently have studies emerged on teachers' conceptions of student engagement (Harris, 2008) and linking student and teacher experiences with student disengagement (Langhout & Mitchell, 2008) or engagement (Archambault et al., 2009). Given the relational nature of teachers' work, one must ask questions such as the following: How do teachers make sense of educational policies and school disciplinary practices that appear to be pushing their students out of school? How do teachers grapple with the aggressive promotion of the completion of Grade 12 with respect to early school leavers, in particular with regards to issues of equity and social exclusion (Taylor, 2002)?

Parents, too, play an important role in the lives of children, and almost no studies, either qualitative or quantitative, have examined parents' beliefs, attitudes, and understandings of early school leavers. In one of the few studies focused in the area, the importance of intergenerational components in understanding educational attainment was pointed out (Boardman, Alexander, Miech, MacMillan, & Shanahan, 2012). Recognizing that students live amidst communities, some studies have examined community and cultural values that influence school leaving. In recent work Tilleczek (2011) challenges the "individualistic, pathological, essentialised and fractured constructs and practices" (p. 264) when understanding early school leaving; she argues for a consideration of early school leaving and transitions as understood in "nested social ensembles" (p. 253) where youth need to be drawn into the discussions of transitions and resiliencies. However, this work is at the beginning stages.

No Consideration of Early School Leavers in Context and over Time

Very few studies focus on early school leavers and families in their particularity and over time. It has been established that family and friends have profound influences over students' decisions to leave school early, but few studies have explored the views of peer groups and families from this perspective. Yet, examining the experience of early school leaving in a larger sociocultural context would allow for a richer understanding of the issues and the phenomenon. For instance, little attention has been paid to how diverse young people frame the issue of school leaving. Attention needs to be paid to subgroups such as lesbian/gay/bisexual/transgendered youths, Aboriginal youth, youth in rural areas, Francophone youth, first and second-generation immigrant youth, and visible minority youth and their understandings and experiences of early school leaving. Beginning work exploring early school leaving in the immigrant population is being conducted (Anisef, Brown, Phythian, Sweet, & Walters, 2010). School-based efforts to prevent early school leaving must address students' circles of influence, within in-school and out-of-school contexts.

It has also been clear that the labor market plays a role in the phenomenon of early school leaving, yet a further in-depth analysis of the influence of changing labor markets and policies on gaining further educational qualifications needs to be undertaken. Some research shows that unstable employment patterns for parents lead to dropout among adolescents. These findings need to be further substantiated and expanded, as they indicate the importance of placing the problem of early school leaving within a larger social-cultural context (Randolph, Rose, Fraser, & Orthner, 2004). There is a need to listen more carefully to what students say about their school experiences and their involvement in their schooling with supportive teachers and administrators (Knesting, 2008); as well as attending to transitions upon entering into high school (Pharris-Ciurej, Hirschman, & Willhoft, 2012). Langhout and Mitchell (2008) suggested that future focus should be to allow for conversations about the purpose and goals of school, as well as the facilitation of teacher and student empowerment.

Methodological Considerations

Tilleczek et al. (2011) point out the need for innovative social approaches and youth-attuned methodologies. Innovative methodologies might challenge and overcome the barriers for the push toward evidence-based research, which further marginalizes the voice of those who are already silenced (Smyth & McInerney, 2011). While methodological advances are much needed, it, too, is important to build the institutional capacities to listen (Smyth & Mcinerney, 2007). This shift in the ways in which researchers attend is also important when we begin to understand the difference between schooling and education (Tilleczek, 2011). Perhaps understanding this shift and the difference between education and schooling from the youths' perspective, would allow communities to find a way to reinvent the institution of schooling and make student voices central to the process of schools (Smyth, Down, & McInerney, 2010; Smyth & McInerney, 2012).

Chapter 3

Methodology

D. Jean Clandinin, Vera Caine and Pam Steeves

To inquire into the experiences of youths who left school without a high school diploma (early school leavers), over time and across different school, work, social, and home contexts, we selected a narrative inquiry methodology. We adopted the following definition of narrative inquiry:

> Arguments for the development and use of narrative inquiry come out of a view of human experience in which humans, individually and socially, lead storied lives. People shape their daily lives by stories of who they and others are and as they interpret their past in terms of these stories. Story, in the current idiom, is a portal through which a person enters the world and by which their experience of the world is interpreted and made personally meaningful. Looked at this way narrative is the phenomenon studied in inquiry. Narrative inquiry, the study of experience as story, then, is first and foremost a way of thinking about experience. Narrative inquiry as a methodology entails a view of the phenomenon. To use narrative inquiry methodology is to adopt a particular narrative view of experience as phenomenon under study. (Connelly & Clandinin, 2006, p. 477)

This definition guided our research process as we framed our research puzzle, located participants, composed field texts, and, through interpretation and analysis, moved to the composition of research texts. While narrative inquiry shares features in common with other forms of qualitative inquiry such as the emphasis on the social in ethnography and the use of story in phenomenology, it is a unique research methodology. Clandinin and Connelly (2000) developed a conceptualization of narrative inquiry as a relational inquiry process within a three-dimensional narrative inquiry space.

The Three-Dimensional Narrative Inquiry Space

Clandinin and Connelly (2000) identified the three dimensions of a narrative inquiry space as temporality, sociality, and place. The first dimension, temporality, draws attention to the past, present, and future of events and people. Events under study are in temporal transition, that is, events and people always have a past, present and a future. In narrative inquiry, it is important to always try to understand people, places and events "as in process, as always in transition" (Connelly & Clandinin, 2006, p. 480).

The second dimension is sociality. Connelly and Clandinin (2006) noted that:

> narrative inquirers are concerned with personal conditions, and, at the same time, with social conditions. By personal conditions we mean the feelings, hopes, desires, aesthetic reactions, and moral dispositions of both the inquirer or participant. By social conditions we mean the existential conditions, the environment, surrounding factors and forces, people and otherwise, that form the individual's context. (p. 480)

A second aspect of the sociality dimension draws attention to the relational aspect of narrative inquiry, that is, the relationship between participants and inquirers. Emphasizing the relational aspect of narrative inquiry, Connelly and Clandinin (2006) wrote, "inquirers are always in an inquiry relationship with participants' lives. Narrative inquirers cannot subtract themselves from relationship" (p. 480).

Place, the third dimension of the three-dimensional narrative inquiry space, draws attention to "the specific concrete, physical and topological boundaries of place where the inquiry and events take place" (Connelly & Clandinin, 2006, p. 480). All events take place in places and the specificity of location is crucial. As they noted, "Place may change as the inquiry delves into temporality" (p. 481), and a narrative inquirer needs to think through the impact of each place on the experience.

Working narratively to study the lives of young people who left school early allowed us to honor the youths' lived experiences as sources of important knowledge and understanding. It was their stories, as they told them in relationship with us as researchers, to which we attended. Clandinin and Connelly (2000) allowed us to see that

> narrative inquiry is a way of understanding experience. It is collaboration between researcher and participants, over time, in a place or series of places, and in social interaction with milieus. An inquirer enters this matrix in the midst and progresses in the same spirit, concluding the inquiry still in the midst of living and telling, reliving and retelling, the stories of the experiences that made up people's lives, both individual and social. (p. 20)

While narrative inquiry begins with a respect for people's everyday experience, we knew that narrative inquiry did more than valorize individuals' experience. Narrative inquiry allowed for an exploration of the social, cultural, linguistic, familial, and institutional narratives within which each individual's experiences were constituted, shaped, expressed, and enacted. However, narrative inquiry begins and ends in the storied lives of the people involved. Narrative inquiry, as both a view of the phenomenon and as a methodology, allowed us to study an individual's experience in the world and, through the study, seek ways of enriching and transforming that experience.

Narrative inquiry, thus, allowed us to relationally inquire into the lived experiences of the youth while staying attentive to the social, cultural, linguistic, familial, and institutional narratives within which each youth's life was embedded. We honored each youth's narrative of experience in the narrative accounts.

Finding Our Participants

As we wrote in the literature review, we selected the term *early school leaver* rather than school *dropout*, which evoked a deficit view of our participants, or school *pushout*, which evoked a negative view of schools. Our criteria for selection of participants were that youth (a) had left an Alberta high school without a certificate, (b) were between the ages of 18 and 21, and (c) had been out of school for two Septembers, that is, for one or more years. Knowing the high number of early school leavers who had left Alberta schools, we anticipated we could find youth through placing posters in schools, agencies, and community outlets. We also anticipated that we could meet the youth who had left school early through contacting agencies who might work with them.

Finding participants was much more difficult than we anticipated. Our first poster was focused on the youth themselves. We put the posters in coffee shops, art centers, employment agencies, and on community notice boards in retail outlets and libraries. When we had limited response we began to question this recruitment strategy. In conversations with people in schools and agencies as well as informal conversations among ourselves and with colleagues, we designed another poster that was directed to others who might know a youth who had left school early. Both posters were also translated to French. We put these posters in the same or similar locations but we also posted them in educational institutions and agencies.

When we emailed the posters to contact people, we also included a letter outlining the purpose of the research, the research team, and the parameters for participation. When we received little response to this initiative, we wondered if perhaps a more direct line of communication would attract more potential participants. We began to also include a more personal letter explaining to potential participants exactly what we were expecting in terms of participation including the number of conversations and other details.

Claire Desrochers and Marion Stewart, two team members, contacted and visited the following agencies in Edmonton and Calgary — Inner City High; Boys and Girls Clubs of Calgary; Calgary Mennonite Society; Calgary Catholic Immigrant Society; Norquest College; Old Strathcona Youth Coop; Pride Centre; YMCA; Outreach Network; Bow Valley College; Canadian Arab Friendship Association; Multicultural Health Brokers; Native Students Association, U of A; Mennonite Centre for Newcomers, Edmonton; Alberta Child Youth Initiative; Aboriginal Youth Suicide Prevention; St. Theresa Pregnant and Parenting Teen Program; Youth Emergency Shelter; Native Friendship Centre; outreach schools in several school districts; and school principals in several school districts.

On the assumption that some potential participants would be in the work force, we also sent posters to employment agencies and to a large local construction company. We also contacted people and agencies outside of the two major urban centers. Many people we contacted thought they knew youth with whom we could talk. We continued to put up posters. Over time we gradually began to reach the young people. Members of our research team also made personal contact with some youth to ask if they knew possible participants. Sometimes participants suggested other possible participants through a snowball sampling process.

We found youth slowly over an 18-month process. As we found youth who agreed to meet with us, we selected individuals from our research team to meet with them. Sometimes researchers asked to work with certain individuals who seemed particularly interesting to them. Sometimes decisions were made on the basis of researchers' time schedules and availability to travel to other towns and cities to meet with the youth.

The 19 youth with whom we met came from all over the province, with a higher proportion from the Edmonton area than from other places in Alberta. We did, however, hear the stories of youth from diverse places across the province.

Challenges in Recruiting Participants

Recruiting participants who are early school leavers was difficult for several reasons. Firstly, there is no institutional base from which to elicit participants. We needed to reach the general population, individuals involved in a range of activities, in order to find people to fit our unique criteria (between the ages of 18 and 21, out of school for a year, leaving an Alberta high school without graduating). Secondly, the youth who have left school early are not easily identifiable, as they have become part of the general population after leaving school. Thirdly, the idea of leaving school early (dropping out) has a stigma attached to it. The phenomenon seems to be treated as a matter that is private, personal, and evokes feelings of shame or failure for some. Fourthly, the experiences around leaving school early is a difficult subject to broach and difficult for youth to admit to, making it harder for our contacts in the community to refer potential participants to us. Some were uncomfortable raising the topic or felt they could risk alienating the youth. Fifthly, some of the youth did not see themselves as early school leavers but described themselves as individuals taking time out for various reasons. It is something we began to understand through the stories of participants. In retrospect, we wonder about the choice of the descriptor *early school leaver* in that we have become increasingly aware of how language does not easily allow us to represent the actual and perceived experiences of youth.

The Research Team

Our large research team was composed of researchers with diverse experiences. Each researcher brought unique strengths and knowledge to the work. As we worked with participants and one another on the team, research relationships and conversations with participants unfolded in somewhat different ways. In narrative inquiries, there are no pre-set interview question guides, and we followed that process in our research. We did, however, create a tentative outline or way of being with participants. To that end, the initial outline for beginning the conversations allowed each researcher to create openings for participants' stories. In this way, we created the possibility for each individual researcher's distinctive imagination and knowledge to shape the relationships.

Narrative Inquiry with Participants

Using a narrative inquiry methodology, with attentiveness to the three-dimensional narrative inquiry space — temporality, sociality, and place — enabled us to work with multiple forms of field texts (data). It was crucial that participants felt comfortable in telling what, for some, were hard to tell stories. We also knew that we were all researchers with multiple university degrees and that participants could see us as somewhat intimidating given they had left school early.

In our initial research team meetings, we agreed that we would begin our conversations by working through the informed consent forms. We, however, wanted a way to begin that would allow the youth to focus on the whole of their life experiences rather than on their particular school experiences.

We set up our meetings mindful of creating comfortable spaces for participants. Because we were trying to build relationships, often our conversations happened around food. Some participants were accompanied to the first meeting by someone they trusted and with whom they were familiar. We met in places the participants had chosen. As researchers and participants, we were somewhat uncertain at first about how the conversations would proceed. As the relationships developed over time, we came to eagerly anticipate our meetings. The time between meetings seemed to enrich the spaces for reflection for both researchers and participants.

The first youth with whom we talked helped us devise a way to think about working with other participants. Although she did not want to pursue more than one conversation with us, her brief participation helped us design an approach to beginning the research conversations with other participants. We did not include her as a participant. We intentionally did not start with the event of leaving school but with the temporal unfolding of their lives in different places and in different relationships. We asked each youth to tell us about their early years, early schooling, and home and family experiences, which enabled us to begin to understand the whole of their life contexts.

In subsequent conversations, we shared tentative annals (Clandinin & Connelly, 2000) or time lines of the youths' life experiences, asked further questions that we had not understood from the first conversation, and often asked them to bring artifacts, memory box items, or photographs. On a number of occasions, they invited us to visit their elementary and junior high schools, and, when possible, we did this. On some occasions, other family members and friends were introduced. Sometimes we attended family and cultural events with the youth.

We saw most participants three times, for two conversations and then a final meeting for sharing the tentative narrative accounts we had written about our conversations with them. Occasionally, we saw participants only twice; on a few occasions, we saw participants four or more times.

Ethics

Relationships among narrative inquirers and participants are at the heart of narrative inquiry. "Relationship is key to what it is that narrative inquirers do" (Clandinin & Connelly, 2000, p. 189). While we completed the ethics review process at the University of Alberta, we often discussed the relational ethics that lived at the heart of narrative inquiry. Clandinin and Connelly (1988) wrote about the central place of relationships in collaborative research. They drew attention to negotiation as understood in terms of the negotiation of entry and exit from a school or classroom. However, they also wrote of the ongoing negotiation of the narratives of experiences carried within the researcher and participant involved in the inquiry, the "negotiation of two people's narrative unities" (p. 281). They described this as a deep experiential process that lives at the heart of the relationships the researcher and participant negotiate. In this way, the narratives of their experiences shape the inquiry.

Ethical matters need to be narrated over the entire narrative inquiry process. They are not dealt with once and for all, as might seem to happen, when ethical review forms are filled out and university approval is sought for our inquiries. Ethical matters shift and change as we move through an inquiry. They are never far from the heart of our inquiries no matter where we are in the inquiry process (Clandinin & Connelly, 2000).

And so it was for our work with the early school leavers. Beyond the ethics review requirements, we knew we needed to continue to think about relational ethical ways as we sought out, met with, listened to, wrote about, and eventually negotiated narrative accounts with each participant in the study. While we felt the long-term relational responsibilities to participants, at the same time we lived with the ethical tensions around the extent to which research participants would engage in the research.

Ethics approval was first granted in the summer of 2007 and was renewed in April of 2008 and 2009.

From Field Texts to Interim Research Texts

For each participant we composed a narrative account (Clandinin & Connelly, 2000). We drew on the field texts (transcripts, field notes, artifacts) and worked within the three-dimensional narrative inquiry space as we wrote these accounts. We were mindful in writing the accounts that it was participants' stories shared in relation with us that we were telling. We realized that narrative inquiry is relational inquiry, and we knew that as researchers we were co-constructing the accounts with participants. We wanted to be respectful of the youths' stories of their experience. We negotiated each narrative account with each participant. At that time, when we, and they, had made the necessary changes and had an opportunity to tell us whether they felt the account was an adequate representation of their experience, we asked them to select pseudonyms for themselves. In the narrative accounts we described home communities and demographic information when it was important to the experiences of the participants. We did not name cities, towns, or schools in order to provide anonymity to participants. Occasionally when we did mention schools or places, we created pseudonyms for them.

As we worked on the move from field texts to research texts, we formed our somewhat large and physically separated research team into smaller works-in-progress groups. The smaller groups allowed us to respond to each other's tentative interpretations and representations in the narrative accounts.

One Version of a Final Research Text

For the purpose of preparing a final research text for the funding agency, we worked collaboratively as an 11-member research team to look across the 19 narrative accounts. We prepared a final report "Composing lives: A narrative account into the experiences of youth who left school early" for the Alberta Centre for Children, Families, and Communities Research. We described the six resonant threads or patterns that we discerned as we looked across the narrative accounts of the early school leavers.

Three Years Later: Another Research Text

The relational nature of narrative inquiry changes both the researcher and participant as we come to be in the midst of one another's lives. The youth often talked of the sharing and composing of narrative accounts and how the inquiry helped them more clearly tell and retell their life stories. For example, Kevlar told Pam as they sat in the restaurant negotiating the narrative account "reflecting on it with someone is different than reflecting on it yourself." Jasmine told Yi Li, in their last meeting together, "I learned to remember." As for ourselves the stories we heard, and later inquired into, both within and across the narrative accounts, shaped new insights and new wonders. Three years later many of us still find ourselves haunted by the narrative accounts of the youth. Our experiences following the initial study have deepened our sense of relational responsibility to the youth drawing us to "look again," to reconsider the narrative accounts, and our research wonders.

As Vera, Jean, and Pam engaged in further narrative inquiries over the past few years, new experiences, along with some older and personal ones, pulled the three of us toward further puzzles around understanding the youths' experiences of transitions and to new questions about the youths' stories to live by. As narrative inquirers we are fundamentally concerned with people's lives and so our wonders around transitions are inextricably linked to wonders around identity, stories to live by. In Chapter 1, we began our telling of coming to edit this book through making visible autobiographical beginnings that lead each of us back to our study with the youth. Polanyi (1969) writes of "attending from" our experiences. All three of us have been involved in narrative inquiries that led us to trouble the ways identities and transitions are viewed in the story of school, part of the larger institutional narrative.

Our autobiographical beginnings in Chapter 1 left us troubled and made visible the importance of acknowledging identities as fluid, contextual, embodied, and shifting. For us, identities are shaped in the living of lives in particular times, places, and relationships. We are troubled with conceptions of transition that do not acknowledge the improvisatory nature of change over time, that are shaped by people and contexts. What kept rubbing away at us was how we might learn more about transitions and identities in relation with the lives of youth in motion.

Three years after the narrative inquiry into the experiences of youth who left school early, and after engaging in other narrative inquiries of people's experiences as they moved into different situations, Vera, Jean, and Pam came together in early July 2012 for three days to revisit the narrative accounts of the youth in order to learn more about transitions and identities as understood narratively, that is, when we attend to lives lived and told over time. We imagined that by inquiring again into the narrative accounts of 11 of the youth we would gain richer, more layered, and more nuanced concepts of transition and identity when youths' lives were viewed in their complexity.

We designed a further method of moving from the 11 narrative accounts in order to pull forward narrative threads attentive to stories to live by and to transitions. We began with five of the narrative accounts we had co-authored with the youth with whom we three had engaged. As we read these aloud to one another, we paused when one of us noted something in the account, often occurring at times and places of tension and uncertainty in the stories the youth had told us. We identified these moments as moments where we might learn something about transition and identity. There was much conversation among the three of us as we pulled forward threads from these five narrative accounts.

We then asked six other authors of narrative accounts to reread their accounts. Pam, Vera, and Jean then met separately with each author/researcher to engage in a similar process. As we undertook this further process we were mindful of our relational responsibilities to the six researchers and to their participants. We had each negotiated the narrative accounts with participants. Each researcher had a deep understanding of the accounts s/he had co-authored with participants. In this way, we gained further insight into each researcher's understandings in relation to transition and identity in a particular participant's life.

After the further rereading of each narrative account, and after the conversations with each researcher, we had identified sections of each narrative account that were related to transition and identity. Throughout, we remained respectful of the whole lives of participants. We were mindful that our intention was not to dissect their lives. We then looked across the sections that helped us understand transitions and identities in the lives of the youth. We considered a number of resonant threads to guide the writing around transitions and identities.

We then began a process of collaboratively writing two chapters, one on transition and another on identity. We developed a rotation protocol such that each of us had opportunities to work on each chapter multiple times. A trusting relationship built over many years enabled the co-authoring of these chapters. The literature review was amended by Vera to reflect an up to date and comprehensive chapter reflecting historic, and current, information and perspectives around research with early school leavers. In what follows, we share 11 of the original 19 narrative accounts.

Chapter 4

A Narrative Account of Robert

Marilyn Huber

I was excited and yet a bit apprehensive as I waited in the customer area of the mechanic shop where Robert worked as an apprentice mechanic. Robert had made arrangements for us to use the conference room at his worksite to engage in our first research conversation. Trying to calm my nervousness, my mind travelled across time and place to the stories I held of Robert from our time together as student and teacher in Foods 10 at West Central. These now nearly 4-year-old memories included:

> Robert ... participating and contributing to all aspects of the foods lab, including clean up.
>
> Robert ... negotiating with group members diverse aspects of the foods lab such as which recipe to prepare, who would complete which tasks, possible solutions to unforeseen situations that bubbled up in the midst, and so on.
>
> Robert ... always saying, "Good morning."
>
> Robert ... telling me that the best parts of Foods were the practical aspects ... he needed to know how to cook, to maintain his health, to budget, and so on.
>
> Robert ... always on time for our class which started at 8:15 a.m.
>
> Robert ... at first seemed quiet but, in time, began to share stories of his life outside of school. For example, I learned stories of

> Anna, Robert's niece, and of how he loved spending time on a farm a couple hours drive outside the city.[1]
>
> Robert ... part way through the term begins to bring with him to class a long, thin, black case. When I ask, he shows me that inside the case is his pool cue.
>
> Robert ... telling me how he often goes to a local pool hall between Foods and his first afternoon class. I know youth in Grade 10 are not permitted spares.[2]

It was memories such as these that drew me to ask Robert if he would consider participating in this inquiry. We had not seen one another for 4 years when we happened to meet one day in the grocery store. When he asked what I was doing, part of my explanation included my involvement in this inquiry. In response, he told me he had not completed high school. We talked about his possible participation and, prior to our saying good-bye, he gave me his phone number. Some months later, I phoned Robert and asked if he might be interested in participating in this inquiry.

Reconnecting in Conversation

Settled into the conference room, Robert and I first read and discussed the letter of informed consent. After this letter had been signed, we proceeded with our first research conversation. As a way to share stories Robert told during this and our subsequent conversations, I composed the following word images by selecting Robert's words from transcripts of our research conversations. Creating word images, as explored by Clandinin et al. (2006), is a "highly interpretive process" which "create[s] a temporal sense" of how a participant stories her or himself or a particular experience while also providing "a more vivid rendering" (p. 99).

> Kindergarten to Grade 6 at Townsend Elementary
> Addison Field for junior high
> High school at West Central

---

1. Robert was in Grade 3 when Anna came to live with him and his parents (Anna's grandparents) and brothers (one of whom was Anna's dad). The farm belonged to the parents-in-law of a family friend; Robert spent increasing amounts of time there, including periods when he lived there.
2. A spare refers to a block of time in a high school student's timetable when s/he could be taking a course but is not.

> I'm the youngest
> Three older brothers
> We're all three years apart
> So knew teachers [at Townsend Elementary] before I went there
> Knew it was a good school
> Was happy to go
> Nervous moving to a new school for junior high
> But my brothers all went there too
> My brothers also all went to West Central

For the most part, Robert's and my research conversations centered on his experiences within school. Yet, woven into Robert's tellings of his school experiences were often stories of his family and family stories. It seemed, as Robert recounted experiences from his childhood and youth, that stories of family and school could not be told separated or distinct from each other. For example, as shown in the word image above, as Robert storied his beginnings at Townsend Elementary, Addison Field Junior High, and West Central High School, he made visible that his knowing of these schools did not commence in kindergarten, Grade 7, and Grade 10 but, rather, started much earlier with stories his brothers told of their experiences on these landscapes. Robert also highlighted how his decisions to attend these schools were informed by his brothers in that it calmed Robert's nervousness to start at a new school knowing that his brothers had previously gone to the school. Exploring the importance of family connections, Robert drew links to how he thought it was similar for Anna, his niece. Referring to Anna, he said, "She can go ... [to school] wherever she'd like but, you know, it's comfortable for her to go down the hallway and see her uncles on the ... pictures. She feels like she belongs there." Just as being able to see pictures of her uncles on the school walls seemed to create a belonging place for Anna so, too, did Robert's older brothers' stories create a sense of comfort and familiarity for Robert within a particular school.

Memories of Elementary Years

> Kindergarten to Grade 3
> Had pretty easy going teachers
> In a split Grades 2/3 classroom for Grade 3
> Probably good if academic child in Grade 2
> But, as a Grade 3 student
> [Message was]

You're not getting it
It's getting a little dumbed down

Grades 4, 5 and 6
Start getting ready for junior high
Your free ride is over

Grade 5
My teacher was Mrs. C.
Made learning a lot more fun
An excellent teacher
Also the Art teacher
More eccentric

Definitely got along better with option teachers
They have fun
Kids have more fun in their classes

Music and Art
Weren't labelled options in elementary
Learned that label in junior high
But, knew they weren't core curriculum[3]
So they weren't as important

Can't remember what my marks were in elementary
Don't think I ever did poorly

Initially, as Robert shared early memories of his years in elementary school, he provided more factual information such as which schools he had attended, the names of his teachers, and so on. However, as our conversation continued and Robert seem to reconnect more strongly with his experiences, he shared that in Grade 3 he was in a split Grades 2/3 classroom. Moving further into the details of this story, Robert explained how "even then ... [he] could tell" the story attached to his being in this split grade classroom was that he wasn't "getting it" and needed the subject matter to be "a little dumbed down."

Storying his memories of Grade 5, the next grade in which Robert's storytelling lingered, he explained Mrs. C. was an "excellent teacher" because she "brought more fun back into [learning]." Recalling enjoyable

---

3. "Core curriculum" in elementary and junior high schools in Alberta refers to math, language arts, science and social. Students have no "option" about taking these courses in school.

experiences he had alongside Mrs. C., Robert drew my attention to that Mrs. C. was the Art teacher at Townsend Elementary in addition to being his Grade 5 teacher and to how "because she was the Art teacher, she was a little more eccentric." As our conversation moved to Mrs. C.'s eccentricity, Robert highlighted how it was during elementary school that he learned "options" such as music and art weren't "core curriculum so ... weren't as important" and that he "definitely got along better with teachers that were option teachers." These teachers, like Mrs. C., taught in ways where they as well as students had "more fun" and where learning was made more accessible because they "changed it up a lot."

Bringing together Robert's sharing of these stories, I wondered about interconnections which may live among them. For example, as Robert realized he was seen by others, particularly his Grade 3 teacher, as being not "academic" and as needing to have subject matter be "a little dumbed down" alongside that the course content in "options" was "not as important" as that in "core curriculum," did he internalize a story of more probable success in "option" courses? As Robert experienced subject matter content in these courses as more accessible and fun, did this contribute to his getting along better with "option teachers?" If so, how might Robert's and these teachers' relationships been shaped by teacher beliefs about who children were and who they could be in relation with each other, with her/himself as teacher, and with subject matter?

> Pushed around a lot in elementary school, bullied
> Kids making fun of my glasses
> Somebody punching my glasses off or whatever
> I'd be pretty angry
>
> Probably in half a dozen fights throughout elementary
> I wasn't the bully
> Was the person getting bullied
> Or, stepping in
>
> Student at my elementary school
> Had skin problems, scabs, stuff like that
> A lot of people picked on him
> Definitely the outcast
> I stood in
> Protected him
>
> I was never really hated by anybody
> School is very segregated
> For example,

In Grade 5
Don't play with kid in Grade 4
That's a young kid
Grade 6 kids looking at you in the same way
That's a young kid because you're in Grade 5

Didn't talk to teachers too much
Not about anything like bullying
Had mom and dad at home
Could talk to them
They talked to the teachers

Storying how he was "an outcast" throughout much of his time at Townsend School, Robert explained he was "pushed around a lot" by bullies in the school. His stories made visible that being positioned as an outcast typically arose from physical difference. For example, he described how the bullying he experienced often began with being teased about his glasses whereas another student became the prey of his peers because of skin problems. Amidst Robert's stories of being pushed around, I learned he felt he had no space to talk directly with teachers about anything like his experiences of being bullied but, rather, could talk with his mom and dad at home who, in turn, could talk with his teachers at school. Regardless, it seemed, talking with his parents and his parents talking with the teachers, the bullying Robert experienced day-by-day in school did not shift.

For the most part, Robert and other children, such as the boy who had skin problems, were left on their own in school to face, and be pushed around by, bullies. Perhaps, then, it was because being bullied made Robert "pretty angry" or because he was learning within his family to live by a story[4] (Connelly & Clandinin, 1999) of needing to be a "good Samaritan" that Robert began to respond to the bullying by "stepping in," "standing up" and "fighting back." While Robert knew it mattered within his family that he live by a story of being a good Samaritan which meant helping another in a time of need, he also knew his parents would not support his fighting. Yet, given that talking with his parents and his parents talking with teachers did little or nothing to shift the stories of bullying being lived out at Townsend Elementary, what was Robert to do? How could he simultaneously "stand in and protect" his peer who was being bullied while not

---

4. Stories to live by is a narrative term conceptualized by Connelly and Clandinin (1999) as a way to understand the interconnectedness of knowledge, context, and identity. They wrote, "Stories to live by, is a phrase used ... to refer to identity, is given meaning by the narrative understandings of knowledge and context" (p. 4).

"fighting back"? In this way, then, Robert seemed caught between family stories, that is, he was simultaneously encouraged to live by stories of being a good Samaritan and of not fighting.

Coming to see how Robert may have felt caught between family stories, I wondered if he might have also been caught between stories at school. For example, I wondered, if some teachers might have thought it was wrong for Robert to step in, stand up and fight back while others, perhaps, thought he should protect peers in need while others, still, might have expected Robert to ignore the issue. Carefully reading the transcripts of our research conversations, I learned "the teachers didn't like it. Especially in elementary, they didn't agree with the fighting at all." I also noted that Robert gave this response along with telling how he had been "put into detention for watching a fight." This led me to wonder if, at least at times, teachers responded to Robert's fighting by assigning him detentions.

> First time I ever skipped school was in elementary
> Was put in detention for watching a fight
> Principal lecturing me and three others
> I'm watching my clock
> I'm rocking on my chair
>
> Principal got angry
> Kicked my chair out
> Dropped me on the floor
> I got up
> And, left the school

Listening to Robert recount this event, his words repulsed me as I considered how such a moment might have contributed to children living out stories of bullying at Townsend Elementary. I imagined as Robert's telling continued, his story would clarify how this incident had led him to skip school more and more. Instead, Robert explained:

> Principal took time to track me down
> Came to my house
> Took time to care
> Talked to my mom and me
> I explained my side
> He listened
> He explained what made him go off
> I listened
> It really stood out to me

He took time to care
Made a good impression on me

Initially, I was surprised when Robert explained that he had understood the principal coming to his house to talk about the events which led to his leaving the school as an expression of care. What stories, I wondered, might have shaped Robert's response. Might it have been a continuation of living by a story of being a good Samaritan? In other words, might Robert have felt responsible to *turn the other cheek* and engage in a conversation in which he and the principal listened to each other's perspectives? Or, might another family story, that is, a story in which Robert "was always taught to respect ... [his] elders, whether they were teachers or police or whoever" have been living behind his response? Considering further Robert's family stories, I wondered, if Robert's thinking may also have been shaped by an intergenerational family story of a strong work ethic, a story Robert's grandfather had taught to his mom which, in turn, she alongside Robert's grandfather had taught to Robert. Explaining this story Robert said, "I have a strong work ethic installed in me, no half job is a job done at all .... You've got to work hard and don't half-ass anything." Might Robert have understood the principal taking the time to "track [him] down" and then coming to his house to talk with him and his mom rather than expecting them to come back to the school as a demonstration of work ethic? When the principal took time to not only explain "what had made him go off" but also to listen to Robert's perspective, might Robert have seen this as the principal not living a story of responding in a "half-ass" way? Did Robert understand the principal's willingness to explain "what [had] made him go off" as a way of taking responsibility? Thinking further about Robert's telling I also wondered if he might have seen the principal as caring because he took the time to listen and to talk with Robert and his mom about events on the school landscape. Perhaps, I realized, this was a profoundly different response than what Robert had received from his teachers either when they had witnessed or when Robert's parents told them about Robert's being pushed around and bullied at school.

Grade 6
D.A.R.E.[5] program

---

5. D.A.R.E. — Drug Abuse Resistance Education — according to the Alberta Teachers' Association website, is a "comprehensive prevention education program designed to equip elementary school children with the skills to recognize and resist social pressures to experiment with tobacco, alcohol and other drugs" ("D.A.R.E Program Keeps Children Off Drugs," n.d.). The D.A.R.E. program was included into Robert's Grade 6 program and was taught by both a local police officer and Robert's Grade 6 teacher.

Taught:
Don't smoke, it will ruin your life
Don't smoke, stay in school
Smokers are not good people
They're hard on the health system
They're hard on themselves
Their second-hand smoke is bad for you

I failed D.A.R.E.
Wouldn't listen [to the messages being presented]
Wouldn't do the assignments
Just didn't want anything to do with the program
Knew then I was going to be a smoker
If I could go back
Would smoke right on front step of school
It was just a joke

As Robert recounted his experiences in D.A.R.E., he passionately highlighted the dominant messages he remembered conveyed within the program — that is, smoking can ruin your life, smoking can lead students onto future pathways of not completing high school, and people who smoke are not good people because they are hard on the health system and themselves and their second-hand smoke is bad for others. Repeatedly, Robert referred to the D.A.R.E. program as a "complete joke" because it did not discourage him from smoking but, rather, seemed to strengthen his resolve to "be a smoker."

Storying his experiences in D.A.R.E., Robert drew links with how his dad, grandpa, and brother — three significant men in his life — smoked. To Robert, then, participating in the D.A.R.E. program by listening to the messages and completing the assignments meant accepting or agreeing that his grandpa, dad, and brother were "not good people," but, instead, were people who had ruined their lives and who did not value children and youth staying in school. Robert experienced the teaching of D.A.R.E in his Grade 6 classroom as having no space in which alternate or additional stories could be considered or told, stories for example in which people who smoked: were cognizant and respectful of the harmful effects of second-hand smoke and, therefore, like Robert's dad, did not smoke inside their home or around non-smoking family members; valued and had completed high school such as Robert's dad made visible when, according to Robert, he said, "You can't even push a broom in my warehouse unless you have Grade 12. You're not allowed to work here unless you have it." So, too, did Robert's grandpa know and share stories of the importance education held in his life. To Robert, in neither of these men's lives did it seem that smoking had "ruin[ed]" their lives.

Memories of Junior High Years

> Pretty much an outcast right up until Grade 9
> Always a couple of bullies in school
>
> Especially bullied in Grade 7
> One kid
> Loved to smack me upside the head
> That was his thing
> Thought it was funny
> (Research conversation, September 2008)

Stories of being bullied seemed even more pervasive and commonplace for Robert at Addison Field than at Townsend Elementary, especially during his year in Grade 7. While there were "a couple of bullies in the school," one boy, according to Robert, seemed to find it funny to "smack" Robert "upside the head" and, therefore, did so regularly. Through Robert's storytelling, he made visible he responded to the bullying and to this boy in numerous ways. Initially, he described, "I told him to stop multiple times" and "I talked to the teacher and principals." He did so, he explained, because, "I ... [was] the new kid in Grade 7. I ... [didn't] want to get in trouble." When neither method of response was effective, Robert highlighted:

> Finally, I told [the administrators], you know, if this happens again because you guys haven't done anything about it then he's going to know what it's like to be smacked. And that was fine by them. You know, like they weren't, they were, "No, you're not supposed to hit him Robert." And, that was as far as it went.... When ... it happened, more blame was put on to him than me.

Unlike in elementary school where Robert did not talk with his teachers about "anything like" the bullying he was experiencing, at Addison Field he tried talking with both teachers as well as the administrators. However, when neither these conversations nor Robert's direct requests to the youth who were bullying him were effective, Robert returned to living out stories of "fighting back." When he chose to teach the one bully, in particular, "what's it's like to be smacked," more blame was placed by the administrators onto the bully than onto Robert.

Teachers, principals don't like fighting
Would tell me
"You shouldn't be doing that"
Get suspensions
Days off
Or, have to sit in the office for the day

They don't tell you what happens to the other kid [involved in] the fight
You don't see that other kid for a couple of days or whatever
Sometimes "Sorry" is said back and forth
That's about it

Inquiring into what happened when Robert fought back as a way to "protect" either another youth who was being bullied or himself, I learned that he was often assigned an in- or out-of-school suspension. Robert referred to "out-of-school suspensions" as having "days off" even though, because one or the other of his parents were at home, he had to "do homework, ... clean and do all ... sorts of stuff. It was a punishment while I was home." He was *punished,* Robert explained, because his parents did not agree with him fighting and because they valued his being in school and attending classes. I imagine they did not wish for Robert to understand or experience an out-of-school suspension as "days off" to be enjoyed. In-school suspensions, Robert described in this way:

The day goes by pretty slow but it wasn't bad .... You got to do your work quietly. You didn't have to deal with all the kids yelling and screaming and the teacher stopping 10 times to calm everyone down. You did what you had to do and you were done .... Sleep if you could sleep otherwise you just kind of sit there and stare around for a few hours .... The rooms] were probably 4 feet by 6 or 7 feet. I used to remember how many ceiling tiles there were in there and how many rivets and screws because I was in there enough times in junior high .... [I'd] bring a dime ... [to] take stuff apart .... They were small little cubicles with a door that opened inward so the room got smaller when the teachers came in.

When I asked if Robert felt he was responded to differently depending on if he was standing up for someone or for himself, Robert explained, "As you go up in the grades, [citizenship] ... matters less and less .... [Message is] don't involve yourself. You know, you're going to get yourself into trouble." It seemed, then, while there was some tolerance given when Robert "smacked" the boy who had been bullying him, standing up for others or to use Robert's words of "being a good Samaritan" was seen as something to avoid. As I pondered how a message of "don't involve yourself" became more prevalent as Robert moved up in the grades, I wondered if this story might have also been shaping the teachers and principals at Addison Field as well as, perhaps, Townsend Elementary. That is, recalling how nothing seemed to change when either Robert's parents in elementary school or Robert in junior high school talked with teachers and administrators about the bullying he was experiencing, I wondered if maybe they, too, thought it easier or safer to not become involved. Might the teachers and administrators have feared their involvement could lead to "trouble" with other youth, staff members, parents, or school district personnel? I also wondered about the tolerance Robert had been shown for "smacking" the boy. Was his action tolerated because, at least according to Robert, the administrators "ha[dn't] done anything" when Robert initially told them about the bullying or when he warned that he would fight back if the bullying continued.

Gym's the worse
More adrenaline
Everybody's active
There's the time to bully
Everybody's spread out, separated from the teacher
Teacher can't watch, see everything
Things happen in the corner that can't happen in a classroom
A ball in the face
Or, slashed with a hockey stick
Isn't fun

So skipped most of Gym

Biked around the neighbourhood
See what's in the back allies
Go to the ravine a lot
Keep myself busy
Not too often, I'd go to the mall

Physical education (gym), according to Robert, was the worst in terms of bullying due to increased adrenaline, opportunities when youths' actions could not be seen by the teacher as well as that some learning activities could be used as a cover for bullying. As already explored, Robert tried many different ways to stop the bullying he was experiencing at Addison Field. When none of these responses were effective, Robert started skipping physical education and health. "Health," according to Robert, "just happened to be a casualty seeing as it was after gym." By skipping physical education, Robert was able to escape the worst of the bullying. During this time, Robert spent most of this time alone biking in the neighborhood and through the ravine. As Robert explored the activities he engaged in, I thought it a bit ironic that even though he was skipping physical education, he was, intentionally or not, engaging in physical activities. I also realized, intentionally or not, by skipping physical education, Robert was defining when and how he would be isolated from his peers rather than letting teachers and administrators have this authority.

While Robert's parents did not like or support his skipping class, Robert said, "I think they could see where ... it was coming from, you know if the kid is getting bullied he's not going to want to be there .... They didn't like it but they knew I had a problem." Perhaps, I realized, Robert's parents knew the different ways in which Robert had responded to, and tried to stop, the bullying he was experiencing. Maybe, like Robert, they also did not know what to do so that Robert could attend physical education without being bullied. I imagine it is deeply frustrating and painful for a parent to see and experience her or his child being bullied day after day in school and to knowingly, then, have to encourage his or her child to keep returning to such places. I also imagine it may be difficult for a parent to watch her or his child learning stories of using physical violence as either a way to get what they want or as a way to protect themselves.

The physical education teacher, Robert storied, reacted to his skipping and failing grades by "complaining" to Robert, his parents and his homeroom teacher who "would try to enforce things a little more .... He gave me detentions and, yeah, I got school suspensions." The health teacher, Robert said, "didn't have a problem with it .... I think out of the whole year I went to six classes and I came out of there with a 90%. When I went to class, I did my work ... he [referring to the teacher] was happy with it."

> Doesn't matter if you come to class
> Doesn't matter if sitting and listening to your Walkman
> Doesn't matter if you're picking on people all day
> If marks are good
> Or, if you're throwing the winning touchdown
> Probably not going to catch too much flak

Exploring with me his skipping physical education and health as well as his grades in these courses, Robert made visible another story that seemed, at least in his knowing, to be shaping Addison Field School. Central in this story was that what mattered or counted in the school was the achievement of "good" grades and/or leading a school sport team to victory by "throwing the winning touchdown." Having one or both of these stories in place meant other stories would be overlooked, stories such as poor attendance, not listening or participating in class and picking on others. As I considered this story alongside other stories Robert told, I was reminded of how all too often in both my student and teacher experiences, a thread of community-making is seen as a way to begin a school year, but within a few days or weeks the focus is shifted away from community-making and relationship-making to getting on with mandated subject matter. I wondered, might Robert's stories of bullying, fighting, suspensions, citizenship, and so on, been otherwise, had he experienced community-making in school such as that which Dewey (1938) and Greene (1995) described? In their understandings, community is necessarily always in the making as it is responsive to, and inclusive of, the ongoing lived experiences of school participants.

Considering this view, I recognized response other than detentions and suspensions would have been needed when youth bullied, fought, or skipped class. Rather than preventing youth from interacting with each other or mandating they say a token "Sorry" to each other, spaces would need to be intentionally created that drew on, for example, Buber's (1947) metaphor of meeting on a "narrow rocky ridge" (p. 218). Attending to communities that have contrasting points of view, Buber saw the ridge as a place where those with opposing perspectives meet and engage in "real conversation" (p. 240). Such a space would be, perhaps, like that which was created between Robert and the principal of Townsend Elementary when the principal came to Robert's home to discuss with him and his mom the events which had led to Robert's first incident of "skipp[ing] school." In this space, Robert and the principal listened to each other tell what I imagine was, at least initially, contrasting and opposing perspectives. Engaging in "real conversation," Robert came to see the principal as someone who cared. Perhaps, the principal also came to see Robert in a similar way. Had such conversation been foregrounded among youth or between youth and teachers at Addison Field, I imagine stories of skipping class as a way to avoid being bullied may have been unnecessary. I also imagine Robert's parents would have been positioned quite differently within the school, that is, rather than being simply informed of decisions, such as Robert being given in-school and out-of-school suspensions, they would have necessarily been participants within conversations.

Memories of Senior High Years

Recounting stories of his going to West Central, Robert began by saying that he "definitely ... wanted to go" to this school and reminded me that his brothers had also gone there. However, as Robert moved further into his experiences within the school, his tellings revealed the school was "just too big. You get lost as a single person. What was it? I think 2000 people at the school. You're a nobody until you make yourself a somebody." Asking how students would made themselves somebody, Robert explained, "You better get on the sports teams ... and get into a certain group, figure out who is the popular group." Thinking about Robert's comments about how the school felt "just too big" and that "you [could] get lost as a single person," I was reminded again of the necessity of community-making within schools. In so doing, I imagined how difficult it might be for each of the 2000 people to "make [him/her]self a somebody," and what might be necessary for ensuring spaces for real conversation?

> Atmosphere is more relaxed
> But, teachers aren't there to babysit
> Not going to hound you
> "Do your work or don't"
> "I don't care"
>
> Run down, beat up school
> Leaking roof
> Water rings all over the ceiling
> Some areas probably still had lead paint
> Others unpainted
>
> Students spitting on the floors
> Throwing garbage all over the place
> Just disgusting
>
> Didn't enjoy sitting in decrepit chairs
> Or, shoddy-looking workmanship around me
> You think, "I'm coming to a piece of junk every day"
> "Don't want to be here"

As Robert's storytelling moved even deeper into his experiences at West Central High School, several of his stories seemed to hold central a focus on care as they made visible not only his interactions with teachers but, as well, how he experienced the physical condition of the school. Many teachers, Robert highlighted, followed what seemed to Robert to be a commonplace way at West Central, that is, they made clear it was not their responsibility "to babysit" youth which included "hound[ing]" them to complete and submit their work. Talking specifically about his interactions with his English teacher, Robert explained her attitude toward youth was,

"Do your work or I don't care." In response, Robert highlighted, it did not "take too long for me to start missing that class" and to "stop doing any homework." In turn, Robert said, the English teacher countered with messages such as, "If you're not interested in doing your work, then I'm not interested in continuing this on .... You can do the course ... some other time dear, you know, next semester." She also added that, perhaps, Robert should take *the less academic and rigorous* English 13 rather English 10. English 13, the teacher explained, was taught by another teacher. Robert replied to these messages by "just stop[ping] to go" to class altogether.

Although less common, Robert storied some teachers as caring because they did "hound" students about attending class and doing their work. One of these teachers was Robert's Social teacher. Exploring his interactions with this teacher, Robert stated,

> I went to class most of the time. It really irked the teacher if I didn't show up. She was an excellent teacher .... She cared about every student in her class. It showed .... I got good marks .... It just really made her angry if I wasn't there to get those same [good] marks every day.

It seemed, then, the stories Robert lived as a student were negotiated in relation with those he experienced his teachers as living. In other words, when Robert felt the teacher did not care about him, he quit doing his work and, eventually, attending class. However, when Robert felt his presence in class and who he was as a student mattered to the teacher he would work toward getting "good marks" and attending class "most of the time." In this way it seemed Robert was unwilling to let teachers whom he felt did not care about him define or shape who he was and who he could become. Coming to this realization, I was reminded of Robert's earlier experiences in the D.A.R.E. program. Perhaps, just as Robert would not listen to and engage with learning the ways in which his dad, grandpa, and brother were being defined within this program, Robert was choosing to "just stop" interactions with teachers who were trying to define him in ways that were inconsistent with, or bumped against, his knowing of who he was and who he could become.

Messages of care were also made visible to Robert through the school's physical condition. Exploring areas of the school that were "just disgusting," Robert's stories highlighted a lack of caring about West Central both by the school district personnel, as well as youth. Thinking about how the school district demonstrated their lack of care through "shoddy workmanship" which included a "leaking roof," "water rings all over the ceiling," and "unpainted walls," whereas youth "[spit] on the floor" and "[threw] garbage all over the place," I wondered about possible interconnections between these stories. That is, I wondered if as youth experienced a "run down, beat up school" they felt it did not matter or perhaps that they were even justified to spit and throw garbage on the floors. Noting these behaviors, why did the school district not bother completing maintenance work such as painting walls and replacing stained ceiling tiles?

Attending to Robert's telling of how he experienced, and responded to, stories at West Central such as those highlighted above, I was reminded again of his learning from his mom and maternal grandpa to have a strong work ethic, one which included a story that "no half job is a job done at all." I wondered if it was, as Robert laid these family ethics alongside those he experienced as living out at West Central, that the feeling "I ... don't want to be here" began to shape his thinking.

Grandpa
Dad's father
Told me
Junior high — time to figure out
Going to university?
Or, going to trade school?

Thought about, "What makes sense for me?"
Know I'm going to work with my hands
Do well at it
Know I'm not going to university
Didn't want to sit at a desk

In high school
They want you to take the *academic* courses
That's what they want

Entering into high school, Robert made visible, he carried within himself a story learned from his paternal grandpa, that is, that a purpose of junior high school was for youth to "figure out" if they were "going to university or ... going to trade school" and that senior high school was a time to engage with courses which supported the youth's decision. Thinking about which pathway — university or trade school — made sense for him, Robert highlighted he knew he was "going to work with his hands" and, as well, that he was good at doing so. He explained his knowing drew on multiple background experiences, some of which were: renovating houses with Allan, a family friend, as a part time job throughout junior high; liking and knowing he was competent in shop class; and, working on farm equipment and vehicles with Allan's father-in-law,[6] a retired mechanic.

However, as Robert moved into high school he soon realized that what was foregrounded in this context was not his knowing and his experiences or his grandpa's story but, rather, what teachers and administrators wanted which, according to Robert, was for him to take courses included in the *academic* track. These courses, Robert felt, did not support his decision to attend trade school. Indeed, it seemed, Robert's desire to enter into a trade was neither acknowledged nor supported at West Central. Explaining further, Robert said,

> If they would have said, "Okay, well if you want to go into the trades, you need to have these courses and so let's open up all these dead, empty rooms in these wings." Because when I went to West Central most of the shops were closed down ... [except] automotives and welding. The machine shop still sits there to this day, as far as I know, full of dust. I got the chance both with teachers and behind teachers' backs to go into these other rooms and find out what was there. It made me pretty angry to know that there was a ton of equipment there that had a lot of potential both in equipment and for students that aren't getting trade trained anymore.

Attending closely to Robert's words and thinking further about storylines, made visible in his tellings, I was drawn back to consider again Robert's learning that "option" courses were not "as important" as core curriculum in elementary school. I wondered if, perhaps, the senior high school continuance of this story was teachers' and administrators' desire for youth to focus only on courses included in the *academic* track. If so, had these stories shaped decisions to shut down rooms and programs that supported youth "getting trade trained"?

Grade 11
I was officially still there
Even though I didn't show up anymore
Can't recall what school did about my not showing up
Don't recall talking to a counselor or principal about my attendance

---

6. Robert storied both Allan and his father-in-law as mentors who had each significantly and positively impacted his life.

Don't remember getting suspensions or anything
They probably didn't care

Perhaps similar to how Robert's desires, decisions, and knowing, as shown in the previous word image, seemed invisible at West Central, so, too, did it seem was Robert's progression from "not showing up" for some classes to stopping altogether to "show up" for school. Attending to that Robert's possible explanation of why he could not "recall what the school did about ... [his] not showing up" was that "they probably didn't care," I wondered how these events might have shaped the stories Robert told of school as well as those he told to himself about who he was and who he could become. For example, as Robert left West Central did he internalize a story that his presence in school was insignificant, that is, that his not showing up would have mattered, and been attended to differently, had he been "a someone," perhaps a someone whose educational goals had fit more easily with that which teachers and administrators wanted or a someone who was "on the sports teams ... [or was in] a certain group?" Had Robert left school with a story that he could or would have been more successful if he had more adequately measured up — that is, if he had: fit within the definition and boundaries of what it meant to be an "academic child" at Townsend Elementary; denied that his preferred learning style seemed to be kinesthetic which meant that he learned best through moving, doing, touching and so on; silenced stories taught within his family such as needing to be a good Samaritan and to have a work ethic which included believing "no half job is a job done at all;" and, so on. Coming to these thoughts and questions, I wondered, then, if Robert might have needed to leave school so that he could hold onto educative possibilities[7] of who he could become. With this wonder foremost on my mind, I looked again at the transcripts of Robert's and my conversations. In so doing, I learned from Robert:

School's school
At the time you don't think that it really matters
As far as I can see now it doesn't
Something forced to do
Didn't have a lot of interest, relevancy to me

All the interruptions in class
The Charlie Brown teacher—"Wah, wah, wah, wah" all day long

---

7. Exploring qualities of experience, Dewey (1938) highlighted that an experience is educative, or promotes growth, when it continues to move us forward on "the experiential continuum" (p. 28).

Not a lot of discussion
A lot of repetition
Again and again and again
For example, learn about a science experiment for 4 days sitting in classroom
Then, in science lab for 1day
The learning—it's kind of lost
Just teach by doing the science lab
Then it's relevant
Then you might gain something from it

Have learned a lot outside of school, in the real world
Way more than in school
Being on the farm
Lots of biology
Working at the hazardous waste dump
Lots of chemistry
All of a sudden chemistry is fun, relevant

People learn better by doing
Active learning
Once I get it in my hands
I understand it

I do enjoy learning.

Chapter 5

A Narrative Account of Scott

Marni Pearce

I remember …
the early learner thing
    a really BIG part of my life
a good elementary experience
nothing too dramatic or tragic
the same struggles that every elementary student faces
pretty generic experience

                                One of the rules was
                        you had to take off your shoes
                  when you come in for recess
                          or change your shoes
                            when you go outside

                                              I hated that.

                                                    So
                        instead of changing my shoes
                    I would go and hug the teachers.
                            I would tell them
                            how pretty they were
                                            or
                            how well I did
                                            or
                        what I was learning.

Composing Lives in Transition: A Narrative Inquiry into the Experiences of Early School Leavers
Copyright © 2013 by Emerald Group Publishing Limited
All rights of reproduction in any form reserved
ISBN: 978-1-78052-974-5

                                         And the shoes?
                                          A non-issue.
                              teachers didn't have to do it
                                          why should I?

I remember ...
    junior high school
that's
where it kind of started
    the whole emotional changing
    started missing a lot of school
that's when,
I guess,
the *bullying*   would have started
    getting personal

I remember ...
I came out of grade 7 with a very high average
in grade 8
down
    to
        the
            60's.

the transition grades, 6 and 9,
are very hard
to go
from a comfortable place
    with comfortable authority figures
        and comfortable people
to a completely new place
    no comfortable resources
        new people
            new social atmosphere
I just remember
    feeling
out of place   young   *awkward*

I remember
at the end of grade 6
finally starting to understand things that made you popular

                                what I wore
                             was important
                          and what I said
                             was important
                         and how I looked
                             was important

I remember ... grade 7
being so self conscious
so fearful that people were judging you
I remember the first day
I remember sitting at the back
        being very quiet.

I remember wearing all black
black sweater
black chunky boots
I thought I was cool

I remember liking girls in grade 7
in grade 7 I still liked,
I still liked girls
that's one of the things
I remember   distinctly
about grade 7.

I knew that I was better
than some
but not as good
as the rest

there's a class system
in junior high school
        you have your top rung
        your middle rung
and then
        the bottom rung
I remember realizing that in grade 7,
being very aware of it.

the kind of friends that you initially make on that first day of grade 7
determines the situation for that day
    for the next 3 years of your life
in junior high school
that's where it starts
right?

I remember ...
being aware of the friends I had
and the company that I held
and what I liked to do
and how I dressed
and how I looked
and what my family could afford
   all of those things

I was also very aware
there was a whole 'nuther tier
I wasn't privy to.

    you could see it
    how happy they were
    how beautiful everybody was
    and how it was great fun.
    I remember seeing that
    and knowing that
    and trying to be part of that
    but
    knowing
    I was different
    somehow.

I remember grade 10 – high school
wanting to go there because
it had
independent self directed learning, ISDL
I really loved that idea
I had some friends
   willing to go there with me
I think "my luck has changed"
No longer fearful.
No more black.
Trying to meet as many people as I can

By the end of the first day I had created my own new circle of friends
Top tier.
I'm feeling good
designer clothes
looking good
Life is good.
    But
I'm still insecure
it's just a different kind
of insecure
the kind
you don't talk about.

We all have cover stories
and
one of the ways
to be popular
is to not talk about
your insecurities.
You make yourself look
like you don't have
any.

In October,
I remember ...
    something happens
there was a falling out
between me
and my closest friend

                                      now, it sounds like we were
                                              playing chess
                                    it's pretty much what it was
                                              ... a big game

she was   the queen   of the group

she knew
I collected
    ancient daggers
I trade them   go to trade shows
    just ... a hobby

I knew
> I wasn't going to win
I wasn't going to come out of this with friends.

that day I was
> planning to trade with a friend
it was in my backpack

She accused me
of
outlandish, outrageous things

a friend warned me
> locker search
I knew
> what she was trying to do
> so
I surrendered it instead

I knew
I hadn't done anything wrong
thought
it would all be solved
sorted out

the vice principal recognized there was
> a lie involved
"go home, take the weekend off," he said.
and then
later that day
the principal, who I'd never even met
leaves a message on our voice mail
saying
I was expelled.

now I know they had no right to expel me
without a hearing
without evidence
without informing my parents
but
at the time
I didn't want to go back

                                    I didn't feel I had any power
                                                       once I left
                                              I had no friends

and then
three weeks
spent sitting at home
waiting for the phone to ring
and finally
I'm at a new school
but
a completely different side of the city
less than half the size
but didn't know anybody
but

I remember

thinking that everybody would know
what I had been accused of
all the teachers would know
for sure
I remember thinking
here we go
teachers that are gonna think
I'm some kind of delinquent

I remember thinking
I'm just gonna try to be as quiet and blendy as possible
the first day
wearing nothing that would make me stand out
staying under the radar.
But I remember
skipping class
My mom would drop me off at school
I'd wave goodbye
and I'd walk to the bus stop
and go home

I remember
in grade 10
later on   spring time

I came out
  to my mom
It takes a lot of courage to identify yourself

                    Once I came out of the closet
                         my whole life was different
                    by identifying myself as what I was
                              it grows you stronger
                         sometimes you get reactions
                           people who are supportive
                                         sometimes
                people are indifferent and don't really care
                                          and then
                                         sometimes
                               they say   oh
                                 you're a faggot
                                    that's gross
                I always knew my life would be harder

I make it to grade 11
because I know
I'm smart
and they can't deny a child the right to attend
a certain class
my mom works for Education
so I know things
and I go to the principal
and the teachers
and said, "you're going to put me in these 20 level classes because I know you have to"
and they did
even though
I didn't
necessarily
pass grade 10.
But I know
all you need to get a high school diploma
is credits.
and you can get credits just by attending
and not necessarily completing
or passing the course
but they don't tell people that

I found out
because I read
the policy manual.
If I was smart enough to read the policy manual
I was competent enough to take
Science 20 and Math 20
obviously.

It was important
because
I didn't want to look like a fool.
I didn't want people
to think
I was stupid.

I loved to provoke teachers

I remember
I had a teacher
who was pro-life
and I'm very
pro-choice.
she was preaching
not teaching.
And I would get her going.
I would get her going and
help her have some personality
and my classmates would encourage me.
"get her going today" they'd say
that was one way for me to make friends.

                        the more powerful I appear
                             or make myself
              people are going to want to hear
                        what I have to say

but she engaged me
when I pushed her
instead of telling me that I'm wrong
or that she was the teacher
she just

pushed me back.
I felt valid
like I had something to contribute
I was worth listening too.

                                    Social
                                Humanities
                                    Drama
        I share a personality with those kinds of teachers
                         Science and math people
                                   I don't.
             I've never had an English teacher I didn't like
               I've always been able to discuss literature
                                or politics
                    or personal values, moral beliefs
                    With my math and science teachers
                   there was never room for discussion
                               I always hated that.
                         couldn't stand those classes.

I went to the classes that I felt
were fun
or where
I liked the teachers
or where I thought
they were necessary.
But
at that age
it was like every class
was pretty much
unnecessary
unless I really liked the teacher.
but
I would convince the teacher
not to report my absence
and
I wouldn't get a phone call reporting to my mom
that I had missed the class
and if I was caught out of class
by one of my vice principals
I would just ask them
not to report me
and they wouldn't

I don't know how I did it.
like 212 days
I missed in grade 11 and 12.
I never even got a letter.
how do you get away with that?
but
even though I didn't have a lot of good friends in school
I was close with many of the teachers
I made sure
to get to know
the admin support
the secretaries
the janitorial staff
    I knew them all by first and last name.
Pretty soon we would have coffee together
I remember ...
being invited into the staff room.
and yet
they didn't report my absences.
and if I didn't like an assignment
I would ask for a different one
and I would usually get it.

I stayed 'til grade 12
I completed high school
I just never
finished high school.
I never set out
to not finish
it was just a by-product of choice
    of choosing not to attend classes
    or not completing enough work.

at the end of grade 12
I just knew
that I didn't care enough
and graduating
wasn't important to me
and going to grad
wasn't important to me

I didn't care
because I always knew
    that I didn't need a high school diploma to define myself

              or to get a job
                    or go to college or university.

I remember
no one ever approached me
and stopped me in the hall
and said   "you can't graduate"

I still don't identify myself
as
a
high
school
drop
out.

that's not who I am
I'm not
a
high
school
drop
out.

I just chose not to finish
high school.

Chapter 6

A Narrative Account of Jasmine

Yi Li

I Had Big Dreams: Jasmine's Stories

> Every child dreams to be a doctor first. That one was gone when I realized that I don't like hospitals. My second goal was to work for the United Nations. I wanted to travel and help people in the third-world countries. The third area I was interested in was pharmacy.

I first met Jasmine on a snowy Saturday morning in mid-March 2008. I had been working on a planning committee to provide newcomer students with additional support in a local high school since May 2007. I came to know a youth worker on that committee and really admired what he had been doing with the newcomer youth. I told him a little bit about this project and how difficult it had been to find youth participants. It so happened that Claire also knew him. Through several emails, phone calls and visits, eventually Claire arranged for Jasmine and me to meet and talk. I phoned Jasmine the night before, telling her that I would come and pick her up. We had agreed to meet on the University of Alberta campus because Jasmine needed to go downtown for a youth group meeting afterward.

When Jasmine and I arrived at the Hope House, it was already 10:40 a.m. I showed her around from the basement to the attic, and she was very impressed by the children's hope artwork. We finally settled down at the small round table in the Jack Chesney Library and began our first conversation. As we went through the informed consent forms, I asked why

---

Composing Lives in Transition: A Narrative Inquiry into the Experiences of Early School Leavers
Copyright © 2013 by Emerald Group Publishing Limited
All rights of reproduction in any form reserved
ISBN: 978-1-78052-974-5

she was interested in participating in this research. "I want to help other youths," she told me.

In the following 3 months, I met Jasmine two more times for our research conversations at the Hope House. As I sat beside her at the small round table in the library with a cup of tea and some snacks in front of us, I listened to her stories about her life in central and northern Africa and in Canada.

Life in a Central African Country: I Could Read Perfectly in Grade 4!

Born in June 1987, Jasmine's young life has been greatly affected by the war in a central African country. She was separated from her mother when she was only 8 months old. The war was getting closer to her birth place, a small city in the south. Her grandmother had to take her to the capital city in the north to join her big brother, who had moved there several months before they did.

> My mom was left behind because she got married again to a man from a small village in a different tribe. Her father-in-law and his tribe wouldn't let her go. Once they take a woman to their village they never let her go as if they own her for good. She and the man had four children. The man died in 1998, but her son and the other people wouldn't let my mom go. She somehow escaped, but she left two older children behind and took the two younger ones with her. She's in another African country right now.

Jasmine has not seen her mother again since then. She and her big brother were raised by their grandmother, uncles, and aunts.

Jasmine cannot remember the exact year when she went to kindergarten.

> ... because back home in order for a child to go to kindergarten, she or he has to lose teeth. It is weird, but children lose their teeth when they turn 5 or 6. So that's when they go to kindergarten. Sometimes a Grade 1 class might consist of mixed-age children, ranging from 5 year old to 13 year old.

But she remembered that she went to a K-9 Catholic School in the capital city. It was a one-story school house with nine classrooms, each with about

20–30 children in it. The children sang songs and recited poems in Arabic, the common language, in kindergarten (Jasmine still knows a little bit about her tribal language). They had to memorize them and pass a test before moving on to Grade 1; otherwise, they would stay in the same class for another year. She cannot remember what she did during Grade 1, 2, or 3, but she knew that she learned to read perfectly in Arabic in Grade 4 when she was about 9 or 10 years old. Besides reading, she also studied religion and math. She seemed to do quite well in school at that time.

> I also remember the students sitting beside me in Grade 4 used to copy me on the tests. One of my friends told me to write all the wrong answers first and let them copy and then erase all and do the right ones. It worked because these students stopped copying from others. They had no idea of whether the answers were right or wrong. They just wrote them down. They did not pay attention in class. They did not study.

Jasmine went to school with her cousins. She also had a lot of friends in school. She liked school.

> I liked school. It was fun to read. My grandmother didn't pressure us. I lived with my brother, grandmother, two uncles and an aunt who were not married at that time. It was fun to go to school. When we came home everything was ready. So we ate the food and went out to play and then do our homework. It was fun. I was not complaining.

The fact that one of her uncles was a teacher at the school also helped. She behaved herself and did her homework. At that time, it was a common practice for teachers to beat students with some light wire hoses if they did not do well or misbehaved in the classroom. She was rarely beaten up because she was scared, she told me. She probably did not want to be publicly humiliated on report card day, either.

> On report card day, teachers used to announce all the students from the highest grade to the failing one, students who passed and who failed. If a student failed and was at the bottom of the class, the rest of the class would chase him or her all the way to his/her house. They would sing a song and call him/her a failure. They found it very effective to those failed students because when they came back the following year they would try to do better. Nobody wanted to be chased home like that or to be called a failure.

Growing up as a Catholic in this African country, Jasmine remembered the religious tension:

> I remember at one time the President came up with a rule that everybody should wear hijabs. But we were Catholics and we wouldn't wear a hijab. The situation went really bad. We wore hijabs for a couple of days and then the President dismissed that rule. They tried to make everything Muslim. They tried to control people. That's why they did that.

Jasmine began her Grade 5 in September 1998 but did not finish it in her home country. She moved to the capital city of a northern African country on March 3, 1999, because of the advice from another uncle. At that time, he was studying in a university there. He thought that schools in that country were better. Her grandmother encouraged her to go for a better education. Jasmine left her home country with her brother, cousins, uncle, and aunt. Her grandmother chose to stay behind.

Life in a Northern African Country: I Was Among the Top 10 in My Class!

After Jasmine arrived in this country with her family, she continued to do Grade 5 in the following school year (1999–2000) at a Catholic school, which was the only school for her fellow students from her home country in that capital city. Because the school did not have enough classrooms, they had to offer a morning and an afternoon session to accommodate all the students. Jasmine went to school in the afternoon for her Grade 5. She switched to the morning session for her Grade 6, 7, and 8.

The classrooms were really big and there were 36 students in her class. They sat in rows. Jasmine did not experience any difficulty moving from her Grade 5 in her home country to Grade 5 in this new country. It was the same system and the same language, Arabic, but somehow she sensed the difference.

> I don't know why, but I could remember better in this new place. It was different. They had different textbooks. Everything was different, but the language was the same. The subject math was lower back in my home country. The learning there was lower than that in this new place. I think that was the difference.

In order to catch up and do well on all the school subjects, Jasmine began to focus and study really hard. She was also a member of a study group of six girls. They were all her friends in one class. They went together for evening classes and communion classes. If they had trouble in math, they would all go for math classes. They were busy every night. When the exams came, they would be given a 2-week break to study. During those 2 weeks, every day Jasmine and her friends would go to somebody's house and study. The next day they would go to another person's house and study. They just studied and studied. They didn't do anything else because they liked to study all the time.

The teachers at that school were all graduates from the same school. They were very strict with the students. Jasmine told me about her teachers: "They would give us homework every single day and we had to hand it in at 7:30 sharp in the morning. If we didn't, we would get beaten up badly."

I was surprised when Jasmine told me that the principal of that school was her uncle, too. He was related to her family. "There was always someone related to me in school," she said with a smile.

Jasmine thrived in this school and was among the top 10 in her class of 36 students for 2 years. She was an academically strong student and she worked very hard to achieve her goals.

> On the report card day, there was a big celebration. The teacher in each class would announce students' names from number 1 to number 10 and gave them presents. For the rest of the students, they didn't call them in front of people. Students would feel good when they could get something. I won two prizes. I passed and I was among the top 10 in my Grade 6 and 7. I missed my Grade 8 exams. If I had stayed, I would have probably received another prize because I always studied hard. Studying with my friends, I found it easier to memorize things. I used to know all the names for the parts of the human body in Arabic for my biology class.

Jasmine's face lit up when she said this. She seemed to remember the sense of pride and happiness she felt at that time. School was a very important part in her life then.

However, in the wider community, there were a lot of tensions between her people and the locals. Jasmine heard many horror stories about how her people working in the local houses as house maids were killed or abused. She used to be very scared of the local people and never made any friends except talking to one girl neighbor. "Our balconies were connected. So when I came out, she came out and we talked. We didn't go out though. We just talked through the balcony sometimes."

That girl neighbor went to a private girl-only Catholic school, where Jasmine and her friends played basketball with the girls from that school in the evening. They had a lot of fun practicing for tournaments for their own teams.

Unfortunately, that was probably the only positive experience Jasmine had with the local people. Most of her other experiences were quite negative, sometimes even frightening. She told me a story about how she was caught up in a racial conflict between her people and the local people on a hot summer day in 2000. At the time, she did not realize that her life was actually in danger.

> One of my school friends and I were walking home from the soccer practice field when she suggested that we stop by our school. She wanted to wash her hands. The church was full of people on that Thursday. There was a prayer for some people traveling to Australia. They also had invited some actresses to perform a play in a traditional way. So many people came to watch that play. When we were going out we saw many of our people coming and running towards the church. We wondered what had happened, but nobody wanted, or had the time to tell us. They kept pushing us because we were walking out and they were running in. Luckily, we met my aunt and she took us right back into the church. It turned out that dozens of local people were chasing after some of our guys because of a traffic accident involving a local bus driver and a pedestrian. It escalated to a violent fight. When we closed the church door the locals started banging on it. They were trying to find a way to get in, but all these men used an African shield to hold the door. The locals burned the pastor's car outside the church and they pushed it to the door. The door was very hot. And then they put gas in a Pepsi bottle, lit it up and threw it into the church. It was really bad. I had no idea what was happening. We were sleepy during the whole fight. We just slept here and there. My aunt kept taking us from the church to the classrooms and then back to the church, just to keep us away from those local people. After hours and hours of fighting, at last the police came. They chased those locals away. They didn't arrest anybody. The police used those big police trucks to take us home. Some people were scared. They were worried that the police would take them to jail. But others thought that it was better to get in there than die here. We got in the police trucks and they sent us home. It was bad.

It was still daylight when Jasmine and her friend went into the church. When they finally went home it was already 1:00 or 2:00 in the morning.

Because of those conflicts and tensions, Jasmine's uncle would not let her work with the locals even though she was begging to have a job at that time. It was too dangerous for young people, he would say.

Jasmine was busy preparing for her final exams in Grade 8 when her family's application for refugee status in Canada was approved in May 2002.

> I was studying very hard. I was doing the study group. We were getting ready for the finals — math, English, social, biology and chemistry. We had five or six subjects in one day. We needed to pass all the subjects in order to move to the next level.

Jasmine really missed those 3 years in that northern African country. She was happy with who she was and felt very successful with her academic studies then. She had a lot of fun with her friends both in and out of school. However, when she moved to a northern city in Alberta, Canada, to join her uncle and his family, her transition into a Canadian high school was not an easy one.

Life in Canada: My English is Not Good Enough!

Jasmine came directly to this northern city in May 2002 to join her uncle and his family. She spent the first 4 months hanging out with other students from her home country who lived in the same neighborhood. They used to play basketball at a neighborhood park, and her uncle was their coach. When school started in September, Jasmine went to Grade 10 at a local high school.

> I started Grade 10 at this school in September 2002. There was no Grade 9 for me. My uncle picked this school for me because his son used to go there. Most students from my home country go there. They like to stick together for some reason.

Previously Jasmine studied all her school subjects in Arabic and did very well. She only started learning English after she arrived in Canada. Therefore, the initial language barrier seemed very daunting for her. She remembers this one incident when her school principal asked her to be a translator and realized how limited/limiting her English was to express her ideas:

> I remember there was this girl, who had just come from the same northern African country. They took her to a different

> high school, where there were no Arabic-speakers. So she couldn't communicate with anyone. She didn't know any word in English. Finally the principal called my high school because he knew that our school had many students from my home country. They called me to go and translate for them. I didn't know anything in English then. I knew just a little bit of English words. But I didn't say no. When I talked to this girl on the phone, we talked for 15 minutes. We talked and laughed in Arabic while the principal and two other people were waiting for me to tell them something. I could only tell them that she did not like it here, that she was scared and that she couldn't understand anything. I only told them one word or one short sentence because my English was not good. They were expecting much more from me. And I remember telling myself, "You thought you knew English and you were just lying".

Fortunately, she met a very good ESL teacher during her first year in that high school.

> I started ESL level one with Mrs. M. I was very comfortable with her. She made a lot of students feel this way. She talked softly and clearly. It helped. She pointed out everything well. Everything was good. I somehow understood what she was saying. I don't know how, but I understood her. She always talked slowly and she used her hands.

Jasmine studied only ESL for that year. The school modified the curriculum and taught them ESL math, ESL social studies, and ESL religion in addition to the ESL classes. She did very well for that year.

For Grade 11, Jasmine studied ESL Level 2 and 3 with Mrs. S, who was just there for a year because the regular teacher was on holiday. In Jasmine's memory, Mrs. S was nice and loud. She taught math, science, social studies, and English. Some students found Mrs. S annoying, but Jasmine thought that she was just trying to push them to do well at school. She liked Mrs. S and didn't have any problems with her.

Jasmine also took Math 14, Science 14, and Religion 15. In addition, she took fashion and cosmetology during that year. The two teachers teaching these two courses were her favorite teachers because in their classes she experienced a sense of connection with her past.

> I found cosmetology fun because of the different hands-on activities. You got to put the makeup on the mannequin and

do some sewing. I loved sewing, but I did not know how to cut. Back in my home country all my aunts sewed and they taught me how to sew. I don't know how we used to do it, but it was really perfect. We used our own hands to sew our own dolls. Here we used machines. I learned a lot from these two courses. I learned to sew with a machine. I learned the names of the threads and the needles. I didn't know the needle or the thread or the bobbin before. I made a quilt, a hoodie, a skirt, a purse and a bag.

In Grade 12, Jasmine began the self-directed learning program at her high school. She had mixed feelings about this unique education program.

I liked the self-directed learning when I got used to it, especially with English. It was good because it made you think more instead of depending on a teacher all the time to explain things. But sometimes it was hard when it came to science and math. I needed a teacher to help me catch up with something. Even if I asked them for more help, it still was not enough.

Jasmine was not very good at math. When she took Math 24 with Mrs. G, she was motivated to learn. If she didn't understand something, Mrs. G would go through it again. Jasmine thought that Mrs. G was a very good teacher because she explained well. However, her other math learning experiences were not as pleasant.

In schools there are some teachers that are not good. In January 2006, I was supposed to take Math 10 pure, but I dropped it because of the teacher. He was not really doing his job. He didn't help when I asked him for help. He would say to me, "Oh, great, a Grade 1 student can even do that. Why are you taking this? You're supposed to be in ESL or something."

Some teachers would tell Jasmine all the time that her English was not good enough to do this or that. She felt deeply hurt and discouraged. I could hear her frustration and anger when she said to me,

Maybe I didn't speak English very well, but for me, I had no problems writing and reading in English. I could understand things. But they just judge you by the way you talk. They would tell you that your English is not good enough so you can't take this. Even my level 4 ESL teacher Mrs. A told me

> that. She even made me repeat ESL level 4 when I passed.
> I got 67 and my friend got 50 something. She kept both of us.

Jasmine couldn't understand why the teacher made her repeat the course. She found ESL level 4 easy because she loved mythologies, short stories, and poetry. She loved reading and writing in English. The teacher brought something new every day and they had exams almost every week. As a matter of fact, Jasmine didn't even notice that she was repeating a class until one of her friends pointed it out to her later.

> The other ESL classes were very boring, the level 1, 2, and 3. We did the same things every day, math, grammar. They would hand us papers and we had to fill them out. It was the same routine every day, very boring. That's why I never noticed that I was repeating a class that I didn't even go to because most of the time she would tell me to go to the learning center to do religion or something else. I didn't understand what she told me. She said that my English was weak. But it was only the speaking. I had no problems with my writing.

I shook my head in disbelief as Jasmine told me this story. I wondered when this additional language support might become an obstacle for ESL students like Jasmine. There seemed to be a glass ceiling — a limit to what Jasmine was expected to be able to achieve at school. Therefore, her ideas of jumping into higher level courses were often discouraged by her teachers. I wondered how many ESL students like Jasmine are being artificially maintained in these special kinds of language-based classes.

At the time, Jasmine was so happy because she thought that she was going to pass her ESL level 4 and to take high school English Language Arts (ELA) finally. She wanted to go to university and become a doctor or a pharmacist or work for the United Nations, so she was eager to take those academic and university-bound courses. That was her dream, her story to live for. However, when she wanted to take ELA in summer school, this ESL level 4 teacher told her not to.

> She even called my uncle and told him that my English was not good enough and that I shouldn't take English 10-2 in the summertime. She told me to go and drop it because I had already registered. She told me to take something else. I said OK, just to shut her up. My uncle also told me not to drop it. So I took it and I passed. I took it in the summer school. I didn't tell her though. But she knew I passed it. I think she

> received the marks when the school started and she didn't say anything to me. She was my advisor and my teacher at the same time. I don't know why she did that to me. I never took the time to ask her or something because I just let it slide. I just wanted to forget it. I wouldn't take it as racist but maybe she had a problem with me.

These negative messages teachers gave to Jasmine, whether it was the low expectations or straight put-downs, or harmful insults, were very injurious to her identity, to her sense of who she was and who she might become. Sadly, the only source of hope for Jasmine at that time was from home. Fortunately, she has a very supportive uncle at home. He always encouraged her to do well at school and spent time helping her with school work.

> My uncle always encouraged me when I went home. He makes me feel good about myself. He believes in me. He is really good. But when I came to school I felt like nothing's going to work out. My uncle used to help me do my homework. He used to tell me that I could do well in school. I remember when I took science 10 in the summer school of 2004, he helped me do my homework every day because the summer school is very short and very intensive and I never took science in English before. He helped me go through it and I passed it. In fact, summer school was the only time that I could take high school courses. If I waited till the school year, they wouldn't give me the courses that I actually wanted.

As Jasmine was speaking, I wondered what was going on with the school and why such decisions were made. I wondered why the school seemed reluctant to move ESL students into regular programming.

When Jasmine came back for her fourth year at her high school, taking Grade 12 again in September 2005, she told the school to get a different teacher advisor for her. They did; Mr. M was very nice to Jasmine. No matter what school subjects Jasmine wanted to take, he would register her in them. At that time, Jasmine was struggling to decide which math to take because she was not good at math.

> If I asked him for Math 10 pure, he would give me the slip. After a couple of days, I dropped it and asked if I could get Math 20 pure and then Math 20 applied. He gave it to me, but I dropped it again because of the teachers. They were no help at all. One day they made me really pissed. I went to this teacher for help. But when he saw me coming he just left and

ran away. He was my study seminar teacher, so he knew that I was coming and he ran away. And then this student teacher, he couldn't even figure out how to put in the graph in this big calculator. I sat there for almost an hour and he was just on the calculator trying to figure out how to put in the graph and he couldn't. I got pissed. That's when I dropped it. Holy! I couldn't take it. And math was my weakness so that's why I dropped it.

I sensed a lot of anger in Jasmine's words. There seemed to be a shift in the language she used to describe this experience. Sadly, Jasmine was not the only student who had those very negative experiences within the school. Many of her fellow students had similar experiences. They often sat together and talked about it.

We were scared. If we told the principal he would tell the teachers and the teachers would turn against us even more. So it would be bad. That's why we just kept it to ourselves. We didn't tell the principal. Actually we had this counsellor, who spoke our language and worked at our school. We went to him and we told him about those teachers. But he warned us not to take any action because if we did it might get worse. We thought about it and agreed that the teachers would turn against us. That was what he told us too. He told us just not to bother. Even if we spoke up they might do that to a coming new student. They might do worse. So that's why it's better not to let them know what they're doing.

I sighed inside as I listened to Jasmine. School was not a safe and comfortable place for Jasmine and many of her peers. Knowing that her uncle was always supportive of her efforts to do well at school through the stories she had told me, I changed the topic and asked Jasmine why she didn't let her uncle know what was happening at school at that time.

But when I went to school, I felt discouraged. Of course, I didn't tell my uncle what was happening in school because my uncle talks too much and he would react. I didn't want any fist fights. We only told the school counsellor. He even agreed with us that we should not tell the principal of the school what the teachers were doing. He thought if we did, the principal was going to tell the teachers, who would still be mean. They were not going to tell us exactly what was wrong, but they would have some changes and we wouldn't like that. The teachers did not treat some of the students well at that time. If I told him anything, he would go to school and mess up everything. He knew all the teachers. He is like a politician. He knows everybody. He's crazy. So that's why I didn't tell him anything.

In fact, Jasmine never thought of telling her uncle at that time. She seemed to have been caught between a rock and a hard place, feeling powerless both at school and at home. Looking back, she thought that maybe she should have told him. She knew that he would have done something about it. He would have pushed those teachers into doing something different. She wished that she could go back and tell him why she decided to leave school, or rather, why she was pushed out of school.

I decided to stay out of school in September 2006. I didn't go back to school since then. I stopped. I felt like even if I did better I wouldn't get anywhere. I don't know. It was only me. I was feeling down about everything at that time. I had a lot of goals, but it felt like I wouldn't reach them even if I tried to work hard at something.

Outside school, the youth community that Jasmine was a part of was also falling apart. With deep sadness, she told me:

All the youth used to be OK. But now some of them drink alcohol, others do drugs and girls get pregnant. Everybody used to be happy and respectful. Nobody used to do stuff that was illegal or bad. We used to be together. We used to have community youth parties and meetings. The president then was very good. She was very creative and talented. She came up with good ideas and made people actually want to come to meetings and talk about things. We had barbecues, played games and had a good time, all kinds of names for the parties, classic parties, dressed and pressed parties, red carpet parties. We invented those names. But then some people gossiped behind her and she decided that she did not want anything to do with us and the community any more. So it collapsed and all of it went down. The last president for the group was very careless. He lost the money that we raised for the community. We would give the money to someone in need just in case something happened in the community. He ate money. He ate people's money. He was careless calling people for meetings. Everything went down. People used to be happy and stay

> together and have fun. Now there is a lack of communication between people and everybody went to the wrong direction. I am just worried about the next generation that's coming. The community actually would love to bring the youth back together. But when they call the children to have meetings with them, the children won't go. They don't like the idea of old people telling them what to do. Yet they themselves can't bring it back together again.

Jasmine thought that if her uncle decided to do something about the situation, it might work because he knew how to be with the children. However, he was busy taking care of the younger children with homework club and activities every Saturday from 1 to 3 p.m. He invited children from Grades 7 to 10 to come, get help, play, and have fun. He had some government funding for that program and the children liked that program.

Although Jasmine's high school has a fourth year program for returning students called Ascension, Jasmine felt that she was running out of time and that she had nowhere to go to continue her education. A dream she had at that time was very telling about how she felt cornered and blocked to move forward.

> I had a dream two years ago around this time. I was sleeping in the living room in my aunt's house after braiding my friend's hair. I hated sleeping there but I did. Then I had a dream that the dining room window was open and that there were three wolves outside walking by the backyard. I saw rain. So I got up to close the window before they got in the house. But by the time I got closer to the dining table one wolf outside the window already started coming in through the window. He was soaking wet. So I tried to run to close the door, but I couldn't move. I was just standing there. I couldn't move back and forth. I couldn't scream. I couldn't do anything. I never saw the other two wolves again. So that dream makes me think a lot about something's holding me back when I'm trying to move forward. That was the weirdest dream, but I never sleep in the living room again. I never had dreams like that before.

After leaving school, Jasmine worked at different kinds of jobs. In fact, she had begun working on a part-time basis since she was in Grade 10. Her first job was a catering job in the summer of 2003. She worked 8–10 hours a day, once or twice a week.

> I did not like the schedule because I worked very late and it was hard to get home. I had to call somebody to come and pick me up and then they got pissed because sometimes I finished work around 2 or 3 o'clock in the morning. Sometimes I just slept over at my friend's. That was not good.

It took Jasmine a while to find her second job at a machinery company. One of her friends found this job and asked her to go and check it out together. They were both hired to start the night shift there. So every day after school Jasmine and her friend went to work. She had worked there for 3 years since Grade 11. "I liked working there, but it was too far away from my house. It took me almost 2 hours to get home, which I really hated because I hated going home really late."

However, Jasmine met a good friend there. This friend came from one of the Asian countries and was her reference. He often encouraged her to go back to school. He himself went to school part time and at the time of our conversation he was promoted to become a manager.

Jasmine also worked at a Dollar Store for 4 months, but she didn't like that job. She then worked at a Tim Hortons before going to a local college in September 2007. She took English 20-1 and math because she was told to.

> Because it was student funding, I felt like they were taking control of me somehow. They decided what I should take. So I didn't like it and I dropped out. There were two courses that I really wanted to take so that I could get into the goal I wanted. But they kept saying the same thing that my English was not good enough and that I wouldn't survive in that field and all this stuff. So I just dropped out. I would just save my own money and go to school and then pay for myself.

So she did. She found another job and worked really hard to save some money for school.

> I get up at 6 in the morning and give myself 20 minutes to shower and get ready to catch a bus at 6:20. The work starts at 7. I like it that way because I finish at 3:30. I go home and just read my books.

Jasmine's aunt had advised her to take business because she could have her own business and work in a lot of places. At first, Jasmine didn't like the idea. She didn't want to do it. When her aunt said that she could even open a salon, she thought more about it. It so happened that one of her friends knew that Jasmine was struggling to find a better school to go to and invited her to come along to talk with an education counsellor at another local college. Jasmine finally decided to go to that college and study business.

> My uncle is going with me to register for the business administration and marketing program at that college. He said the form is hard to fill out. I think he just wants to make sure everything is correct. I can't wait to go back to school. September seems really far away.

I was so happy and relieved to hear the excitement in her voice as she shared this great news with me. She wanted to go back to her home country and open her own business one day.

> I am trying to open my own business back home when I am done. I want to go back home. My uncle thinks if I go there I will have better opportunities and better jobs. My uncle is a businessman too. He is in ... He said this is going to be good. The English-educated people will have better opportunities than the Arabic-speaking people. I know both English and Arabic now. So it's better. It helps in the workplaces in my home country. Most of the African countries use either French or English as one of the official languages. So it will help me to communicate with them.

Jasmine wondered why it had taken her so long to apply for Canadian citizenship. She just sent in her application package on January 28, 2008. She wanted to have a Canadian passport so that she could travel safely back to her home country.

Toward the end of our third conversation on June 17, 2008, I asked Jasmine what it had been like for her to participate in this research study. She said,

> It makes me feel good to talk about these things that I have been keeping for so long. Nobody ever asked me to talk about these things and I thought I don't remember anything from way back. It helped me to think back. It was a good experience for me. I learned to remember.

It was very difficult to say goodbye to Jasmine and I didn't know how and when to tell her that I was moving to Winnipeg in a week for a new job. So I took Jasmine to my office in Education North, which was almost empty except several psychology textbooks that were left behind on the shelf. I broke the news to her there and she was very surprised and asked me why

I didn't tell her earlier. She was very sad that I was leaving. But she also told me that she felt happy for me that I had this new job.

I was very surprised when Jasmine showed great interest in the psychology textbooks and asked me if she could have them. She took almost all of them. I gave her a shopping bag to hold the books. She said that she was very interested in studying psychology at university, but was told that she wouldn't be good at it and that it was very difficult to find a job in that field. Someone couldn't get a job in 20 years. I asked who said that. Some teachers at her high school, she replied. I shook my head and sighed.

I walked Jasmine to the bus stop and hugged her goodbye, wishing her good luck for her studies at the college in September 2008.

Chapter 7

A Narrative Account of Andrew[1]

D. Jean Clandinin

Our first meeting (April 16, 2008) was in a coffee shop, a noisy, friendly spot where the cappuccino machine hissed and steamed in the background. Sean, a high school teacher on sabbatical, knew Andrew and invited him to participate in our study. Sean had offered to introduce Andrew and I, and we had planned to meet the week before (April 11, 2008) at this coffee shop. However, Sean and I waited for an hour or so and Andrew had not come. I had been nervous the week before and even more nervous this time. I worried that Andrew would not be comfortable telling his stories to someone who was part of an educational institution. I wondered how Andrew felt and wondered why he had not come the week before.

Sean had come along with Andrew this time and, after he introduced us, he retreated to another spot in the café and left Andrew and I to talk. After we went through the ethics materials and Andrew signed, we began to talk. This was the first of three talks that Andrew and I had. Each one stretched past an hour. Our meetings stretched over about 6 months, from April to October, and we had talked briefly again. This first one was in the coffee shop but subsequent ones were in my office at the university.

Andrew was about 19, tall, with the height of a basketball player. Even dressed in jeans and casual clothes, it was hard not to notice him and I learned to listen very carefully as he spoke softly and carefully. As we came to know each other a bit, we often laughed together and I began to see his

---

1. A version of this chapter also appears in *Engaging in Narrative Inquiry* by D. Jean Clandinin @Left Coast Press, Inc.

gentle sense of humor. When we met again in the fall of 2008, Andrew's clothes had become trendier and I sensed he was changing his style.

While we began with his stories of school when he told me he had gradually drifted away from school in the middle of his Grade 12 year after he was kicked off the basketball team, I came to see the layers of family and community support in which his life was nested. He had been out of school since about January of 2007, more than a year at the time of our first meeting.

Relationships

As Andrew and I talked, I began to see his life as situated in complex nested relationships. Over the months of our conversations, Andrew gradually shared more and more about who he was in his family. At first I learned he lived at home with his mother, a nurse, and often spoke of his two older brothers, now both married, who owned a restaurant. His brothers both finished high school and also were involved with sports. He spoke fondly of his nieces and nephews and of spending quality time with them. He said,

> I have a lot of like kids in my family and me and one of my cousins we're like the oldest so usually ... there's babysitting that needs to be done. We obviously have to do it so I'm usually like around a lot of kids and both my brothers have two kids.

As we spent more time together I learned that his mother had come to Canada from one of the islands in the West Indies and had first settled in New Brunswick before moving to Edmonton. He was born in Edmonton. His father was no longer a central figure in his life.

He spoke of being close with his brothers but also of being "close with cousins." As he spoke more of his life, stories of a family that was spread from Edmonton to an island in the West Indies began to be told. He spoke of how his mom, grandmother, aunts, and cousins had traveled to the West Indies a couple of years ago to visit cousins and aunts and uncles who still lived there. They stayed with his grandmother's sister and, as he described his time there, I learned that family, sports, and a strong church connection held the family together over the distances. He spoke of cousins who lived there who also played sports, "soccer, basketball, cricket." As he told me about these cousins, he spoke of cousins who also moved to Edmonton about 6 years ago and how the strength of family connections persisted over the years and miles.

Andrew indicated "all of my mom's sisters and brothers are here" in Alberta, mostly in Edmonton with one in a community just north of

Edmonton. Later he said one was in another place in the Caribbean. He is also still connected with his father's family who also live in Edmonton. As he spoke, I learned of his mom's cousins and one of his grandmother's sisters and children who also live here.

Family matters to Andrew. The layers of relationships run deep as they stretch across generations and miles. While there was no doubt that family mattered to Andrew, Andrew also mattered to his family. In our third conversation, I was just beginning to understand all the people who lived in Andrew's extended family. As Andrew said, "We're pretty close all of us. We hang out pretty much every weekend." Church was one of the places where they all came together. Family and the church were bound together.

Being a Responsible Member of His Family

As Andrew shared stories of helping out by taking care of his brothers' children, of working in the restaurant his brothers own, of helping out with the foster children who came to stay in his home, and of trying to support his extended family members, I had a strong sense that he had learned to live a story of being a responsible family member.

Paying his own way appeared to be part of this. Since he was old enough to hold a job, Andrew has worked to earn money to support himself while living at home. While he was in high school, he worked at a store in a large mall. When he left school, he worked first for a grocery store, and, for a while, also worked in construction. Eventually he quit the grocery store and kept working in construction. By the time I saw him in the fall of 2008, he was working at a car lot.

Belonging to a Church

The church connection was a strong influence in the stories that Andrew learned to live and tell in his family. His extended family has a strong connection to a particular faith. I sense the church has been part of the extended family's life from before they came to Canada.

I learned of the church connection in the first conversation when Andrew told me that his mother had moved him to the Logos school. He said,

> Well, my family is Christian so my mom thought it would be good for me to go to a school like that so she moved me from elementary to that 'cause that was the first year it actually opened up so she decided to put me into there.

In our second conversation I spoke of his faith and he responded by telling me, "I always have been going to church since I was little and I still go." As we talked he spoke of how "the youth pastor and me get along really well ... and we always play basketball every Sunday ... so it's good." As we spoke more of the church connection he began to speak of how his whole family goes to the church. Later, in the third conversation, he spoke of the church as the place where his extended family connects on a weekly basis.

He also spoke of bible study groups and church events on Fridays and "then usually on Sundays a bunch of us will go play basketball at the school associated with the church." As he said, "They let us use it, like they let all the church members use the gym that they have to do sports and whatever it is. So we usually do that on Sundays."

As I listened to Andrew's stories, I began to see how his life with basketball and the church were interwoven. As Andrew tells his story, sports was a major thread in junior and senior high school but also in his life in the church and in the community. Even after he left the high school, he continued to play basketball at the YMCA, in the community, and at the church.

Playing Sports

Andrew's love for, and ability in, a range of sports created connections for him in his family where his cousins, both here in Edmonton and in the West Indies, also played sports. His mother and his brothers approved of, and encouraged him in, his love of sports. His love of sports also connected him to the church where his youth pastor encouraged him to continue to play and to develop as an athlete.

Sports seemed like an intergenerational activity that cut across the places and people of Andrew's extended family. The first mention of sports was when Andrew said "I was playing soccer when I was around, in Grade 4 I started playing soccer. I was just playing that on the school team and a club team." He played soccer "until Grade 7 and then after that I started playing basketball ... that was part of the junior high school and the community. I was playing both." He played both sports until he was at the end of Grade 8 or the start of Grade 9. He stopped playing soccer, because

> two sports was just too hard 'cause in school I was playing basketball for the school and then soccer I was playing for the community and the club teams, and it was kind of hard to do two sports every day.

Andrew said he liked both sports,

> but I just figured that I was playing basketball in the school so that could have got me better than playing soccer outside of school. If I was playing both of them in the school then it would have been a tough decision.

His intention was to "figure out which one I want to do and just focus on that one and get better at that one sport."

As I listened to Andrew tell of the place of sports in his life, he said, "It has always been about basketball in junior high too, but, like the teachers in junior high, they seemed more caring and understanding so I kinda like got along with them, like really well." Sports were the central thread in his life and it was being able to play sports, particularly basketball, that kept him involved.

> I'd just go to school and play basketball and I had good times in doing like school stuff, so, and in high school, it was a big change from how the teachers were in junior high to high school so then that's like when I was, I just like really focused on just wanting to play basketball.

Andrew continued to play sports, mainly basketball, both in and out of school, during his junior high school years. He spoke of the support of his junior high school gym teacher whose daughter he met while playing "club basketball." By the end of junior high school he had to choose one sport and concentrate on it and he chose basketball. He did, however, mention that when he was in Grade 11 he played some volleyball on the school team "for fun."

When it came time to choose a high school, Andrew selected the high school because of their interest in having him play basketball. As he said, "'Cause I just liked the, I had been talking to the coach since I was in, like Grade 6, so, kinda like had a bond there so I decided to go there." He agreed when I said, "So it's been about basketball for a long time." Andrew's story of himself was composed around being a basketball player.

In all of our conversations, sports, particularly basketball, came up repeatedly. He spoke of playing basketball on the university campus with his cousin who was studying there, of playing at the Y, of being recruited by professional teams. Even after he was out of school, he continued to practice,

> with, like guys that I know that play on the college teams so I just, so I keep up with them and like, then I can keep up with

anybody else and once a week I go and practice with the team that they have now. My cousin plays on the university team so I practice with them.

When we talked in April and May, he said he continued to play basketball 3 days a week. Even as he began compose who he wanted to be and what he wanted to do in his future career, he wanted to continue to be involved with sports in some way.

While it is difficult for Andrew to speak about how talented and skilled he is at basketball, I learned from listening closely that his high school team has traveled extensively to other countries to play and that Andrew was an excellent player on the team.

Sports, particularly playing basketball, provided the coherence that held his life together. Without understanding his desire to play sports and his excellence as a basketball player, it is difficult to understand his stories of school.

Making Sense through Music

As he spoke of his love for Rap and Hip-Hop, Andrew told me that in the music

> people like to talk about their life and like how they went to school and things happened and they had to drop out whether to like take care of their family and stuff so, like listening to that, it makes me think that I'm not the only one who had, like the problem where I got unfortunate and had to deal with all that stuff. So it keeps me going too.

Andrew himself does some rapping and was part of a musical group when he was in Grade 10. They performed at the opening ceremonies for a big basketball tournament when he was in Grade 10. I can only imagine the confidence he must have felt performing in front of such a large crowd.

Going to School

Andrew's whole school career was spent in Edmonton. He went to one elementary school up until Grade 5 when his mother moved him to an academically oriented, publicly funded Christian school. Later Andrew told me that his mother wanted him to gain something extra from the program as he had been doing well in school. He said,

'Cause it was like really, a lot of like people were really smart and I like, I was doing really good so she just decided to test me and see how I would do in there and I did good.

I wondered whether he wanted to move to that school but, as he said, "It didn't really matter to me. A school is a school." I wondered whether he was concerned about losing his friends, but he said they "all lived in the same area so I still got to see them, so it wasn't that bad." While he said little about the program at the school, he did like the teachers there and made "friends and got along well." He liked being in a special section, the Logos section, of the school. As he said,

> It was a good school. It was easy to meet new people 'cause there was like your own section compared to like the regular program so you were associating with like all those kids and you were in all their classes all day so it wasn't that bad to meet people.

He returned to a neighborhood school for junior high school. As he said,

> Junior high, well it was like all of my friends that went to my previous elementary so we all went to the same junior high 'cause that was close by our house so I still got to hang out with them too.

He described his junior high experiences in positive terms noting that

> in junior high the teachers, they would go out of their way, like if they see that you were like struggling or something, they'd go out of their way to help you. But when I went to high school, they just seemed like, if you wanted to get something done, you'd have to come after school, they wouldn't really help you during class and like, that's when you remember most of the stuff, so it was kind of difficult.

Two junior high school teachers were particularly noted: the gym teacher whose daughter he met playing club ball and his construction teacher. He said the gym teacher told him he could "go to her and she'd help me out, it doesn't matter when, so that's why I kind of liked her." His construction teacher told Andrew he saw him as "really dedicated to what I was doing so he said if I needed anything like through construction or homework wise he would help me too."

In junior high school Andrew spoke of liking mathematics because of "how the teacher taught it. He made it more fun than just teaching it."

The junior high school basketball coach was, as Andrew described him, "just strictly basketball."

> He wasn't really like anything during school wise, 'cause I remember a couple of times I, I wouldn't, I'd uh, have a basketball game the night before and then I'd like sleep in during school and I know I'd skip, uh, skipped a day and then we'd have a basketball game that same day and I wasn't planning on going to school so then he called me and he asked me if I was going to go to the game and he'd know I didn't go to school so I think it was just strictly basketball.

He selected the high school because of the encouragement of the basketball coach and was there until mid-Grade 12. Andrew chose this school because he was recruited to go there.

By the time he was in high school, Andrew was not particularly interested in any subject area. As he said,

> I was interested just 'cause I know I needed that to go somewhere else with basketball, but it wasn't really something, like I'd make sure I'd get like a high percentage, I'd just make sure I'd get like the passing grade just so I could keep playing. So I wasn't really putting all my hard work into it.

Interrupting his Stories to Live By

In mid-Grade 12 Andrew was kicked off the basketball team because of "a situation."

> A couple of guys on the team went to the coach and told him a couple of things that weren't necessarily true and then there wasn't like, I really didn't defend myself in the matter. I just kind of let them say what they said and just left it at that. So then that got me off the team ... I really only went to the school 'cause of basketball-wise. Then I get to play at the end of the day, so when that was taken away, I didn't have any real motivation to keep going to school.

As I pushed to learn more, I learned that, for Andrew, he

> did not go deep and defend myself 'cause it's, they were captains of the team so it was their word against mine I

was really just there to play basketball at the end of the day, so when that was gone then I was like, nothing else to really stay for school 'cause that was really what kept me in school was knowing that I got to play basketball at the end of the day.

As I pushed to try to understand why he did not resist being taken off the basketball team, he said,

It was really two against one 'cause two captains against me so really, that really, it was like a lose-lose situation. Even if I said my point, two against one, not really a matter of, I didn't really think I'd get believed so I didn't really figure I should just explain myself so I just let them say what they had to say.

When I asked about his mother's response, he said, "Well I didn't really tell her like how the situation went 'cause I didn't want to escalate so I just like, I just left it at that." I wonder about how he told his mother and how difficult that must have been for him to speak about being taken off the basketball team and for her to hear about it. Andrew spoke of being angry, and at one point, said,

I was like more in a state of shock than anything that they would actually say that because we were like supposed to be like a team and when you're a team you're like, if anything you stick up for each other, not try and do things like that.

Later, in our October conversation, Andrew spoke of how he

was getting more playing time than some of the seniors who had played before (he and someone else who had come up with him). So I was getting more plays than the seniors and some of the rookies, so those guys kind of like plotted together and they said whatever they said.

I had a sense that Andrew was beginning to name jealousy as one of the motivating factors behind the other players' story of him.

His Grade 12 had been filled with courses (social, math, science, English, com tech, welding, gym) but, without basketball, he described his experience in the following way:

I just eventually like, I'd keep going, but like time after time I'd miss a class here, 'cause I had the morning, then it was lunch, then I had one class after lunch and the rest of the day

> was my spare so really I'd go for the morning, then after lunch I wouldn't go to the next class 'cause I thought it was pointless to go for the next class and have a spare so I just stopped going to that class and then after that I'd miss like maybe the first class. I'd sleep in and miss that and then I'd figure I have really two more classes to go to so then I stopped going to that so just time after time I just went and missed one class and keep missing, missing, missing.

As he said,

> After a while I was just like, well like I'd see like people when they were like going to basketball practice 'cause the lockers are like in the same areas so I'm like, just like, it's not really worth it anymore. Why they got to do what they liked to do when I can't do it because of, like the reasons that it happened, so I just like stopped going.

When he was kicked off the team, "that left me nothing to do in school, 'cause everything else at school was just to play basketball."

As I listened to Andrew tell his stories, I could hear how difficult it must have been to still go to a locker located alongside those of the basketball team but to be there as an outsider, someone who no longer belonged to the team. Losing his membership on the team must have rendered him almost invisible as he would have been excluded from the conversations and privileges that went with being a team member. He would have no longer been seen as who he still saw himself as, that is, as a strong basketball player. Andrew tells a story of himself as a good student who "knew I could do it if I just put the effort into it." Holding onto the story of himself as a good student is one that helps him feel confident about returning to school.

Stories of Becoming, of Being on the Way Back into School

Andrew does not tell his story as one in which he has dropped out of school but rather as one in which he is going to finish high school and "just going to college and keep doing school and playing basketball." Even with the interruption in his Grade 12 year, Andrew kept planning to somehow finish his Grade 12 and go to a postsecondary institution where he could play basketball. As he said in our first conversation,

> I've just been working and then I've just been talking to a bunch of coaches and then actually getting a scholarship to go

to a community college to play there if, well, one of the coaches that I've been talking to, after watching one of their games, he came up to me and asked me if I wanted to play for them, which is this coming year 'cause he saw me in Grade 11 and we talked about my situation and how it went off. So he invited me to practice with them for a day and then after that practice he was, like, well I want you to keep coming in on these certain days. It was 3 days a week. So I kept going to that and then he just asked me if I wanted to play next year and he said he would offer me a scholarship. But then he might be transferring so if he's transferring, I might not get to play but if he is still the coach then I've for sure got that chance.

While he wavered about his choice of what to study, social work was what he seemed most interested in. When I asked him about social work, he said,

> Just 'cause my brothers have kids and I usually like to take care of them, when they, one of them owns a restaurant so I take care of his kids a lot, when I'm not working, so I'm usually around kids so might as well just do that for a living.

For Andrew, social work meant working with kids who had trouble in their families. He knew something of this from his mother's practice of taking in foster children over the past three years. His mother had begun this work because as Andrew said,

> One of my aunts does it and so she just told my mom 'cause my mom's home in the afternoon, so she's like why don't you do that. So my mom just took a course and then she did it. She's the one who gave me the idea about it [becoming a social worker].

Playing Fair: Living by an Ethical Code as Part of a Team

What it means to be part of a team is part of a deeply lived metaphor for Andrew as he used it to think about how to act. For example, he said, "Well, I said it wasn't true but I didn't really like, go deep and defend myself 'cause it's, they were captains of the team so it was their word against mine."

Carr's (1986) words help me to understand something of Andrew's unfolding life story. Andrew sees himself as in search of narrative coherence, of a plot line that helps him to make sense of his life. When the narrative coherence of his life story was interrupted by his expulsion from the basketball team, Andrew began to search for ways to rebuild that coherence.

As he turned to examine his experiences and to try to rebuild a sense of narrative coherence, he drew on his strong feelings about what it means to be part of a larger collective, an extended family, or a team. For Andrew, belonging to a team or a family means thinking hard about who he is as a member of the team or family, of being responsible for who he is as part of the team. He did not feel he could judge others but rather could only try to live up to his own code of personal ethics.

As I noted earlier the interruption of Andrew's narrative coherence caused him to try to restory his life. When I asked Andrew if he was sorry that he was off the team, he said:

> I am and I'm not, like I am 'cause it was my last year and it would have like gave me more opportunities on like where I wanted to go, but then I'm not because it made me look at life in a different way.... it made me more responsible and made me look on like how you should treat people and like what to expect and you know like even if you are a team, and like you are close as a team that there might be even a couple of people who will hate on like how good you are and stuff like that.

Chapter 8

A Narrative Account of Billie Bob

Claire Desrochers

> One diploma exam short of a high school diploma, Billie Bob left to become a mother...

I caught my first glimpse of Billie Bob from a distance as Sean and I waited outside her place of work at an inner city shelter. Now a high school teacher on sabbatical, Sean had come to know Billie Bob when he worked as a teacher's aide at her school some years earlier and he had kindly offered to introduce us. When Sean pointed her out to me, she was walking down the street, alongside a fragile-looking woman. With an arm draped around her and her head bent toward her in conversation, Billie Bob guided the woman through the crosswalk. Once on the other side, she paused to watch the woman walk away. Earlier that day, Billie Bob had called Sean to delay our meeting so she could accompany a client to a medical appointment. I wondered if this was the client in question. As soon as she turned around, Billie Bob spotted Sean and waving excitedly to him before quickly making her way over to where we stood. Out of breath and smiling broadly, she apologized for the delay and confirmed what I had been thinking. With her client safely on her way, Billie Bob was now free to join us at the restaurant across the street.

As I think of this vibrant 22-year-old woman I have come to know through conversations which took place over a five month period, I often come back to this image of her at the crosswalk. I think of it as an early glimpse of the care and commitment Billie Bob brings to her work with some of the neediest people of the inner-city community. I think, too, that the image speaks to the sense of connection she feels today to a community she has known and cared for all her life.

Growing up in the Community

Billie Bob was born in the inner city, or as she put it, "right on the corner of a bad area of town" where she lived with her mother and half-brother until grade nine. Born of a previous relationship, her brother is four years older and is White. Billie Bob describes herself as mixed race, born of their White mother and her West Indian father who came to Canada at the age of 25. Soon after her birth, Billie Bob's father left the family, remarried, and had two more children. In later years, Billie Bob learned from people in the community that from a number of subsequent relationships, he had fathered eleven more children now living in several other Canadian cities. Largely absent during her childhood, Billie Bob remembers her father showing up now and then with child support payments and birthday presents. His pattern of occasional visits continues to this day. Through most of her childhood, Billie Bob remembers her mother working two or three jobs simultaneously, primarily in daycares and catering. Billie Bob often accompanied her mother to work in the daycare, becoming the helper in the "babies' room." As she got older, however, doing so became more difficult and she spent more time at home, alone.

A Sense of Community at School

Billie Bob was delighted when I suggested that we hold our third conversation at the neighborhood school she had attended. While her time there had ended after Grade 9, she spoke of having attended this school her "whole life." Her choice of words suggested this had been a very special place for Billie Bob, a place where she had felt a strong sense of connection and belonging. I couldn't help but notice the enthusiasm and energy in her step as we entered the recently renovated school and she remembered how thrilled she had been to start school.

> I was really excited because I had an older brother who had already gone to school. So for me it was like oh! Now I get to see all the fun ... I had known the excitement that was there.

She recalled rising at 5:30 a.m. to be ready for a 7:30 a.m. start to the school day. "School was fun ... there was nothing to do at home ... at least there, there's people." As we made our way through the entry, she pointed out where students from every grade level used to line up and wait for the signal to enter the school in the morning. Describing herself as "a good kid in school who never got into trouble," Billie Bob particularly enjoyed science and math. "I loved science and math. I hated English and Social ... I don't know, too much reading and writing...numbers are my [fave]."

In the main hallway of the school, she pointed out where the science lab had once been; this was where she used to come visit the menagerie of animals, another reason she loved to come to school. Across the hall, there had been a large aquarium full of fish she loved to watch. School, it seemed, had indeed turned into the exciting place of discovery she had expected.

As we made our way down the hallways past classrooms, Billie Bob took pride in letting teachers and students alike know she was a former student. Peeking into various classrooms she remembered from her time there, she pointed out how different the student body looked today. She felt there were many more visible minorities represented than in her time.

> When we came, there [was] only Asian kids, now there's Black and White ...it's mostly immigrants and Blacks...Now it's like everything, which is good...cause me, I was the only Black kid. I'm not fully Black but I was the only Black kid.

Although she did not talk much about it, I sensed that Billie Bob had grown up feeling less accepted than her White sibling.

> When I was growing up it was me and my brother and my mom who was White. So my brother used to tell everybody I was adopted, that I wasn't part of the family. I don't know if it was a joke, like he tells me today it was a joke, but when I was young, it's different because I looked different; I was a different color so it was easy for me to believe that I wasn't a part of this family. And back then, we were in touch with his whole family and then there was me, this little coloured kid, so it was odd. I don't know if it bothered me, like I got older, and then I just knew that my father was Black. Did it bother me? I think I would have remembered that but I was so young. Though if he had told me when I was 6 or 7, it might have been different but I was already going to school then. There were lots of kids that were in foster homes, like Native kids in a White home, or an Asian child in a Cambodian home, so there were lots of different nationalities.

Looking around at the diversity represented among the students in the hallway today, Billie Bob felt things were probably easier today for children of difference.

I learned this school had also been a safe place for Billie Bob. When we reached the upper floor, she took me directly to large windows that offered a commanding view of the community in two directions. From there, Billie Bob pointed out where she had lived, where her friends had lived and other landmarks of interest. From this window, Billie Bob and her friends would watch life happen in their community. "We used to always watch here and you can see everything going on ... fights, prostitutes, drug dealers." I learned that this window had been a vantage point from which Billie Bob had planned her walk home everyday. "I used to watch how you gonna go home, who's on the corner." The particular corner to which she was referring was where "bad kids" would often pick fights and steal clothing. Billie Bob told me that her brother had been beaten on this corner and had his shoes stolen. Asked whether the teachers knew about the problem corner, Billie Bob shrugged her shoulders and explained there was little teachers could do because these incidents happened after hours and off school property. This upper floor "window on the community" had provided a way to cope with the sometimes scary and dangerous streets of her community as she navigated her way home.

"Sports Made Me Want to Go to School"

A strong plotline in Billie Bob's story of school was her connection to sports. Although she excelled academically at the junior high level, sports were her passion. She spoke of spending hours and hours before and after school training and competing in soccer, volleyball, and basketball as well as in a school-based running program. "I was a real athlete...Sports made me want to go to school. I played every sport — anything I could get involved in I would 'cause there wasn't much else to do."

Billie Bob was drawn to all sports that were "active" and the various championship banners she showed me in the school gym were evidence of the success she and her teammates had enjoyed over the years. Billie Bob spent most of her spare time in the gym with her friends, all of whom she described as "pretty much jocks." This, thanks to a basketball-playing custodian who quietly bent the rules to allow Billie Bob and her friends access to the gym before and after school, sometimes even joining them to play. In addition to providing academic and athletic opportunity, Billie Bob's elementary junior high school had also served as a contact point for social opportunities she and her friends could otherwise never have afforded. School was a place to connect to professional sports events and concerts thanks to the generosity of a local sports team owner who was a friend of the principal and who would regularly provide the school with free tickets and transportation to events at a major sport facility located not far away.

"I Helped Out at School"

An honors student and star athlete throughout her junior high school years, Billie Bob was also recognized for her leadership skills. Typically chosen as captain of her many sports teams, Billie Bob grew to be recognized as a leader around the school. In Grade 6 with the help of one of the teachers at school, she became involved with an agency that partnered disabled youth with friends. She was trustworthy and teachers often called on her to help with younger or less able students. By Grade 9, she was giving up her art time to help out in a behavioral class taught by her running coach. Asked why she engaged in this kind of volunteering, Billie Bob responded:

> Most of the people we went to school with came from nothing so they knew what it was like to give back...most of us, we helped out...what else was there to do? I guess I made a difference, a lasting impression...I don't know, [I was] like, you know, that cool kid who acknowledged the geek.

She particularly enjoyed working with kids from the behavioral class; these were students who became easily frustrated because of their low attention span. Ever since she could remember, Billie Bob recounted, these were kids who got picked on, which was something she felt "wasn't nice." Billie Bob's commitment to and support of these students garnered her numerous leadership awards throughout junior high, including a scholarship valued at $2000. During our walk through the school, Billie Bob was unable to locate the plaques on which her leadership accomplishments were recognized. Although they had once lined the main hall, they were nowhere to be found since the renovation.

"Teachers Have Known Me All My Life"

In this small school setting, many of Billie Bob's teachers doubled as coaches and she got to know them very well. These close relationships were evident that day when we ran into one of her former teachers in the hallway. Billie Bob almost squealed with delight as she introduced me to her former running coach, Miss Gazelle. As I listened to them reminisce and inquire about each other's lives, I could begin to see the depth of relationships Billie Bob had forged with her teachers during her 10 years at this school.
"I had teachers who had known me for 10 years... my math teacher taught my brother when he was in kindergarten...so my Grade 9 math teacher had known me my whole entire life."

I found it particularly telling that, as we worked our way through the gallery of class photos, Billie Bob pointed her teachers out to me (identifying each of them, save one, by name) before her classmates. The classes, I noticed, were small; by Billie Bob's count, never more than 15 or 18 students per class. The close connections she enjoyed with her teachers and coaches would serve her well as she moved into her last year of junior high.

In Grade 9, a dispute with their landlord forced Billie Bob and her mother to move to a different area of the city. It was a long bus ride from this new home to the school and Billie Bob hated waiting for the bus, particularly in winter when she had to travel to and from sports practices in the dark. She began to skip school and eventually "just stopped coming one day." Her absences were quickly noticed and Billie Bob remembers how persistent teachers were in their efforts to contact her mother.

> My mom was working all the time...she was gone and she couldn't see what was happening. What [the school] would do is, not like high school, not leave a message, like they wouldn't give up until they got a hold of her, and then like, 'cause the school's so small, I would come into the school my teacher would be like: "What's wrong? What happened? Something's wrong. I know you. What's wrong with you?" It was really hard to fool them. They talked to everybody. Everybody knew everybody, we'd all been there so long that if we skipped...they'd call your parents...they would be like right there, right in your face to understand your absence.

Even the principal got involved in figuring out how to reconnect Billie Bob with school.

> He'd call my house then I would answer the phone. He's like "how come you're not in school?" I'm like "'cause I can't get to school. I can't get there it's too cold." And he used to live in the west end so he used to drive the road by my house and pick me up.

For the next three months of winter, the principal and Billie Bob travelled to and from school together and her teachers collaborated on an attendance plan to make sure she stayed in school. Then, once winter had passed, "school became ok again."

Billie Bob's Stories to Live by Interrupted

> I liked junior high — I just didn't like high school...I went to a different school every semester.

Intent on staying connected to one of her junior high teachers and coaches, Billie Bob registered for Grade 10 at a large high school where he had been hired to teach the following year. Her plans were thwarted before the start of the school year when her mother was promoted to a new job in a city three hours away. I couldn't help but think what a shock it must have been for her to move from the intimacy of her neighborhood school to a high school of 3500 students in a new city. Billie Bob did not have good memories of her first semester of Grade 10. "I didn't make very many friends, started doing very bad in school."

Her stay in this school was short lived. In the second semester, school authorities forced her to relocate to another school when they discovered the house she and her mother had moved to was located outside the first school's catchment area. She referred to this new school as "the far school," which she would have to reach by bus. Billie Bob had faced a similar problem in Grade 9, only this time, her frequent skipping went mostly unnoticed. She rarely attended classes but unlike the friends with whom she skipped, she remained committed to completing assignments. One teacher noticed and rewarded her efforts.

> There was one teacher...she was really nice; she was the one who actually, I should have failed because I missed almost every one of her classes; I would only go to class once a week, but I aced all my assignments so she couldn't really fail me, but attendance-wise I failed so my mark was like 67, but attendance, I got a zero. So all my marks were based on just my assignments, which was good for me...she couldn't fail me cause like the other kids would skip and wouldn't do the work...even if I wasn't there...she would still get my assignment...I always did the work, I just wasn't there.

At the end of summer following her Grade 10 year, Billie Bob and her mother moved back to her home city and she transferred to a third high school setting in as many semesters. "Mom wanted to move back to Edmonton...I was mad at my mom and I hated the world, just hated everybody because I had to make all new friends over in high school again."

I could not begin to imagine the academic and social hardships Billie Bob had to deal with in moving to a third high school setting in as many semesters, Having missed the deadline for high school registration, she began Grade 11 at an outreach school behind her home in the downtown area. Billie Bob particularly enjoyed this learning environment because she could complete assignments without the expectation that she spend much time in class. Working part-time to support herself had always been part of Billie Bob's life and the outreach program delivery allowed her to combine work and schooling in a way that suited her.

> That ... worked for me, not being in school but doing my work, so I excelled a lot, because I worked full time and went to school two hours a day. I passed all my courses and got the most credits ever in one semester.

At the end of this very successful semester, Billie Bob had a falling out with her mother and moved back to the other city to live with a girlfriend. Transferring back to the second high school she had attended there, she completed grade eleven in what would be her fourth high school setting in as many semesters. When her girlfriend moved unexpectedly to another city at the end of that school year, Billie Bob returned home to begin her final year of high school. Her mother had since moved to the suburbs where Billie Bob registered at a large high school. She found friends there whom she had met through sports but shared no classes with them as they were a year behind her. Skipping classes provided opportunities to connect with these friends at a large mall nearby which Billie Bob remembers was a constant distraction; she and her friends began to engage in shoplifting as a way to "get an adrenaline rush." She was eventually caught, charged, fined, and left with a criminal record that made it difficult for her to find a job until she managed, several years later, to buy a pardon.

While in her last year of high school, Billie Bob moved in with her boyfriend, the man who became her common law husband. At 24 (seven years older than she was), he was already working as an engineer and had a pre-school aged daughter from a prior relationship. The night before her final diploma exam (English), Billie Bob was admitted to hospital in severe pain with a suspected gallbladder problem. The following morning, as her classmates sat down to write their diploma exam, Billy Bob found out she was pregnant. Six months later when she had another chance to write the exam, she recalled being "about ready to pop" with the baby and a diploma exam was the last thing on her mind. And so, only one diploma exam short of her high school diploma, Billie Bob left high school to become a mother.

A Family Story of Education

Billie Bob's daughter, Danielle, now three years of age, has been very much part of our conversations. Each time we met, she would pull out her cell phone to show me photographs of a child I found strikingly beautiful whose heritage Billie Bob described as *Dogla*, part Black, and part *Coolie*.[1] By contrast, Danielle's half-sister, now 7, was part *Coolie* and part White. Looking at photos of the two girls side by side, I found it interesting that Billie Bob's daughter was growing up with an older lighter skinned half-sibling, just as she had. I wondered whether Danielle's mixed heritage was an issue in her father's family. Billie Bob explained that while her father-in-law would have preferred a *Coolie* daughter-in-law, Danielle's position as first-born grandchild trumped all such concerns.

The importance of school surfaced in our conversations around Danielle's future and brought to light what I understand to be a strong family story around the value of education. Looking back over her experience of school, Billie Bob insists education had always mattered to her. "I always cared — just didn't like having that person nag...I liked you to give me my work."

In her culture, Billie Bob explained, education is very important. Despite being largely absent from her life, Billie Bob's father had always supported her education. To this day, she believes he is still mad at her for not finishing her high school. He has paid her tuition through two college programs and she knows she can count on him to support any further studies she might undertake. As Billie Bob talks about her daughter's future in school, I see how this plotline of the importance of education lives on in the family. Finding her daughter particularly bright, Billie Bob has already obtained special permission from the board to have her start school early.

> Why waste the year in daycare when they could be learning something, right? And like, I had to friggin' talk to the school board, I was so frustrated, 'cause she was born on March 7, and the cut off was March 1st. and I was like, "You're gonna make my daughter wait, be a year behind, for 6 days? That's not fair. And two of those days are on the weekend." So

---

1. *Coolie* is the term Billie Bob used to describe Danielle's father. She explained it to mean "a person of Indian descent from the Caribbean." According to Billie Bob, although *Coolie* is considered a pejorative term in South Africa, it is widely used and accepted in the Caribbean.

they're going to allow her to go, she'll be able to start when she's 4.

In an ideal world, Billie Bob would have her daughter attend a school that requires uniforms. Asked why, she responds,

> I don't think school is about fashion, like, at all. Or who got the Nike shoes, and who's got the track suit...there are children whose parents just can't afford it, so those kids are picked on and it's not fair. And where we're from [in the Caribbean], everybody wears a uniform, everybody looks the same, everybody is the same, and the only thing that separates you is your brain.... I think that's important because at school, you won't have nobody stealin' nobody's shoes, or stealing nobody's new jackets, 'cause everybody's the same. I always thought that was important...it's not about dressing up; if you want to dress up, go to a party.

At this point in time, Billie Bob would like to obtain her high school diploma to set an example for her daughter. Given the time gone by, this would mean retaking her final high school English course, an onerous task for any single parent working full-time, let along one who "hates to read." Her current life circumstances make this unlikely to happen. Now a single mother in the process of divorcing Danielle's father, Billie Bob has taken on responsibility for her mother, who shares her house and helps care for her daughter. Furthermore, Billie Bob sees little practical value in pursuing that option given that she has managed to complete two college programs without her high school diploma. On the basis of a successful college entrance exam, Billie Bob was able to complete her training as a health care aid. (She had always dreamed of becoming a nurse — becoming a health care aid worker was an attainable alternative under the circumstances.) When she realized this work did not suit her, she returned to college to train as a medical office assistant and landed a part-time job working in a dermatology clinic. In order to spend more time with her daughter by day, Billie Bob took on a night shift at an inner-city agency, later switching to full-time day-shift employment as an outreach worker.

Reconnecting with Her Community ... and Making a Difference

Today, Billie Bob is an intake worker for an addictions program in a homeless shelter where she works with some of the most vulnerable people in society. Her clients are women living with mental health issues who need help from the basics of personal hygiene to support in getting to medical and court appointments. I hear compassion in her voice as she tells me of the time she tried to stop a client from beating her head against a wall to chase away voices she was hearing. There have also been times she had to prevent suicidal women from jumping out into traffic as she accompanied them to appointments. Her face lights up as when she speaks of activities she has planned for the crafts group she runs as part of the recovery program. As we sit together in the restaurant across the street from her place of work, a siren sounds prompting Billie Bob to run to the window. It is clear to me that she worries about her clients; these women matter to her. "I care about them, if I don't who else will? ... A lot of people turn their face...I grew up here so I've seen this for so long ... I know the issues and I can do good here."

I ask Billie Bob why she thinks she connects so well with her clients; she tells me it's because she treats them like people. One of the necessities of her work, she believes, is to smile and treat clients like people, not frown and look them up and down, especially clients with no self-esteem wondering if they're ever going to get clean. Billie Bob explained that she treats them not as clients, but as friends...she cares for them. And it seems they too care for her; some women, she tells me, walk up to 10 blocks to receive a morning hug from her. She works with them because she wants to be here. "Clients just want somebody not to judge them, to be honest with them, but work with them about how we are going to get their life back together."

Billie Bob's commitment to her clients is evident in her choice of pronoun as she talks about how "we" are going to get their life back together. She worries that clients get very different approaches from some of her colleagues. Not everyone "gets it" she tells me, and Billie Bob finds this lack of understanding challenging. She is dismissive of people who are superficial or afraid of homeless people.

> I treat them like people. I smile at them, hug them. [The clients tell me] you make us laugh, you listen. My managers are the kind of people who show up with their notepad to see Billy and write down something about Billy but they would never remember anything about him. And then there are managers who are like "Do you know how many clients I have?" But to me, faces, memory and info go really [good] so I'm like "Oh, what happened? How is your son? What happened with your son's court? They're like 'You remembered!" I try to remember things about their life. People need to go to AADAC. I will help them, I will hold their hand, I will visit them, I will never find them a place and leave them because

then they fail, and they'll fall through the cracks and end back into the shelter... Helping one to the fullest is better than helping ten. Some other people I work with don't get that.

As she speaks of her work, I am deeply impressed by Billie Bob's humanity, compassion, hope, determination, and sense of responsibility. I find it hard to imagine how such a young woman with so much on her personal plate continues to bring such energy to her work on a daily basis. Most people would find it overwhelming to work with such a high needs clientele in this area of the city. I wonder how she sustains her energy and commitment. Billie Bob explains that it's her connection to the women that keeps her coming back.

> That's what keeps me coming back. Those ladies still remember me. My reward is to see one of my clients be like, I want to go into your recovery program... I'm ready to give up getting high, prostitution, the money. I'm ready to let the Lord do his work; I'm getting my life back. And that's why I come back, 'cause all it takes is one lady that will make me wanna come back... I work with women who are, you now, the worst of the worst... the most passed out... the biggest prostitutes, HIV, tuberculosis, Hep C, they got it all, they got nothing going for them, and then it's like they care. Life means something now, you know? And to let somebody see that life is meaningful, life isn't all about getting high and partying. Yeah. Cause like my thing is I can't change the world but I can change one person at a time.

Billie Bob tells me she finds her work rewarding because it provides a way for her to give back. Hearing her use the expression "giving back" reminds me that she used a similar phrase when referring to her volunteer work in the behavioral class at her junior high school. Interestingly, Billie Bob told me recently that one of her newest clients in the shelter recognized her as the girl who had volunteered in her behavior class many years earlier. I saw this as a way Billie Bob was continuing to live a familiar story of helping others.

Has Billie Bob come full circle, I wonder? Found her way back to a place of comfort and purpose? She enjoys her work as a mental health worker in the inner city; I think of her as having found a rewarding way to reconnect to a community she has known all her life, a place where she "knows everyone by name."

Looking Ahead

While Billie Bob shared very definite ideas about how she thinks the shelter should be run, she has no aspirations to take on more responsibility at her work. Management, she insists, is not for her. When asked where she imagines herself in five years, Billie Bob responds without hesitation that she will still be working as an outreach worker because it is where she feels she can best contribute.

> I love what I do. I would like to retire from here...for me the biggest thing is helping people... I could work plastic surgery where I used to and all I'm doing is helping somebody look pretty...or I can come here and make a difference in somebody's life. I'm making somebody want to live.

What does the future hold, I wonder, for this early school leaver? Perhaps further training in the mental health field to learn how to help these people to the best of her ability Billy Bob tells me, or perhaps even further education to become an addictions counselor. And while she imagines her father's offer of tuition still stands, Billie Bob now has living expenses for her family to think about...and she has a plan. In a little over a year, she will have accumulated enough years of service at the shelter to apply for a scholarship.

Chapter 9

A Narrative Account of Kevlar

Pam Steeves

Fortune Cookie

Awash at Sea...

Wandering past closing store fronts inside the downtown mall on Thursday evening in late September, I arrived at the escalator down to the deserted food court below. Empty chairs and tables filled the vast open basement floor, but where was Kevlar? My eyes scanned up and down the vacant space to get a first glimpse of my participant for the early school leavers' study. My heart was pounding a little, perhaps he would not be there, but then I saw him at the credit card kiosk where he had stood since mid-afternoon that day, trying to make sales. I was delighted to meet him, a nice young man. We chit chatted for a minute. He was bored and hungry, he said. Then I waited a short distance away until his official job time ended. Kevlar thought he should stick it out even though I realized there was no one around to check on him.

I planned on inviting Kevlar to a nearby hotel restaurant, which I had scouted out earlier as being quiet and private enough for a meal and conversation with a tape recorder running. Kevlar was personable and talkative. He wanted to be part of the study. He noticed it on an Internet website he came across and he made contact by email. Kevlar thought we would be interested in his story of leaving school early because it might be quite different than most. For him it wasn't about school but about his "screwed up" upbringing.

While waiting for menus, we engaged in lively conversation about politics and the upcoming U.S. election. Kevlar struck me as very bright and savvy for his 18 years. The menu was a disappointment ... for Kevlar. He wondered if we could go to a restaurant just across from us that might have "real food." I began to think about restaurant food in a brand new way. Fancy hotel pasta and seafood dishes are light, probably just right for business people traveling and arriving late evening for a bite to eat. The food isn't hearty enough if you are actually really hungry. The other restaurant offered shepherd's pie, a big enough portion.

In preparation for the taped conversation, I handed Kevlar a blank piece of paper and pen whereby he could create a kind of annal or time line of events over his life reflecting the story of his early school leaving and beyond. Points on the annal might trigger stories he'd like to talk about. I told him he could create the annal in any way he liked.

He began at the beginning ... his life story as he composed it, drawing and doodling events over time as he talked. Drawing the annal while telling me the stories gave Kevlar a sense of authority over his soon-to-unfold haphazard life. I noticed that events around significant "troubles and confusions" led to a great deal of intense picturing.

For this narrative account I chose to create word images of Kevlar's early school leaving story interwoven within life stories. The word images are drawn from Kevlar's actual words in the transcripts, filled with emotion, hope, and tension that speak to who he is and is becoming.

Apart

And the day I was born my dad and my grandma came to the hospital
They actually took me from my mom.
He didn't believe I was going to be safe with her
And then long story short I, I met her when I was 13
But that's later down the road.

Living in Rivenmore Grade 1 or something...
My dad, the trailer company, he was working on top of it
A really hot day and he actually fell — passed out
From heat exhaustion and,
So that's like permanent, constant pain

I would go every weekend up North
To visit my grandma and then about Grade 3
I ended up just staying with her for a year
Cause my dad's back got really bad.

Aspen Road School. It was fine
And I had this teacher named Miss Fensminster

If you did something good you got this little mark,
And like if you collect a certain amount
You got ... stuff or whatever.
It worked really cool.

And um then in Grade 4 I moved to Easton
Have you been to Easton at all?

Kevlar wanted to know if I knew where in the city the community of Easton was located. I knew it could be described as a rough and tough neighborhood. I recalled a city school district considering some schools in the area as "inner city" even though they were located on the outskirts of the city. The tone of my reply seemed to give Kevlar the signal he was looking for and he continued his story.

Well in this place, it's called the Plainview Motel,
My dad basically thought that since he had a small kid
And couldn't really clean and do anything,
That living in a motel that had maids would be a good idea.

I went to Easton for Elementary
It was really difficult going to school
I couldn't really tell anyone where I lived
I'd come home and play on the computer
Yeah. I grew up on the computer
I didn't really fit into anything
Like fit in with the popular kids or anything

But that's school

The perfect situation

Grade 7, That's St Pauls I think
The most unpopular kid in school
Completely alone, definitely embarrassing
Cause in schools
There's always the people
Who have the perfect lives, the perfect parents
And they rocket directly to the top
They're practically favoured by all the teachers
Because they get the best grades,

Because they're not even stressed at all
School is built for them

And it just doesn't work out well for anyone that's not in a perfect situation

But for Grade 7
I learned how to play the saxophone and stuff
It was quite awesome
I loved the saxophone

And then Grade 8 at Walton
An email from my mom
Found me through my uncle
Military records — Googling my last name
And she would come over sometimes
And I got to see my brother and sister.
Yeah it was really awesome.
I talk to my sister all the time now.
We're so close.

I started despising the way my life was here,
And how I basically hated it.
She brought up the idea of moving back in with her
She was engaged to a man who had a good amount of money
Apparently they really had a good life
And my dad agreed

Because we all thought it would be a really good situation

Finally I thought, Kevlar's fortunes seemed to be changing for the better. How amazing it must have been for Kevlar to see his brother and sister and mother for the first time. What perhaps I take for granted ... an actual semblance of family was coming together for Kevlar.

Fraying at the Seams

Two days after I moved in with her
She ditched him,
Will was swearing around Cindy (his sister)
A great guy otherwise
Probably the greatest guy I know.
He's helped me so much in the past few years

She took us to a women's shelter in Morgan
And then a different one in Shaftsbury (outskirts of Rivenmore)
And eventually I found a really neat little house
The exact one that was perfect

I remember how Kevlar described finding that perfect house. He said it was "really weird actually." He had been looking for a rental property for a really long time and then just as he was about to give up, he sneezed and his eyes fell on this "exact" one that he described as perfect. Kevlar then told me that a lot of things in his life worked like that.

I went to school in Shaftsbury Plains
Grade 8 was pretty much finished
I missed a good chunk of it
Like half of it

Then my mom decided to move us again to Rivenmore
No idea why
A little place near Rivenmore Mall
Another junior high school, Valleycrest
It was a really cool school
Shaped in a circle

I don't remember teachers but I remember doing home ec class.
Cooking — it was really fun — I still cook,
Especially now that I'm getting my own place
And a good little group of friends
I met hanging out during breaks and stuff like that
Not a bunch of rich kids
Yeah

But we were room mating with my mom's friend
He had a really bad gambling problem
She had to find a place she could afford herself
So we moved to Ash Rd

I finished Grade 9 at Valleycrest
I just barely passed
They can't actually fail you in Grade 9

Despite this downturn and turmoil, I imagined Kevlar as getting a break, a second chance. Whatever gaps in his schooling Kevlar was enduring as he moved from place to place and school to school, he would not have to fail

Grade 9. I wondered how he knew about this policy and what part the school system plays in providing second chances? Or was this simply a serendipitous occurrence, one that can be taken advantage of when perfect situations are few and far between?

Summer after Grade 9 — A Life in Pieces

And then it happened again

We were living in the apartments
Me and my Mom had an altercation one day
My freezy melted on her table
Her tiny little octagon table by her bedside
One little corner was peeling
Oh, no

She went crazy — I don't know why
Like she had pent up rage or something
She walked into my room just kicking my computer and smashing it
Saying how would you feel if I broke your stuff

She f'...ing grabs me and threw me on the bed,
Sorry for swearing, but she grabs me.
She thought I was going to throw her TV out the window
Makes no sense
She starts chasing me, so I go out to the end of the hall
She closes the door and locks it.

I walked outside and tried to yell to her from the window
I'm not even wearing shoes
No shoes, no socks, nothing

Then Kevlar stopped for a minute in the midst of this outpouring to look down at the audio recorder and to ask if it was still turned on. The recorder was digital so no moving tape was visible. I assured him the recorder was working and he said O.K. and went on with the events of the story. He wanted me to hear it.

I finally coerced her to bring me my shoes
She walks into this bus stop and sits me down
She throws two or three bucks on the ground and tells me
You better get used to getting money this way

Cause this is the way you're going to get it from now on
And well, I don't even get what that means
Because why are people going to throw money on the ground — right?
It was just ridiculous.

And from there I walked,
To Rivenmore Mall
The only place I knew,
Knew anyone would be

Seeing my friend Kenzie
Went back to her house
Her mom called social services
I gave them my Mom's phone number so they could talk to her
She told them she would let me back in

But she told me to f...off.
She doesn't let me back in.

Throughout his telling, I noted Kevlar often shifted to the present tense. He became very animated and detailed in his drawing and scribbles portraying the graphic account of these events on his annal. The intensity of Kevlar's telling made me wonder how many people have ever heard his story. Was this a second chance for Kevlar...to be heard? Yet I was shaken as Kevlar continued — was this a story just too hard to tell?

Forsaken

I went to a group home. It was O.K.
But I was practically traumatized
There's a probationary period
For the first two weeks there are chores
You have to follow all the rules and stuff
And if you don't you are out
But I was like a 14 year old kid that just went through all this

So I ended up just a-wol ing from it
To try and go see my friends
And it created a kind of chain
Of going from group home to group home.
I ended up in a parented home that I actually liked
A Pre SIL (Supported Independent Living)

But I never got that far 'cause
'Cause I don't know.
I just was in a really bad time I guess
I would leave on the weekend
And get back a day late
Social services is so packed with people.
There was a time
If you were even a minute late
Your bed was closed and they put someone else in it.

During this time I started Grade 10 at George Wood
And I kept trying to do it as much as I could
Living in random places
But it's really hard to do school when you don't live anywhere.

I could do the school…
Its just like after school.
I would have to do my homework
Figure out where I'm going to stay
Figure out if I'm going to make it through the day

A lot of the time I ended up just going to the mall
Staying all night
Cause it's open
24 hours

And so some nights I would have been awake all night
And going to school
And practically passing out
And it just stopped working

I ended up completely going the homeless route
Chilling and hanging out at Rivenmore Mall
With other people in roughly the same situation
I got stuck in that

There were random times that I would see my sister and brother
But I wouldn't even want them to see me
Cause of the stuff that was going on

Kevlar often used the word "random." It makes me think of serendipity and chance. Luck is random. Being "down on your luck" at certain times leaves a space to be lucky at other times. It might be viewed as a stroke of luck that Kevlar had been able to connect with his sister and brother in the first place, through his Mom browsing military records. Listening to Kevlar I realized I was needing and inventing a way to see hope in his story.

Resilience

And then Grade 11, George Wood
Just giving up — going to a group home
Accepting what it was
I just decided to change things
Cause I was going to die if I didn't

And then things started picking up.
I was doing better in school — a really good group of friends
And then from there I moved back with my mom
Back to Shaftsbury
Around mid Grade 11 before the second semester

My mom got back together with her boyfriend and a nice big house.
And it was "you're back," "you're back," "la la la," open arms.
And this is something that's still between us to this day
She thinks that I ran away
It's not running away

It's almost like nothing happened
Everything just kind of went back to normal I guess
As normal as it could get.
Never actually brought up what happened in that entire period.
Went to Lansdowne High School
Finished Grade 11.

Grade 11 was probably the greatest year of my school
Both schools — the friends.

Kevlar could see from my reaction that I was thinking that things were getting better. Grade 11 at George Wood High School in Rivenmore and Lansdowne High in Shaftsbury were his greatest school experiences. A kind of sigh of relief must have shown in my body language. But then I heard the words "But it gets worse."

Summer after Grade 11 — Abandonment

Right before I turned 17, the summer

We all have different Dads
And one day a phone call
Saying you have a daughter, 14. Here she is. She's on her way.
My mom took her in when she could barely support us all
The sisters started fighting
Created a really giant rift in my family.
My mom couldn't take it. She kicked Mia out
She wanted to move to Rendall — to her new love in Rendall

Me and my sister and brother thought it was a stupid idea.
There was no way we were going
And the moment I brought up the word abandonment
The gloves were off

She dropped off my brother at his Dad's
My sister got kicked out because she was defending our viewpoint.
And she dropped me off at the fair grounds
Where I was working at a booth with a website
My 17th birthday.

I didn't see her again for over a year.
She just left.

My sister and I returned
To the basement [the nice big house]
In Shaftsbury

Jenny (a friend) and some roommates
We let them in
But it went sour
Cindy (his sister) ended up leaving.
And then I left and eventually Jenny left.

And this was in Grade 12, at Lansdowne
The best school I've had

Yeah, I learned German both years.
Lansdowne's an amazing school
'Cause it's in Shaftsbury
Everything is

The people are a lot cleaner.
They're from a higher grade
Like they're just more upscale I guess
And there's just not all the bullshit ghetto drama
Like the city has.

Three quarters through the first semester of Grade 12
I just couldn't handle my roommates anymore.
Basically our roommates had already graduated
They're already finished school
So every single day they'd party to 4:00 or 5:00 in the morning
I ended up moving out of there

And I left school
And ...It really sucked
'Cause that was probably my favourite school

And in Alberta it's almost impossible for a kid to get a 4th year at a public school
So I just had to stop school.

I had registered
I tried going to T M Rogers
To do another year of Grade 12.
They wouldn't let me.
I tried going to a lot of schools in Rivenmore
I just couldn't do it.
But I am actually registering for virtual school.
It's really awesome

Kevlar told me he would need $70 for registration for the online courses. I wondered how difficult it would be to get the money. Maybe someone would help him out with this if necessary. Maybe there are student loans. Maybe this would work. I was beginning to enter Kevlar's world.

After I moved out
I went back to Kenzie's (his friend) house

Her Mom let me stay
Eventually I moved to Murray Road
To Walton, it's just like a community.
A three-storey apartment.
Everyone in the whole building ended up meeting everyone else
It was cool. It was really fun. It was like a frat or something

After Walton I finally got in contact with my Mom.
I stayed with her a month to save money for a place
A little house with Kenzie
Across from the fair grounds
And also my cousin and Jarret from Walton
This past summer
2 months ago

Fortune Cookie

I listened hard as Kevlar told this story, traveling with him to a world so different from my own when I grew up. Kevlar's story took centre stage. There were nods and a few checks for clarification but I did not want to slow the momentum, the words igniting as he moved the pen across the paper. But now I felt I was coming to a place where I could ask Kevlar questions and where Kevlar might reflect on things past and tell me more of his hopes and dreams for the future.

To begin with, I was startled wide awake to realize Kevlar had been able to stay in school so long, making it to mid-way through the first semester Grade 12. He told me, "It sucked changing so much but my mind's built that way now I guess." He added "I've always known that education is the key to life and I think it's ridiculous to not get it." He is planning to redo math and physics, taking Math 20 and 30 because they are pure and because he loves quantum physics. In fact on his own he feels he has learned more from researching on the Internet than his entire education, "'cause it's practical knowledge. It's not like trigonometry. Like honestly I think the only thing I've used from school that I've learned is multiplying and adding."

Kevlar showed me his I-phone. He enthusiastically explained to me that he can answer any question, get any phone number, and "find out anything about anything in the entire world." He showed me how he could find out where to order from and find the nearest pizza outlet. I thought about how significant an I-phone would be if you were on your own — the sense of connection it might give you. He told me it was costly but well worth it and was purchased during the time of his credit card kiosk job.

He also talked to me about libraries, and how he had always used them. He loves the computer access but also the reading. He has four library cards, and although he can't take out any materials because of fines he is able to use the computers there. He also recalled the library at Lansdowne High School and was impressed with how much money they had recently spent in replacing computers and electronic equipment there. He loved the computer and media classes while he attended. It was interesting for me as a former teacher-librarian that when I asked him if anybody in the schools ever tried to figure out what was going on with his haphazard life he recalled that it was a librarian who would talk to him. "They're more human." Certainly I remember conversations with a few children who seemed to think of the library as a kind of escape. The possibilities to attend to children's interests were always high, whether choosing a book to read, choosing a research topic or just hanging out after class.

Kevlar shared with me that because his life had "ended up" the way it did he had learned a lot of life skills. He has the ability to move around and be fine. He said he's met so many people and had to "accept them as who's going to be around me." He feels this has made it easy for him to talk to people he doesn't know. He wondered aloud if it would help him in the future with his plans to go into media and broadcasting. I was taken aback with what he said next. I had never really given enough thought to the idea that it might be better not to have any influence of your parents. Yet I know of situations and circumstances that parents could be in that would be untenable for a young and growing child...

I have chosen to capture Kevlar's words in a found poem portrayed here:

To be honest
I really am actually so grateful for the way that I grew up
Most people end up just being the clone of the parents
That brought them up.
The sum of what their two parents are.
Whereas I grew up without any
Almost any
Influence besides my own.
So I could actually grow up and be myself.
Not many people get that opportunity.
To be honest

Kevlar's words prompted further questioning at a later date to ask him about resilience. He agreed that he did seem to bounce back and that if something didn't work out he "would make something else work." But he also told me that "the bouncing" was tiring and he was getting sick of it. I responded that I thought he was very young for living through all of this.

He later told me that sometimes he'd just like to hop on a plane and disappear. I wondered whether there were people he could name that have helped, supported, or encouraged him. Kevlar told me there was "sparsely" Will, but no one else. He told me he wasn't in contact with his Dad and his Mom didn't have the money. Will (whom Kevlar described as being awesome and having helped him so much recently) was formerly married to his Mom and was very involved with bringing up his sister Cindy. Will supports Kevlar's plans to finish high school courses online and go on to post secondary. Kevlar sees Will fairly regularly when he visits with his sister. When I asked Kevlar about support from friends he told me they were there but "friends can only go so far…because they're not in the same situation." Counselors and staff at his various high schools did not seem to have an impact. Kevlar's understanding from school people was that "in Alberta it's almost impossible for a kid to get a fourth year at a public high school."

Since the summer of 2008 Kevlar has explored options for finishing his education online. He only needs to come up with the $70 to register. In September, with his credit card kiosk job and a magazine project job slated to start in October, he figured he would have the money to pay for his place and living expenses and save for future education. In the meantime, he excitedly told me about the magazine project which came up when he was living on Murray Road. It was a federally funded program to enable "like groups of people to come together that are having trouble staying in their jobs because they're not built for that kind of thing." So people "having trouble in their lives" can get a "booster shot" by learning how to write a magazine article, do layout, graphic design, and photography to create a magazine for distribution in the city. The magazine would give exposure to aspiring clothing designers and other arts-based entrepreneurs. Kevlar was thinking of doing something on a number of DJs he knew in town. Afterward Kevlar said the project tries to fund you and lead you on the right track for where you want to go. Kevlar had a copy of the latest magazine with him; he showed me some of the layouts. He wanted to give me the copy but I told him to save it. He could bring me one next time if he would like.

Later in the fall when I spoke to Kevlar again he told me the magazine project had ended; the funding pulled. He had to move again by the end of the month. He was staying with friends for now. Kevlar also had changed jobs. He no longer worked at the down town mall at the credit card booth but at a music venue on Murray Road that had a bar. He planned to get a bachelor place near his work so that it wouldn't be far to walk home at 3:00 in the morning. Kevlar likes music and the money is good with tips.

But it was talk of the design college he hoped to get into some day that lifted his spirits. He wondered if I had heard of it, Sagen College of Design Arts, a teaching college for drawing, photography, cinematics, animation, and the science behind graphic design. He told me the day before he had decided to walk in there while he was downtown and "check it out." He struck up a conversation with the marketing director who told Kevlar the history of the college, and he in turn showed her "a lot of stuff I'd been making lately" and how long he had been using technology. The dean of admissions got involved and told Kevlar he could be accepted as a mature student in January if he was able to pass the admissions test, but would give him a chance to take the test first so he could find out what he needed to learn. Kevlar was thrilled to think he could be going to college "on time." He asked about the online courses with Alberta Education. But the dean suggested that the design course was an intensive 6 months and he'd be too busy. Kevlar mentioned the expensive tuition but said that he thought BGS could fund him up to $10,000. Once he is finished with the program he told me the people at the school would help him look for a job in the industry. He knows there are opportunities in Rivenmore especially in the arts, but there are also many hard memories for him here. Kevlar imagines himself going to Vancouver or Toronto. Or maybe just getting a car and driving out to California to see what he could do.

I turned the tape off. Our second dinner conversation was ending. This time we were at a restaurant on Murray Road, one of Kevlar's choosing. There was lots of music, friendly staff, and delicious "real" food in big portions! He thanked me. We began talking again about the U.S. election. Kevlar was well informed and also pleased about the outcome. On my first meeting with Kevlar he showed me his tattoo — a lotus flower. I told him a story of the lotus flower of hope in Vietnamese culture — that no matter how long it took or how muddy the soil, the dormant seed will eventually bloom in beauty. Kevlar's stories are hard to hear and imagine. I feel very inadequate. I can only offer my hope that things will come together. It is the end of the meal and the waiter has handed each of us a fortune cookie.

Afterward

I had mixed feelings as I prepared to meet Kevlar for the third and official final conversation for the study. I would be presenting Kevlar with my narrative account of his story of leaving school and he would be invited to make changes to suit him. I was a little nervous of what he might say but also it was hard to think I would not be meeting him again. I had been drawn in by his sincerity and good will and I was moved by the stories he told.

It was early evening but getting dark and cold as I raced past storefronts and eateries looking up at signs for the restaurant of Kevlar's choosing while all the while looking down at my ticking watch. I couldn't find the place and it was getting later. A few blocks further down the road I bumped into Kevlar going the other way. I was grateful to see him. I had walked right past the restaurant. It wasn't a place I was expecting, based on our last few meetings; this one was more upscale. Kevlar seemed more at ease to see me this time. As well, his clothes seemed to indicate a cooler sophistication, black jacket with collar up. I began by ordering coffee and water as I usually did and this time Kevlar did the same.

At this visit I found out Kevlar was working at an Internet café. He told me about his boss whom he admired as someone who wanted to expand his service to companies in town to provide free Internet access throughout the city. I imagined Kevlar at this place, being personable, assisting people with their computers, selling snacks, and pop behind the counter.

I wedged the narrative account among the cutlery, linen serviettes, water goblets, and coffee cups on the high café table we were sitting at. I planned to go through the account page by page with Kevlar. We both had pens to change things. As we began, he told me it was good to see his story of leaving school on paper, "reflecting on it with someone is different than reflecting on it yourself." He felt it gave him perspective, underlining for him a more objective way of looking at the events of his life. He liked the way he could see "tiny little moments that changed the rest of my life." He appreciated the titles I gave to portions of his account and suggested, "Maybe we should title this (the whole piece) Fortune Cookie." He talked about the stories as "something out of a movie."

Reading through the account he paused to wonder what the week was like for his sister and little brother after he had been kicked out. He wondered how his grandma would describe her taking him away at the hospital when he was born — that she might see the whole thing differently. He wondered if his mom would ever realize what had happened. He also said that lately although some things had gone well "I'm almost waiting for everything to fall apart again."

Kevlar felt his plans for Sagen College of Design Arts were going ahead. He had the funding in place through BGM (related to the magazine project Kevlar had been involved with in the fall but whose funding had collapsed.) He plans now to take the entrance test in July so that in the meantime he can "pick off" as many Grade 12 courses as he can, in order to get his diploma on line. Kevlar told me he wants as much knowledge from high school as possible because most of those attending the college will be people who have graduated.

My thoughts have returned to Kevlar many times since then. At the same time I remember our first meeting when Kevlar showed me his Lotus flower tattoo. I am struck again by the simplicity and power of this symbol of hope. I imagine it as something that helps hold him together as he composes his life out of pieces, out of fits and starts.

Chapter 10

A Narrative Account of Ben

Vera Caine

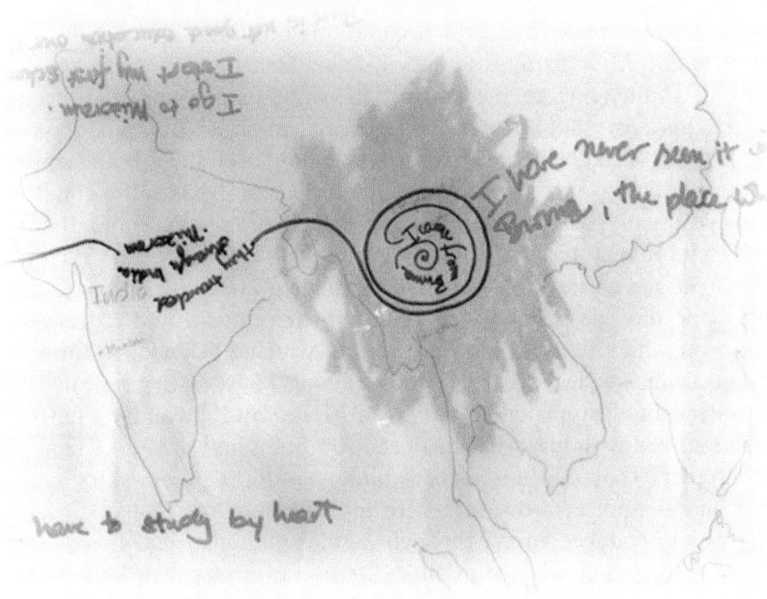

Figure 1: Map 1.

... Where I Am From ...

I will try and just write from my memory for now—no notes, no transcripts—just a couple of snippets taken from a larger map of Ben's life

(Figure 1). It is the image of a map I return to, both in actual and metaphorical ways, as the image of maps seems to live in the stories I remember of Ben. His routes of migration both geographically and through different school systems and cultural experiences have greatly influenced his stories of school. Ben and I only met once at an urban shopping mall—a perhaps somewhat stereotypical North American meeting place—as well as we had a few very brief telephone conversations; scattered among these were fragments of sentences with his mother and what I assumed was his older sister. These conversations happened when I was trying to connect and stay connected with Ben. Ben and I lived some 300 kilometres apart in the same Canadian province and while we managed to meet once, our lives became too busy and complex it seemed to meet again. After many attempts I called Ben one last time and while he finds it challenging to meet again to negotiate his narrative account, he wants his story told. As I hear myself talking with him about the many insights I have gained from his telling and life I can sense his body straightening out, his voice becomes clear and has more tonal variance ... 'yes, really?', a mix of pride and disbelief. I reassure him about the use of pseudonyms and that his story is one of other stories and will be told in a larger context of school leaving. We end with a promise that perhaps one day we will have a chance to meet again and to revisit the occasion on which he told and the times in which I listened, restoried and relistened to his stories of early school leaving. My memory returns to our conversation that happened several months ago and I wonder what of his story has stayed with me, what has been forgotten and how do I remember Ben. Wonders that opened up new understandings of his story, a story that resonates only at a distance with my own.

Ben was introduced to me through a colleague, who had made contact with Ben with the help of a counsellor. Before I ever met Ben, I knew he was an immigrant from Burma who had left high school and was now working for many hours each week. My attempt to piece together an initial story was marked by my struggle to understand a life I knew little about. I lacked the social-political, historical and cultural context of his life. I recall my anxiety and worry, my franticness in attempting to find friends who could help me ... as I struggled I began to wonder about my franticness, about my futile attempts to compose a storyline. Amidst this I began to wonder: would I be able to hear Ben's story as he told it? Would I be able to retell his life story? Who was he? What would he think was important for me to know? Where would he begin to tell? Would it be OK to ask personal questions that revealed my not knowing, yet were questions that didn't position him? I remember my sweating hands.

I arrived several hours before our planned meeting and I wandered the mall. The mall was a meeting place Ben had chosen, because it was close to his home and a place he had been many times. I remember walking in endless circles, looking into people's faces and wondering if Ben too would pace like I did. How would I recognise him? Getting closer to the meeting time I wandered to the agreed upon place and each time someone unbeknown to me would pass I would smile... there were many smiles that day.

Finally I heard this timid voice say 'Hmm, hello'. Ben made no eye contact, and so, ironically, my smile probably wouldn't have made a difference. A few quick words and I followed Ben up the escalator to the food court on the second floor. I pointed to the far corner, a place away from the constant interruption. Ben nodded, which I read as agreement. He declined my invitation for lunch, coffee... I was hungry, but I could wait too. We turned quickly to the research protocol and the signing of the consent form. I wanted him to know and I wanted to be able to begin recording our conversation. Remembering becomes difficult at times, particularly when I am nervous. Ben never looked up the entire hour, the only time he raised his head was when he looked out the window to point in the direction where he lives and where he works. He looked up to point, however, I am not sure he ever looked at me. The conversation was fragmented, yet rich and filled with many wonders. Our conversation started and ended in many places it seemed, always simultaneous.

I Have Never Seen it in My Eye — Burma, the Place Wherever I Go

How did Ben learn about Burma? Where was he from? Was that the beginning of his life? He had never seen Burma with his eyes, but it was there in his stories, in who he was (Figure 2). He kept making references to it and his entire life was told in relation to Burma. I started thinking about my own life as an immigrant woman and how much of my own telling continued to reflect my motherland, my home. Do others hear these stories? And how do they hear them? Do others encourage us to tell these stories? And if they do why do they want to hear? My mind starts drifting as I listen to the transcript again. I recall Ben's story of his teachers in Canada.

> Uh, I don't really like asking people personal stuff, so I just ... some teachers they just, I don't know, they ask me like personal stuff, like in front of the kids. And they share my story, like he came from that country and they can say. But

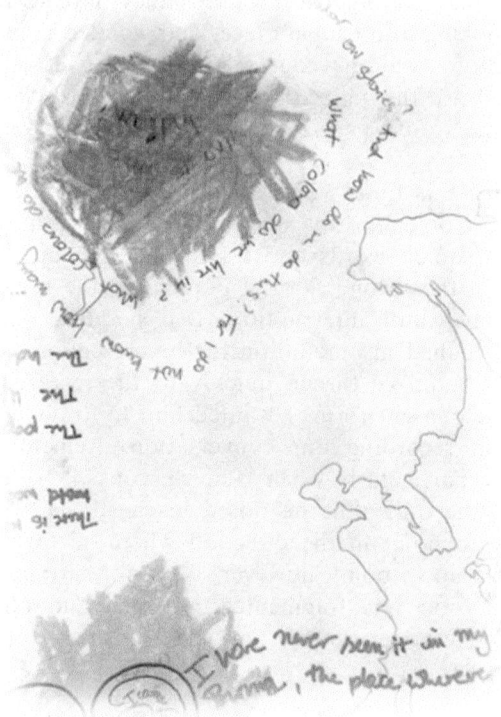

Figure 2: Map 2.

> I don't want that thing to be out but the teacher like asked me, from the teacher so I have to answer ... it was embarrassing for me.

Ben never talked about his embarrassment or his discomfort of being asked personal questions by his teachers or his counsellors; he felt the authority of the teachers and an obligation to answer. I wondered where and when Ben had developed his notion of authority and his lack of agency. Home mattered to Ben and as Ben kept returning to his stories in other places, I began to see how strongly his ability to relate, his sense of obligation, authority and discomfort might be shaped by this. Ben left Burma with his parents when he was two years old and at the time his family settled in India, or more specifically Mizoram. Yet, many relations of his family continued to live in Burma. Ben talked only in fragments about this and about the historical political events that shaped his families' journeys and extended relationships.

I Have Been Drawing Since I Was a Child, Even Back Home, Whatever, Even in India

I am getting confused. I sometimes don't know what Ben calls home — Burma, India, Canada — perhaps it is a search for home yet (Figure 3). I return to the transcripts to read and make sense of this. Ben talks about the comic strips he has drawn now for a long time and I return to the conversations about these comic strips to search for his understanding of home: 'I don't do trees, house and stuff. I do, pretty much draw humans, like humans and the clothing'. This helps me understand better what home might be for Ben; home as located in family and in the context of geography. His words are reminders of how important his family stories are in all of this. His family creates the line that provides continuity across oceans, countries, different social-political contexts. He works now many hours so that his sister can pursue her dream of going to university. Perhaps one day she too will support him in his pursuit of education and schooling. 'And then continue my study later when my sister and my brother they are done. They might have a good job and then later on they help me up, you know'.

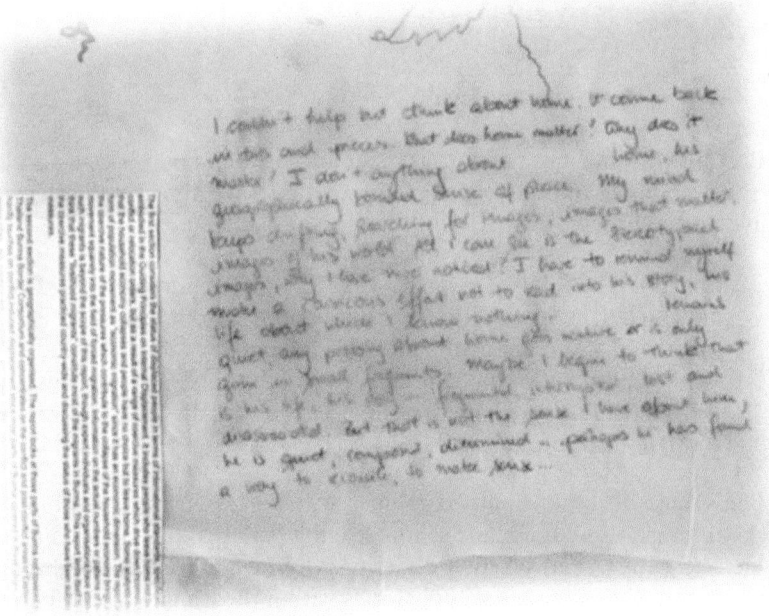

Figure 3: Map 3.

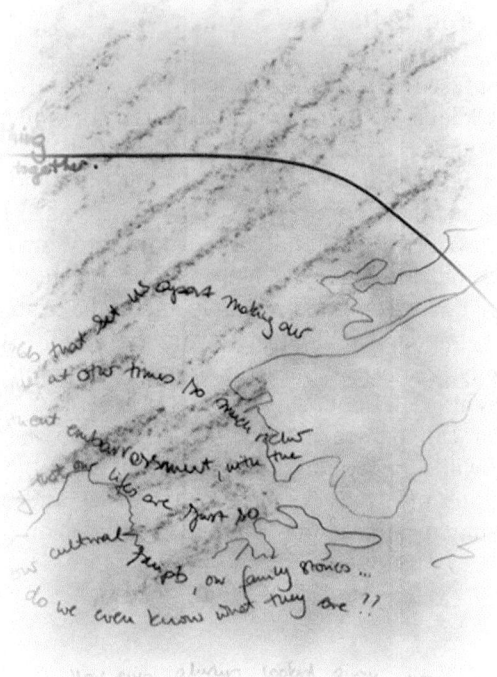

Figure 4: Map 4.

Ben talked some more about his sister and brother and parents and I can see the deep bond and the responsibility that rests on him and that he wants to live up to (Figure 4).

> She [sister] told me to go to, like do the upgrading, but I always tell her like, uh then what are you gonna eat? You know and those kinds of stuff. You have to pay this rent and all those stuff. We can help each other later on. So I think this is Canada so we all have this chance. Like maybe study is not too late for, you know.

Ben's sense of responsibility combined with his beliefs that possibility still exists to return to school made school leaving perhaps easier and in a way a viable alternative. Yet, I kept wondering why he could so easily disengage from school, what were his school stories within the Canadian context. And as I listened to his words (Figure 5):

Ben had completed Grade 6 in India and given his age was placed into a Grade 10 classroom in Canada, a place where he still was older than all of

Figure 5: Map 5.

his classmates. 'When I first came to Canada um I don't know pretty much English so I have to take ESL and I started from Grade 10'. He didn't seem to have trouble adjusting to the academic challenges and when I asked him he said: 'Back home we have to study by heart and then over here the exams, everything is in multiple choices and so it's much easier. Once you read up you, it keeps in your head'.

There were some teachers Ben speaks very highly of, teachers who he felt understood him and could alter their teaching style to better help him. And there were others and, as Ben struggled, he tried to talk with them. 'And then I fall behind and then the teachers start talking to me so I, I tell them out, I was coming from ESL and all that stuff, and then so they understand me in their heart'. Yet, the response of the teachers is something that Ben didn't expect. 'But after I told that some teachers say it to the class, right. So that's when the problems drop in ... but and then, I don't know, but I don't feel comfortable. I was all looking down'. Ben's words of looking down now as I sit here re-counting his life's story are a reminder to me of how I came to know him. Did he too see me as someone in authority, someone who might tell his story without asking him first? I am still left to wonder about this, yet he assured me that I could tell his story, perhaps our story reflective of the brief time we met. His sense of discomfort also grew in other places.

> But somehow like I was already old for the school so I wasn't feeling comfortable or something, you know ... and then the teachers kinda ask me for my age and then I have to say and it kinda not feel normal. And they ask me like personal stuff, like in front of kids. And they share my story like he came from that country and they can say. But I don't want that thing to be out but the teacher like asked me, from the teacher so I have to answer. And then it was embarrassing for me.

Yet, there are also other teachers.

> Uh, well, he like kinda understand I'm a newcomer and then he doesn't tell my personal stories to people, you know. And then he, he just like helped me out when people kinda ask me some stuff and I don't know how to reply.

Ben remarked about this particular teacher, '*I think he's been there in our country*'. I inquired into this and Ben didn't really know, but he sensed that he might have, or at least he seemed to understand Ben's story as that of a newcomer, his shyness and embarrassment and longing to be like others in the school, not one whose story stood out. In all of the stories Ben shared with me, he reminds me that he is not from here, he is not from Canada. The fragmented way in which he tells his story is perhaps indicative of the multiple struggles of a newcomer, of entering places that are unfamiliar and to which we are unfamiliar. While his telling is fragmented there are strong pieces of continuity at the same time, the continuity of his life amidst his family and the continuity of his art work. Ben did share some excitement about school; he continued to draw and got into animations. He volunteered many hours to learn not just the artistic drawing, but also the videotaping and audio-video components. 'So then we get along together and then spend after school. That's what I spend my time mostly, after school ... and then they removed that course'. Just as Ben begins to find a place within school, it gets disrupted and the disruption this causes becomes yet another event in his story of leaving school.

> I was waiting for that one. And that's the reason that I didn't even feel like going to school anymore you know. That was the only course that kept me still going to school. So it was not much students [in that class] ... Like every day when I wake up in the morning it's hard, like when I don't have arts I, you know, oh there's no point of going.

Chapter 11

A Narrative Account of Truong

D. Jean Clandinin

I first met Truong when Sean, who knew Truong from working with him in junior high school, brought him to the university. As Sean, Truong, and I stood in the doorway of my office, I knew that Truong was deciding whether or not he wanted to talk with me. Was I someone who he could trust? I knew his relationship with Sean had enabled Sean to interest him in the study but now Truong wanted to check me out. After all, I was the one with whom he would have the conversations. I was careful to maintain eye contact as I sensed there was much to learn from Truong's story. I could not help but notice, though, the tattoos on his arm.

Truong let Sean know that he would participate after meeting me. We met about a week after that first encounter on October 15, 2008, and again a week later on October 22, 2008. Three weeks later, Sean arranged for Truong, Vera, and another study participant, and Sean and me to meet up at Hamilton School so Truong could show us around the school. I knew from our first meeting that Hamilton School was a home place for Truong, a place where he felt he belonged.

It was as we began our second conversation that I asked Truong about the tattoos engraved on his arm. Truong described the first tattoo, the tiger, as his "Chinese Zodiac animal." He described the second tattoo, the dragon, by saying "in the Chinese tradition, it's like protection." He began to have the tattoos engraved on his body when he was 16 and, over the next 4 years or so, he added a koi fish that "represents prosperity." One artist did all the tattoos except for a Japanese demon mask that he now regrets having done. In response to my wonder about whether having the tattoos done hurt, he said it was "a burning sensation and a cutting at the same time. So almost

---

Composing Lives in Transition: A Narrative Inquiry into the Experiences of Early School Leavers
Copyright © 2013 by Emerald Group Publishing Limited
All rights of reproduction in any form reserved
ISBN: 978-1-78052-974-5

like a knife and a lighter at the same time." The pain he described helped me realize how important these tattoos were for Truong.

Moving Around: Returning Home

Truong went to one inner city school for kindergarten and moved for Grade 1 to Hamilton, a kindergarten to Grade 9 school, and, except for 2 years when he was in British Columbia (B.C.), he was there until he completed Grade 9 and went off to Smith for high school.

At first Truong spoke of going to British Columbia with his dad but in a later conversation spoke of being in Nanaimo in Grades 3–4 with his "mom and siblings" and having "family friends" there. He said, "Like they were our neighbours and I think they came over to Canada with my mom, so like they knew each other from back home in Thailand." Apparently they moved to Nanaimo from Edmonton earlier than Truong and his mother and siblings, as he said, "They were there for a few years already." His time at the school in Nanaimo was challenging at first because Truong said he "was picked on by the cool kids" as he was "the new kid." He described how one boy

> got his little brother Tyson to come after me and try to beat me up but I ended up beating him up ... and then they kinda had a grudge against me for the rest of the school year and whatnot, but I kinda kept my own, like I stood up for myself and I made my own friends and then we, we did get into, you know, clashes with them and stuff but they were little kids right, it wasn't sending each other to the hospital or anything like that.

The year in Nanaimo was marked by incidents in which Truong became involved in needing to protect himself. As he described these incidents that seemed similar to some of the incidents in Edmonton, he said,

> I've had a pretty exciting life as a kid 'cause I, like I wouldn't want my kid to go through that or my little brother or anything, that's why I kind of, I'm more protective about things that I have, right, just 'cause I've been through it and it sucks getting stuff taken from you, especially from people you don't even know and you're walking down the street and not being safe.

When I asked how it was when he left Hamilton school again, this time for Prince Rupert with his brother and father, he said, "at first it was kind of, it was like going to Nanaimo again, right, it was like 3 years and then a year and then back for a year, and then away for another year" but he said he was "kind of glad it happened because I did make more friends." He described how when he first "moved there, yeah I didn't have friends at first but then I started making friends with the big kids, like Grade 7 kids, Grade 8 kids and stuff and we hung out and had a blast." Even though he had a good time there, he is "always excited to come back home. Edmonton was always my home ... I love coming back home ... 'cause I always come back to my friends and ... the life that I know."

The Time of His Life

Truong described Hamilton School as his "most memorable time of school." When he speaks about his time in Hamilton School he describes times with friends like Kirk and others.
As he said,

> My whole life I was kinda, I thought I was the cool kid, but our school was so small that we knew everybody so there was, like the guys that played sports or whatever and they always hung out together, then the girls, they always hung out together, and there was maybe a few outsiders I guess you would call them, but we would always interact with them right, but we wouldn't be kind of best of friends with them but if they wanted to play basketball, we'd play basketball with them, 'cause we all knew each other, right?

The way Truong described his experiences at Hamilton helped me realize he felt he belonged in the school and had relationships with the other students there.
As he said, Sean and his principal "put a big impact on my life because of what they've done for me personally anyways. Like a lot of teachers, like when I went to high school, they didn't care about me or anything like that, it was like, well my gym teacher cared because he knew my older brother." The caring he felt in the school from the teachers clearly mattered to him. For Truong, teachers who care, always care about his "outside life, and what we've been through outside or what we do go through." He said, "'cause it's like if I got beat up the day before, I'd go to school in the morning, [the principal] would be there and try, like what's wrong, what happened and try to solve it."
Now, some years later, when he met up with his former junior high school principal he described the feeling as "awesome, just seeing him

again." He acknowledges that his junior high school principal "always told me to stay out of trouble and stuff, but it came to me and what had to be done was done ... I'm happy ... he came back into my life as the same positive guy that he was before."

Playing Sports as a Way to Make a Life

Truong describes playing sports throughout his time in school. He said, "I was in soccer all the way through" except for his two years in B.C. When he was in Edmonton he said, "I just kind of played school yard ball with my friends, after school, I'd hang out with my friends and play soccer or whatever. I played community soccer in Edmonton." He said that he played in "under 9 and under 12" in community leagues. As he says, "And then junior high came around and I played for the school and we were, yeah, I got Athlete of the Year in Grade 9 and Rookie of the Year in Grade 7." In junior high he "was more of a soccer guy and I was like, when I was in Grade 9 I was the team captain and we won the championship that year and we won, actually we won a lot of championships and I was captain for most of the teams."

When we went to visit his junior high school, Truong insisted we go to the gymnasium where he showed me the pennants of the teams he played on. He also told me a story of a wealthy sports team owner who awarded him a scholarship for his skill in sports that would have enabled him to go to university. However, the wealthy man went bankrupt and the scholarship promises were not fulfilled. Truong thought he still had some of the awards and he wanted to show me. When we entered Hamilton School that winter afternoon, it was a bit like entering Truong's life memory box as we looked at class photographs, stood in hallways as Truong described where he used to play and as we visited the gymnasium where he showed me the pennants which marked the times and places where his excellence in sports was recognized.

When he went to high school he played on the volleyball team and he was awarded MVP for high school volleyball. For him, sports allowed him to not only to care for others and his own safety but allowed him to develop his skills. Playing sports in junior high also created some problems for, as he said, "sports kept me out of trouble and kind of got me into it too, 'cause I would have to go home at night and I would be walking home at like 9 at night and stuff" and, while he described the fun of walking home with a group of friends, there was the ever present possibility of violence on the streets around his home and school.

He described his life as "so I just kind of lived my life and played sports and just living, trying to survive."

The Spaces between Home and School

The inner-city context in which Hamilton was situated created places of tension for Truong and other students. When Truong and I met at the school and he showed me around, we stood in the places where some of his stories were situated. From the windows of the school Truong showed me the places just outside the school walls where Truong needed to be constantly vigilant about protecting himself and others. While he spoke of getting "into a lot of confrontations in the school" with "students that are from the other gangs," he mostly situated the violence in the spaces between home and school. When we looked out the third floor school window, he pointed out a house across the street where older kids had lived that did not go to Hamilton. He said,

> We had a little bit of a problem with them too for awhile. It was like almost you're either with them or you're with us type of thing but we weren't really a gang ... it was just us kids trying to stick up for each other because we're friends. And a lot of things happened to that school too, like neighborhood gangs and stuff would come to the school and bang on the windows and try to get in and stuff like that. Like I remember this one time we were in class actually. Everybody was in class and probably about 10 Native and White kids from around the neighborhood came to the window and doors and stuff trying to get in with bats and chains and stuff.

While Truong describes how the school building was under attack in the above quotation, it was the spaces between home and school that were most frequently fraught with dangers. Truong lived a story of being someone who would protect those who were weaker and might be bullied and beaten up.

> Like I walked this one kid home, it was just me and this one kid and we walked through that alley that they, that they live in, because he lived in that ally. So we had to walk through there and they came out of their house behind the store with saws and bats, like I saw all these weapons. And all I had was a hockey stick because we played hockey with Sean and stuff. This kid was like, can you walk me home and I was like yeah. And he's older than me, he's one year older than I am, but he's asking me for help. So I walked him and then this big kid came out and he, like you guys are walking in our territory, blah, blah, blah, blah, and I was like, you know what, do something about it right and I just kinda stuck up for myself

and they're like, they just kept going on and I was like, well, you know, you want to do something, then do it right. And they didn't do anything and they let us go, so I walked my buddy home, walked back to the school 'cause I was going to play hockey again.

From the Thai Refugee Camp to the Inner City

Truong grew up in inner city Edmonton. He came to Canada from Thailand after a time where his mother and father

> kinda ran from country to country just 'cause of the war. Because my dad got kidnapped by the army and stuff like that, and he escaped and then he would get kidnapped by another army, and then he would escape them and then run away to Thailand. And eventually he got kidnapped by the Thailand army, the Thai army, and then somehow they got out and came here, something like that so, yeah, my mom was left alone a lot because of my dad getting kidnapped.

Truong and his older brother were born in Thailand and he thinks he must have been about one and a half years old when they arrived in Edmonton. At first they stayed in a hotel and then settled in the Hamilton neighborhood that has since been Truong's home place. He told me that while other people also came to Edmonton with them, no extended family came, "just our immediate family."

Truong heard the stories about his family's experiences.

> We'd ... just kind of sit around, like our family would just sit around and chat and she [his mom] would tell us stories and my sister would be very interested, so I didn't care much for it because I didn't know, right, so, but I do like knowing about it 'cause it shows how strong they are. It makes me want to do better for myself so we don't have to go through that kind of stuff ... it makes me kind of sad thinking that they went through that kind of stuff and that they made it.

While he was growing up, he did not think much about living in the inner city. As he said,

> 'Cause my neighbourhood that we grew up in was, I thought it was pretty, pretty bad, like I didn't think it was bad when I

was living there but then I would talk to kids from out of the inner city or they would be oh, my neighbourhood is so scary and whatever and when I went there I was like this neighbourhood's so peaceful and everything's nice here right? Like there's no bums walking around or like hookers on the corners and stuff.

The stories he told seemed to revolve around a plot line of survival in what he now recognizes was seen as a "bad" neighborhood. As Truong said, "Just growing up in the inner city was, it made me tough."

While Truong has spent his life watching out for others and taking care of what came to him, he now says,

> I don't want to fight anymore, well I've never really wanted to fight but ... when that kind of stuff comes around I'm just you know that, I don't, I don't want it. 'Cause I lived, I lived there right, like my whole life almost.

He described robberies and house break-ins as well as violence on the streets.

> It was just kind of hard but that's the stuff we had to go through. It was kind of harsh so never really had nice things or anything. Just kind of had to survive. That's why I relied on sports a lot so that's when Sean came to Hamilton School and stuff and we had like sports night and I always, I always went to it, every time he had it open, I was there 'cause I loved playing sports.

Truong relates who he is today to his experiences growing up, because

> it made me who I am today, and I know that the street is an unsafe place because the police that's supposed to protect you isn't always going to be there for you, so you've got to be your own protector and what not, you can't really depend on somebody to be there ... 'cause they're not always going to be there for you.

I heard in Truong's voice a sense of how he learned that he could not count on others, even the police who were "supposed to protect" him. He learned early to take care of himself.

A Family Home Place

Truong grew up in what he called "a broken home basically since I was like a kid." Truong grew up knowing stories of the escape to Canada and the stories of

> how bombs would just go off and my dad would hide in like these holes and stuff that they had, like trenches that they had to dig up just for that situation, and they would stick my family, like my mom, my parents and my brother and I would be in those trenches and stuff.

He and his brother learned early to take care of themselves. His stories of his early experiences in a war zone (which he says he does not remember living through) as well as his coming from a "broken home" were stories that shaped how he learned to take care of himself. The dragon tattooed on his arm speaks to how often he needed protection as he walked to and from school and around his neighborhood.

> My mom worked double jobs, four of us so like, you know nobody really, nobody could have got a job yet, 'cause we were young, right, so nobody could help my mom really, and my brother was kind of in and out of jail a lot, and then my little sister that's 2 years younger than me and then my little brother, who's 16 now, is 6 years younger than me. So we didn't really have a great start I guess.

Faced with needing to be responsible for himself and his younger siblings, Truong learned to be a protector and caregiver while his mother provided the financial support for the family. Truong speaks now of how much he loves his mother "because she's been through a lot and she's still surviving and so she's, I knew she was a strong woman and that's why I'm trying to make her life as easy as I can."

Truong went back to Cambodia and Viet Nam with his mother when he was 17. He met "his cousins and auntie that I never knew." He met relatives from both his mother's and father's side of the family. Truong's mother would like to go back to visit and Truong "was going to pay for her and the family this year" but the cost was too great. Truong knows enough Vietnamese "to kind of have conversations, just not deep conversations about things ... everyday conversations I can have." I assumed Vietnamese was his first language as he was very young when he arrived in Edmonton. However, when I asked when he learned to speak English, he said, "I'm actually not too sure how I actually learned English but I'm pretty sure it was through school."

Truong does not have connections with Vietnamese cultural or friendship groups in Edmonton, saying "I'm not too worried about other people's lives, 'cause it's hard enough to kind of live my own life."

Truong became a father to a daughter two and a half years ago. His daughter lives with her mother, but Truong and his mother have access to the child on the weekends. He describes his daughter as putting "joy in my life."

> When I see her laughing and playing around it's just like the greatest thing. So when she like, you know, she gives me like kisses and hugs and stuff, it's like it's a good thing to me right because I'm not used to it, like I've never kissed my mom in my life that I can remember. I've never, I've maybe hugged her once my whole life so I mean this kind of stuff is different to me. But she is my daughter and I do love her. And she is, she is the joy in my life.

I wonder if his daughter has, in some ways, interrupted the stories he was living and telling. Did her arrival and his knowing he was a father shift the trajectory of his forward looking story?

Losing the Coach, Losing the Team, Losing Interest

As we talked, Truong spoke of his experiences of leaving school. He had played on the volleyball team in Grades 10 and 11 and had experienced a great deal of success. But Grade 12 was different.

> And then Grade 12 came around and there was no more volleyball ... and so I was like, whatever, I don't really feel like going to school anymore. I got kicked out second semester of Grade 12. Like I did go to my classes and stuff but I was more of, oh I'm late, forget it, I don't want to go anymore or you know, stuff like that and I just didn't have motivation to go anywhere.

In Grades 10 and 11, he said,

> If I was late I'd still go to school, if I didn't have a ride to school I would bus to school but in Grade 12 if I didn't have a ride I was, ah, I'm staying home today. If it's cold or like I

bussed to school in Grade 10 a couple of times during the winter and stuff, right, and like, you know, but that's 'cause I had a game or practice or something after school so I wanted to be there.

As he looked back over this time in high school, he said,

I didn't care about the teachers, I didn't do anything, I didn't really have motivation to go to school really except for when I had volleyball ... because my coach was my gym teacher that cared and he kind of kept me out of everything but ... the only things I really cared about in high school were basically my friends and volleyball.

He had a "distinctive hair style" and was described as "the Asian guy with the bangs 'cause I had like spiky hair with two long strands coming down the sides."

He spoke of his teachers in high school in the following way:

Like a lot of teachers, I don't know if they liked me ... but a lot of coaches and teachers and stuff knew who I was. They knew me for, like the person that I was and stuff but the principal or the student counsellor or whatever didn't really care, didn't, like I've known a lot of kids that got so many chances, like they, they fought or whatever, they got kicked out of school and then they would come back and everything's good and stuff, right, but with me it was like OK, come to the office, you're expelled because you skipped too much. And I'm like OK well, what am I going to do, I'm not going to cry about it right?

As Truong told me these stories about not being given second chances as others had been, I sensed he had learned to accept such treatment and to not fight back. He described that he "was like my own person with my own friends." Truong has tried to complete high school. He tried to register "when I was about 18 or 19" in order to "finish up." He attributes his desire to complete high school to the birth of his daughter. He has

70-some credits, so if I finish my Grade 12 I know I can graduate, and I really wanted to when I was 19, but then money came into play and all that stuff, and I was thinking like student financing and stuff, but I went to do it and they were like, No, you're one day too old. So they cut it off at

September 1st and that's when my birthday is. ... I didn't really try again 'cause money's still in play, like money's still an issue in my life, right.

He became a father at 19. "That's why I kind of wanted to go back to school and finish up too 'cause she was my motivation for it."

Taking Care of Others: His Mother, His Siblings, Kids Who Are Weaker

Truong has spent his life taking care of others with whom he has relationships. Truong recently moved out of the apartment that he shared with his mother and two younger siblings and into a three-bedroom house with a friend. When the friend moved out, his mother and his siblings moved in when their apartment "kinda fell apart."

He worked from when he was about 15, at first with "under the table pay" when he "washed dishes and stuff for the restaurant" where his mom was the cook. The money he earned then was to "just kind of take care of myself and my mom didn't have to worry about me too much right, like I'd have lunch money or whatever." He learned early to help out with the finances at home, to take care of himself to save his mother from even more financial worry.

Truong has been a watchful big brother to his two younger siblings. "I built the rep of people being scared of me and stuff like that so my little brother and my little sister can go through school peacefully." He learned to live and tell stories of himself as a tough guy, someone to be scared of, in order to provide his siblings with protection from harm. As he said,

> I kinda lived the life that I lived basically for them to go through school and I've tried, I did everything that I can for them to graduate and stuff right, to go through school peacefully, you know get rides to school and stuff, 'cause I knew what I didn't have is what kind of caused me to not to go to school. But for them, like I kinda told them, well my little brother more, to actually motivate yourself, to find something to go to school for.

In his words, I sensed he had learned, from his own stories, to live in relation with his younger siblings in ways that would provide them the support he lacked while growing up. His sister graduated and his younger brother found dancing and is well known in his school and in the community as a hip hop dancer. As Truong said,

> I want him to get something for himself so he wants to do it all the time, right? Like with me it was I, I loved volleyball so much in high school. Like I had invitations to play for Team Canada and practice and try out with them but money was always the issue. I didn't have the money but now that I have a job and, you know, I'm trying to get money and stuff, whatever my brother needs for his dancing career or whatever, I would get it for him.

A Spiritual Life

Truong has spent time thinking about his philosophy of life. An "atheist," he believes others should be free to choose their beliefs. At one time he believed in "Buddha, the way people believe in god or a higher power." He still wears a Buddha necklace "because he believed Buddha was "a peaceful kind of guy" and Truong, too, likes "peace in my life ... and my family's life ... Buddha represents peace to me." Truong "just wants to live this life that I have as peaceful and as well as I can without suffering." He no longer prays to Buddha but he does "pray that somebody doesn't hurt me because it would be bad."

Truong also spoke of a Chinese god who represents righteousness and loyalty. Truong relates his thoughts about this god to the importance of being

> loyal to your brothers ... or your family. And that's what I believe in ... don't hurt people for no reason or don't do bad stuff for no reason but if it comes to you, then do what you have to do ... I'm loyal 110% to whoever ... that I like in my life.

As Truong shared his philosophy around loyalty to friends and family, I asked where he learned about these ideas. Triggered by "gangster movies and violent movies, like action movies" that mention gods, he uses the Internet tools, Google and Wikipedia, to just read up on this stuff. He went on to say,

> And then I read on, like that's why dragons, I've read things about dragons. Like there's a red dragon, yellow dragon, blue dragon, green dragon, and they all represent different things.

A black and red dragon is a fierce dragon so they're more aggressive and, but then I think the yellow one is more passive and more about peace and stuff like that. I just kind of, just kind of read up on it and then just kind of do it.

He says he never talks to people about this but just does it on his own. He spoke of karma too which he see as a kind of "common sense" which he describes as follows:

> If you hurt somebody obviously they're going to come and try to hurt you. I mean that's supposedly karma but that's how people are, right? And then, but you know, if you hurt somebody's family they're going to hurt your family. So everything comes back full circle ... I believe in karma a lot and that's another reason why I don't do bad things for no reason. So if people come and hurt me then its bad karma on them because I'm coming to hurt you right after. And some of that can be a bit more spiritual. But I just live my life more physically than mentally ... I just live my life day to day. You know, if you're good with me I'm good with you, and if you're not good with me.

Truong is very aware of how he

> loved the fast life before. It was always go do whatever you want, you know, if it came, then it came. You didn't really care. But now it's like, you might pull out a gun today and that's the end of my life ... like everyday somebody gets stabbed or some crazy person out there doing stuff to old people or young kids or whatever ... You can't save the world but I can save myself and my friends, my kid, my family.

Looking Back, Looking Ahead

As Truong reflected back on his life, he said, "just the life I lived was almost like I could have gone to jail any time basically." As Truong now turns to compose a forward looking story, he speaks of both himself and his daughter. He wants her to live her life almost like how I think about life, just peacefully, and try to get away from whatever you can but stick up for your own ... just show people that you're not going to get stepped on ... so be your own person and do what you got to do.

Chapter 12

A Narrative Account of Lynn

Joy-Ruth Mickelson

I learn from Sean that Lynn is shy. Sean was a youth worker from The Red Cape Society and has known Lynn, her two brothers, and her family, from the time he had met them at Orange Way School where he was a liaison worker for families and their youth. Lynn tells Sean that she will meet with me only if he is present. She will have a look at me and perhaps talk with me and decide if she feels comfortable. Only then will she agree to being a participant in the research. She also needs reassurance that Sean will be nearby during the first "official" interview.

This first "look-see" occurs in a bustling Tim Hortons. Lynn is dressed warmly and her smiling face is friendly as she greets Sean with a hug. She and I shake hands and the three of us tuck ourselves into a corner to chat informally.

Sean's presence is powerful for Lynn; he knew her when she was at school, knew her family well, and kept contact with many of them over the years. They begin to talk about family members animatedly. Lynn seems comfortable when I join in the conversation and make a comment or ask a question or two about a family member she has mentioned. As this is a "look-see" meeting nothing is recorded. I feel that, at this juncture, it will interrupt the easy flow of conversation if I take notes. I wish it was different because Lynn details eloquently names and contexts and I worry that I may not remember. Sean discusses grief and Lynn talks about not having grieved properly over the death of her grandmother, Christine, in 2003. Lynn explains how everything in her family fell apart when this happened. She talks about her grandmother's partner, Peter.

Composing Lives in Transition: A Narrative Inquiry into the Experiences of Early School Leavers
Copyright © 2013 by Emerald Group Publishing Limited
All rights of reproduction in any form reserved
ISBN: 978-1-78052-974-5

As Lynn is telling me about Christine and Peter, her voice resonates with surety, and even though Peter died in 2007 and Christine 4 years prior, the strength of shared memories shine. I know that I want to explore the quality and depth of their relationship at our next meeting. Lynn talks of a goal of hers: to place a headstone at Peter's grave to honour his memory, "He was my dad."

I share what the research is all about and, if she is willing to participate, what is expected of us both including the signing of a consent form. Lynn says that she wants to tell her story and will sign the form next time but that she would like Sean to be nearby during the interview. We arrange the time and place to meet.

Lynn tells us that her boyfriend, Edward, will be coming to meet her at Tim Hortons. We have been talking for three-quarters of an hour when she sees him at a far door. Sean asks to meet him and they both leave the table. I observe the introductions from afar. Lynne has acknowledged Edward as significant in her present life and I wonder whether I shall meet him. We arrange a quiet place for our next meeting.

Sean and I meet Lynn and we make our way to a large table in a library. A nearby window looks onto a courtyard. Lynn and I watch a group of young men kicking a ball and we laugh at their antics as they communicate by gestures with someone in the library. Sean moves to a place where Lynn is able to see him. I wonder if she will feel comfortable to stay and tell her story. She does and tells it fluently and with feeling. The emotions associated with incidents that were painful are evident to me from her body language and facial expressions. Similarly when she told of joyful times and positive relationships she smiled and her voice resounded warmly. I read the consent form and review the research. Lynn signs. I also sign and Lynn will take the form to her Probation Officer who needs to know Lynn's whereabouts and activities. "It really sucks."

Lynn had spoken in our "look-see" meeting about her family and their importance to her. We talk more about her maternal grandmother, Christine, and her partner, Peter, whom she refers to as "my dad. They were together, on and off, for 32 years." She reiterates, "He was my dad." Jane, Lynn's mother, is one of Christine's seven children. "She never raised us but she always came to visit. I knew my mom since I was a little kid. She lived her own life." Jane cared for Lynn when she was an infant for almost three and a half years, but when she was five, Jane left Lynn and her two brothers, Kevin and Carl, with Christine. The overwhelming thread that emanates throughout Lynn's telling and retelling is that Christine and Peter were her guides, the ones who nurtured her through good times and bad, hers and theirs.

> Our house was so homey, so when you walked in you just felt, you know, it was home. And everybody loved our home ...

> she made everything. If we wanted something she would get it. I know we lived good for her being on assistance and watching over us.

Lynn talks about her school, Orange Way School, in glowing terms. It is a junior high school.

> I loved it. I miss those days. I have a lot of friends from when I was growing up as a kid. And we still talk about Orange Way. Like we're always "Oh. Orange Way." All of us still, to this day. We reminisce. I'm one of the most responsible out of all of us. I grew up around boys so I was always playing boys sports.

Lynn lists floor hockey, soccer and football and in Grade 7 volleyball, badminton, soccer, and "tackle sports. I was sort of like a little tomboy." She tells me about her two favorite teachers, Mrs. Smith and Mrs. Jones. "They listened and you could talk to them. I loved Social and LA." Despite the positive experiences she had lived at Orange Way School Lynn's feelings about continuing her schooling change dramatically and she was encouraged to enroll in a store-front school for Grade 10. "[When] I was in Grade 10, my grandma found out she had lung cancer and that's when I dropped out. Decided to help out with my auntie and them at home, because she was really sick." Christine, even though her prognosis was poor, was still "watching over" Lynn. "My grandma wanted me to finish. She wanted me to go to school. But I felt I didn't have to, or didn't want to be there, dealing with that alone put a lot of stress on my family." Lynn tells me that the program didn't work for her. She couldn't get engaged in any courses as there was too much else on her mind. She did go back for a couple of months in Grade 11. "But that didn't work neither. I wasn't interested."

The stress of watching Christine become progressively sicker, which eventually led to hospitalization in an active treatment hospital and then in a long-term care placement, had its effect on Lynn and the family. She described the cooking and cleaning and hospital visiting and coping with extended family members who came from afar as adding to the stress.

> We were angry at the whole thing that she was sick. It wasn't our fault. It wasn't anybody's fault. But we were blaming each other at the time. It was just so different with our whole family. We were all grieving and we were all grieving in the wrong way. I started drinking lots. My dad started drinking every day … we all just turned to alcohol. And after she was in

hospital for months and then she passed away our house
fell apart.

Lynne talks of respect. It is an important value of which she is aware and
it upsets her that she, too, becomes disrespectful.

People weren't respecting our house the way they were when
my grandma was alive and we weren't respecting our place the
way we should have. And it just became gloomy, really, really
gloomy ... like from 6 months before to after it was a big
change in everything.

The dark side of drinking was ever present. "I grew up around alcohol all
my life and I've seen everything." The darkness overtook family members,
and for some, addiction to drugs was added.

And that's just the way we seemed to grieve. And it didn't
help. It just hurt more and it took me a real long time to
realize that it hurt more. Like it wasn't going to bring her
back. The crying wasn't going to stop.

Nor was the drinking. Lynn and Peter, consumed by grief, quarrel and
argue. "He lost the love of his life and we didn't get along at all. We'd fight.
All of us were so close all the time and we're all just splitting and it was so
hard for all of us." After Peter, Lynn, Kevin, and Carl had been living
separately for one year, in different parts of the province, Lynn makes an
important decision because she misses them all. "I finally realized that I have
to grow up, have to get my dad back here. I want to take care of Carl now.
I feel lost. I need somebody and I want my brother with me."

Peter's death 3 years after Lynn and Carl had been living with him causes
another upheaval for her. She was cooking, shopping, and working to pay
the bills. The importance of coping, with very limited funds, led to her
involvement in criminal activities.

I despise drugs and I was a hypocrite because I started selling
it. It was a way of me taking care of my family, That's why
I did it. I know I chose the wrong thing to do. I made the
wrong decisions, but when you have no income. When you
have nothing at all. And when you have to take care of your
family, sorry that's just part of life. That's just the way some
people have to go. And that's the way I chose. I know it's
wrong. I knew I was in the wrong. I knew I was doing wrong.
I knew I was hurting others ... I know I'm hurting people's

> families. I know I'm doing all that but I need to take care of mine. I need to support my family. I was taking care of my family. That's the only reason why I did it. ... I got greedy. I started getting money hungry.

Lynn is charged, her freedom and activities are curtailed and, rather than stay at her home, she discovered a day program for youths. The program has learning components which require group discussions and problem solving exercises "life skills sort of thing and it's prepping me for work." It arranges experiences in the workplace. For the youth there is no choice for where their "work exposure" placement will be.

> I want to go back [to school], last week we were doing school testing to see what grade I was at and I'm surprised, 'cause I thought, like I haven't been in school in years. I was at Grade 9, 10 level. I thought I'd lost it ... Like I'm really bad at math. I love Social and LA you know. I was a straight A student for that ... but when I started doing it, it all came back to me.

Lynn has had a significant person in her life for a year. Lynn names him as "my boyfriend, Edward." Edward has a good job and comes from the same rural area as does Lynn's family. Lynn has met his mother who shows her approval of Edward's choice by giving Lynn jewelry. Lynn is wearing the diamond and sapphire ring that Edward's mother had given her when she stayed recently with Lynn and Edward: "I want you to have this ring." Edward's mother also asked: "When am I going to have a grandbaby?" I wonder whether Lynn feels pressured, but Lynn tells me: "My time-clock is running out, and "Anyway, we want a baby. He's always saying to me, 'Do you think you're pregnant?' He's just waiting." Lynn sounds sure about their relationship. "He's a hundred percent committed. I know he is. He even talks about marriage. 'I just want to be with you.' He looks for the future and our baby." Who will Lynn use as a "sounding board" to reflect on her options?

After our meeting when the recorder was not on we went to have a pizza. Lynn understood that I needed to take a few notes and she reflected on my interpretations of some parts of her story. For me, her sense of family, immediate and extended, was an important thread throughout. Her need to rescue them from addictive behaviours seemed a critical motivation for some of her actions. This speaks to her sense of responsibility which was often nested within divided/conflicting options. "I'm like that. I never learned [about responsibility]. I had to be." Her sense of self-knowledge, her wish to continue her schooling: "I just don't want to feel dumb. I will go back. I want to go back." Lynn now wonders — shall she upgrade her schooling or get a job? She has hopes of being involved in health care. Will she be able to manage a job and schooling? Will she be accepted into a licensed practical nurse or nursing aide program? She knows she has to make choices. She knows she has to rely on herself. When we wonder together about who will guide her in these choices, she says, "No one."

I am aware how complicated these choices are. Lynne has shared that returning to school and completing her diploma are important to her. She wants to graduate from a post-secondary program — perhaps in the field of health care. The tensions for her may explain a reversal of her position when she responded to a question about who, recently, she had been seeing/ speaking to in her family. Lynne replied, "No one. I am not speaking to anyone. I rely on myself." She also realizes that she needs to earn some money for the future. She says that her work exposure placements have been good — she has worked in the kitchens — and, although hard, her work attitude was reported as positive. As a constant backdrop to these choices is her wish to parent a child with her partner.

At a meeting with Lynn on December 3, 2008, I suggested to her some threads that I had pulled from her words during our time together. I continued with a few wonders of my own. Our time and place to meet were muddled as Lynn had fallen asleep and was awoken by me. I shared the threads I had pulled. Her responses made me wonder whether she was still sleepy or whether the following threads I was suggesting did not fit for her and/or were making her uncomfortable.

Caring for Others

Lynn agreed that caring for others was important for her in her life. At school she was always concerned about her friends.

Learning from Others

Her role models were Christine and Peter, and from them she had learned much. Had addiction to substances been perceived by her as a way to ease pain, an escape, or will it have a deterrent effect? She felt she had learned much about its dangers and that learning will be a force in her life. She has also learned that it is important to grieve losses in a constructive way.

Learning from Self

Lynn acknowledged that she had learned much about herself, especially that side of her personality that responded to crises. Lynn has had to grow up fast and has faced multiple challenges. She has experienced relationships that have been meaningful and knows how to give and receive within them. A sense of yearning permeates her story.

Where School Fitted in My Life

Tied to these wonders were — what did school mean for Lynn then, and what did it mean now? A constant refrain for Lynn is how much she loved her school: the familiarity of the building, the friends, the teachers, and the opportunity to play all the sports. Had her world outside school not fallen apart would her reentry into a store-front school have been different? Would she have found friends and teachers there and have become engaged in school learning?

Post Script — March 11

We meet to negotiate the narrative account. Prior to reading it Lynn shares an event that was very significant for her. It was the death of her uncle, her mother's brother. He was murdered. When she went to his funeral, she remembered the warmth and fun of their relationship and she felt the loss deeply.

Lynn is enjoying her present job working in a kitchen and says she is given extra responsibilities and receives positive feedback from her supervisor. When/if the chief cook is away Lynn is responsible for preparing/cooking the meal for approximately 40 residents. We discussed how anxiety-provoking this can be. Lynn told me that she is hoping to move to an apartment nearer her work that is a little larger than the studio one she now has.

Lynn chose her own pseudonym but I had chosen those of others in her story. We laughed together as she commented on those pseudonyms. Most of them had significance for her and she wanted them changed. She chose the names and they have been changed. Lynn read the narrative account with great care. She clarified some incorrect dates which have now been changed. She felt that her grandma and dad, Christine and Peter, were not given the importance that they had for her in her life. I read the last paragraph of page 2: "The overwhelming thread that emanates throughout Lynn's telling is that Christine and Peter were her guides, the ones who nurtured her through good times and bad, hers and theirs." Lynn accepted that this did encompass their importance in her life. I said that the account was written from the transcripts and she reminded me that we only really met for three times. She observed that her career choices have probably changed now. She is definitely going back to school in the fall and may choose cooking as a career option.

I said that I would email Lynn with the corrections. We had been emailing and phoning each other regularly when trying to arrange meetings. As I dropped Lynn off at her apartment, she asked me to phone her. Our relationship has not ended until it is mutually agreed.

Aware My Tense is Everpresent

    to present your story my tense shouts present
    you know the past, yours and theirs,
    I know it too, have heard you tell
    also of future, you give the due to temporality
    the tension creeps and sometime magnifies
    wondering why? oh why?
    examines the space between, borders its liminality
    verb ends question — is tension too high

    and this is why, here's my credo.
    Your vibrancy and life writ in all tension give me no choice
    to present your story my tense screams present

    our sharing
    Faces matter, color matters, places matter
    it's hard to choose the one that fits your comfort.
    we walk, we walk, we walk,
    at last we find,
    black face, white face, red face
    we seat ourselves
    eat pizza, words spring to lips
    kalamata olives shaped in circles stick to melted cheese.
    wind chill extreme freezes outside faces barely seen
    bodies brace and stumble, angles sliced.
    here we sit and eat, uncertain it's the place for conversation
    a private conversation for all the world to hear.
    the place is loaded, party group, singles, and we two.
    Our bodies hunch toward each other.
    Someone greets me, rushes over, starts a lengthy story on and on and on
    a half-formed raise of eyebrow quizzes
    will it ever end?
    It does.

We talk. You tell the ins and outs of contexts and of time
of ups and downs, advances and retreats, of wonders and dismays
and more. I listen. and listen.

Respond then talk too much

have I destroyed momentum and your flow of telling
my search for threads too tautly strung.

Chapter 13

A Narrative Account of Christian

Vera Caine

I was introduced to Christian through Sean, who had worked with him as a teacher and coach in elementary and junior high school. All three of us met, and it was Sean's relationship with Christian that opened up the possibility for me to engage in conversations with him. Sean was always part of our conversations, either by joining us for lunch for periods of time or because our conversation returned to Christian's experiences of school. Sean, too, arranged for me, Christian, Jean, and Truong to return to the elementary and junior high school for a visit. Returning with Christian to this school, a school to which he felt a strong sense of belonging and ownership, opened up many backward and forward-looking stories for Christian and myself.

Christian was a very striking young man, quiet and with a very soft-spoken voice. I was struck by some of his references to violence and the expression of the same in his drawings and tattoos; it was this tension between his demeanor and his stories that drew me into his stories and his life. Perhaps it was in our last conversation when Christian talked about why both the Phoenix and the dragon are representatives of his life that I began to understand. The dragon, symbolic of strength, protection and power, and the Phoenix, representative of rebirth and change, in combination represent his life.

As a way to reflect upon our conversations I began to write postcards to Christian over the span of several weeks, which included two of our conversations and our visit at his elementary and junior high school. I then met with Christian again to reflect upon those notes and we engaged in another conversation, where Christian shared many of his drawings with me. In our final conversation we talked about some of his drawings, all of which are included in this narrative account. The different texts are representative of different stages of our conversation, yet, as a whole, perhaps they reflect some of Christian's experiences and the context of his life, a life in which school leaving is a part.

Figure 1: Christian's Drawing 1.

Dear Christian, yesterday Sean told me for the first time about you... the usual descriptors mixed with the memories Sean has of you. I am not sure how much I listened to Sean as my mind began to wander back to the inner city, a place I hadn't been back to for so many months. I was afraid of my own sense of loss, friends who had disappeared and friends I can no longer locate. Did I really want to go back? Yet, something was already drawing me into your story, Vera.

We sat in the same restaurant again, a place that is starting to feel familiar. A place where the waitress knows you, but not me. She smiles as she takes our order, yours without asking and mine with an inquisitive look that reveals she doesn't remember me. Talking with you now seems so different from when I first met you... the ease with which the conversation unfolds is different, partially because the parts of your life that you have shared with me then have become a way of knowing you now. Your drawings are spread all over my office desk and I am in awe of your abilities and your thoughtfulness as you reflect on both your art and your life.

> For the first time this is a picture that has a story behind it. It is my first picture before I got serious about drawing. It is a story about me and I turned myself into an animated character (Figure 1).

Dear Christian, I can still smell the sausages and bacon mixed with the smell of coffee. A place you come to every morning for coffee/breakfast after working the night shift at the local casino. Your small build and shy demeanor hardly let me guess you worked as a security guard, but then again I know little about that ... the lifestyle, the people, the craving for fortune just once. Who are you amidst this? It was hard for me to imagine where our conversation would go ... there was little for me to connect to. Your life was so far removed from school, it was a place you had been, a place as I heard in your and Sean's recollections that carries many good memories ... of basketball and baseball, of friends and amazing teachers ... I will keep writing and I am so glad we will get to talk more, Vera.

Figure 2: Christian's Drawing 2.

Tattooed on your arm are Chinese characters, characters that reflect what means the most in your life. I listen intently as you translate these characters for me: family, forever, friend(ship), companion. As you put all the words together I hear you say — "forever family and friendship." As you say the words slowly, my mind returns to our previous conversations and I can see the tattooed characters are alive and embedded in all of your life stories. The leaving of school early was in parts the story of longing to be with your friends, of feeling isolated and lonely in a place that paid little attention to you. "I stayed for 5 months in school just to prove a point to someone, yet I wasn't enjoying myself and I had no friends. Stuck in the same classroom ... it made me miserable and I switched high schools because of friends." And I so strongly hear your family stories too, of the responsibility you carried from a very young age.

Wrapped around the Chinese characters is a dragon to provide strength and protection. I wonder what kind of protection does the dragon offer you and protection from what?

Soon after Christian began to draw he started getting into traditional Asian art. This is his first drawing of that kind and "it is based on some of the things I saw before." It is his first attempt at drawing a koi fish, dragon, as well as flowers. Inscribed into the clouds is his name in Mandarin (Figure 2). Christian took Mandarin classes in Grade 10 and when he registered in Grade 11 he felt he had forgotten much of Mandarin and that it would be too difficult to keep up given that he did not speak the language in places other than this class.

Christian, I tried calling and e-mailing and we just didn't connect. Your tattoos have stayed with me, the half-marked pieces on your body, the pieces that mark who you are ... the joy in creating art that lives and breathes much like you do. There is no finality to your body art, always slight changes in the inscriptions of the final meaning. The changes in the transfer from paper to body are amazing, the layers of skin marked by a pencil stroke ... Vera (Figure 3).

Figure 3: Christian's Drawing 3.

"In grade 10 I had to go to the attendance board for the first time and I was really scared and afraid of being judged for my looks." In an effort to not be judged, Christian cut his hair. He had many questions about why he had such a strong sense of being judged. He thought "if they get to know me they are having no reason to judge me." He wanted to show them that he was serious about school and he went for 5 months to school without missing a day. He wanted to show them that "people can work their way through school, that people can change." At the end Christian realized that he was only attending school to prove a point to someone! He switched schools and, after being at a new high school for 2 days, his grandmother passed away and he became very depressed and started to withdraw from school.

Christian, finally we get connected again. It all evolves quickly and tomorrow we plan to meet at the school, your school, the school where some of the happy memories live. A place you and Sean connected. A place your life mattered ... I want to know where you have been, become aware of your memories and experiences, yet I, too, am hesitant.

What will it be like for me to set foot into your memory box? Will I see/hear/smell amidst the fear of opening up my own memory box? Will I understand the communal context of your school? Will we meet people you know and those who know of you? Vera.

Figure 4: Christian's Drawing 4

After some of his initial attempts at drawing, Christian's pictures soon became embedded with symbols and stories; symbols that speak of his cultural background and also about the community and people who surround him. After a fight with his girlfriend and nothing to do, Christian spent hours drawing. He shared comments others have made about his drawings with me, that "the skulls have character and look aggressive," and in retrospect Christian thinks that he has been unable to draw skulls as good as these.

The skulls do look aggressive and portray a seriousness that is often associated with the human skull, perhaps a warning to those who fear putting their lives at risk, or perhaps a reminder of the transience of human existence, or in a way to remind others that one must die. Yet the skulls also remind me of the challenges that face many young adults and a challenge that perhaps also lives in Christian's life, the wish to be taken seriously. The skulls might also represent defiance; the aliveness of Christian's skulls certainly makes me wonder about the defiance of death and perhaps authority. Yet others might read the skull as a symbol of nightmarish youth, of violence, substance use, and promiscuity (Figure 4).

"Evil looking that is what I draw when I am mad" (Figure 5).

Figure 5: Christian's Drawing 5.

Christian, I could see your eyes returning to every inch of the building, the changes in its physical structure, and always the seeking of the familiar.

There was the desk/space you spent much time in, while remembering the stories you never spoke, the stories of the acts of disciplining. At least I never had the sense of punishment. Walking through the building was much like walking through an old Fort ... a sense of protection, but also a separation from the inside and outside. My own footsteps still echo in my ears, the old brick and stone floors ... your life somehow shaped by the building and the peoples, Vera.

"My father is Asian, a Chinese born in Vietnam. I don't know the language, but I have been interested since I was a kid. I loved it so much that I started to explore this. I got some support from my art teachers and near the end of my schooling I became interested in tattoos."

"I was hanging out with older kids, like my brother. It was OK, but I got into things that were not good."

Christian, my mind so often returns to the class portrait and for the first few years you and G. always appeared together ... a foundation for a long and strong friendship. The photos almost appear comical now, the neatness and order that school/institution demand. You moved on from grade to grade, much like any logical progression ... your size and facial expression change, but I can always recognize you and I learn to recognize G. You become part of other families' lives and I have a sense how school shifts who you are in your own family, Vera.

Figure 6: Christian's Drawing 6.

"I started off with stuff in the middle, cartoon images with me and my best friends. We all had similar hairstyles." When I asked if the guns refer to some of violence in his life, Christian responded, "I thought it was cool when I was younger" (Figure 6).

Christian, you talk so proudly about your involvement in the suggestions for changing the school and the installment of sinks in every classroom.

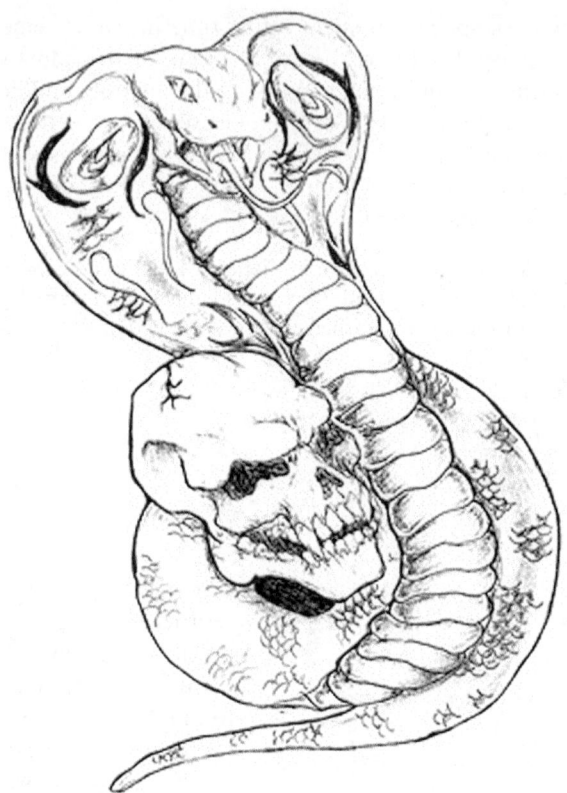

Figure 7: Christian's Drawing 7.

I sensed the ownership you took in your life at school, that this school greatly mattered to you; that you were thoughtful about your recommendations and how they would make the other students' lives better, I could see your eyes glancing over the banners and floor at the gym and I tried hard to imagine you here — day in and day out practicing basketball and soccer, being there with Sean and N. and J. learning his first dance moves, Vera (Figure 7).

Christian started to believe he didn't need high school and that he could just "live to work. But once I had money trouble, because my mom got really sick, I realized that we never really had enough money." Christian realized he needed school to better his career and now wants to study car mechanics and he is motivated to get back to school.

Christian — it was good to talk after the visit to the school, to get to know a bit more about who you are now and where you are from. I can see how complex life became after that first school, but there are many things I still don't understand such as why they kicked you out of school. Are there policies that school administrators indiscriminately apply? Why would they enroll you when they already had too many students? Why did they draw a line between you and your friends? And then to ask for money to enroll in distance education, to force you to work even longer hours, just so you could be told they didn't even have books for you; that you should come back weeks later. How did they think this was going to work? Somehow you were left to balance your future, your mom's, your sister's, your dreams with that of people who neither seemed to care nor knew you. There was no room for negotiation, no basketball scholarships, no room in the classroom, no place to sit beside your friends ... not because you chose to. Your mom too has needed your help and support and I can see in your story how much she has struggled in her life with mental health issues, poverty, violence, and loneliness, Vera.

"People really like this because of the positioning of the dragon and the phoenix" (Figure 8). The phoenix was the first tattoo Christian got at the age of 16. "The phoenix represents a lot to me. That is why I got it on my arm; it represents rebirth and change and the female side. The dragon also represents a lot of me, strength, protection and basically power. Together, the phoenix and the dragon represent life. I used to have a really bad state of mind, and I used to do bad things and always got into trouble. Now I changed that, I started working, I support my family and now realize right from wrong."

Figure 8: Christian's Drawing 8.

Figure 9: Christian's Drawing 9.

Koi fish — The final image combines this drawing with digital coloring (Figure 9).

Christian — in all you told me about your dad — his coming and going and eventual absence in your life, his substance use and jail time — I can see how much you still care for him and how much you care about your own history. In all these times you have always still recognized him, even when he told you he didn't recognize you. I can't imagine what happened in that moment... the hurt, anguish, the long absence accumulated, yet you talk so fondly of your cultural background, your care for your family and the importance of your father despite it all, Vera.

Christian — that day we also talked about your sister and how school was slowly becoming less and less important to her. You waking her every morning, your constant conversations of why it mattered — going as far as disciplining her, limiting her time with friends so she could focus and achieve at school, to stay with it. You left because there was no choice, there was your family to look after, to help your mom survive... you seem so much older than your age or maybe it is that I understand so little about your life in its actuality, Vera.

"This is a Japanese warrior dragon, aggressive looking, all puffed up. I studied on-line about dragons. This Japanese dragon holds a crystal ball, which is supposed to carry everything close to the person, the most meaningful things" (Figure 10).

Christian — I still remember the end of our conversation that day when we talked about friends and children. You told of how you had held T.'s little one and said, "I was so scared," and I remember how your body and face looked so gentle, so caring and I was reminded of all the responsibility that rests on your shoulders, Vera.

"I was at work really bored and a friend suggested I draw a Cyclops — so I started with an eyeball and shading, to try and give more depth to it. Then I traced

A Narrative Account of Christian 187

Figure 10: Christian's Drawing 10.

Figure 11: Christian's Drawing 11.

the face and placed it in position and then I set a light source. My friends call this the friendly Cyclops, because it has a cricked smile." I could see from his books of drawings that many of the pages had been turned many times and Christian informed me that many of his friends look at his drawings and make comments. Christian too shared his art work willingly with me, providing me with insights about the symbolism and at times the stories behind the drawings. The image of the Cyclops stayed with me for days, there was something so unbalanced and decentring about his (Figure 11).

Figure 12: Christian's Drawing 12.

As I turn the pages of Christian's drawing book, I can see that his art work is more and more reflective of his interest in tattoos. He is playing with shading and scales, the intricacies of color (Figure 12).

Christian, today I too went back to my own school, the school I left when I was in Grade 12. It seemed only like yesterday and as I stood there at the bottom of the stairway I could feel tears welling up once more. I felt so alone at the time and the place was too big to be noticed, no one would have heard my screams of injustice, of feeling boxed in. I wanted to paint, to write, to find space to listen and express, maybe one day I will find them. Hang on to your drawings, your body, love, Vera.

Dear Christian, I am so looking forward to Tuesday, to sit down with you again. I have thought much about you in the past few weeks, your incredible dedication to your family ... to fight but to also always find ways to move forward and live alongside you so closely. I can hardly wait for us to meet to take some photos of your tattoos and to get a better sense of their living on your skin. I hope we get to talk more about this. We started a bit in our first meeting with Sean, the differences between paper and body, maybe one day Sean can help us think about his again, but I know his stories of his skin are very different from ours. I often wondered about your mom and what stories she tells of you. And your lives together, her anxiety and what sounds like some depression are hard to cope with even with possible resources ... Thank you so much for allowing me to hear some of your stories, I really am in awe of all you have accomplished, Vera.

Figure 13: Christian's Drawing 13.

For now this is the last picture in Christian's book, a Japanese half dragon and koi fish (Figure 13). "It is a koi fish on a Japanese enchanted river; if the koi fish is able to work itself over the waterfall then it turns into a dragon. koi fish become almost magic — overcoming certain paths, reaching goals, much like swimming over a waterfall. It is almost impossible to swim over a waterfall and perhaps it is symbolic of my life. It represents my life a lot." This was Christian's last drawing in his book and these were also the last words he told me. It is in this story I recognize how important the tattoos and drawings are in his life. It is his drawings and thinking about tattoos that speak to his strong sense of visuality. Christian's life does reflect his effort and perseverance in the face of adversity, yet it also reflects wisdom, knowledge, longevity, and loyalty. In Christian's story the koi fish perhaps also symbolizes this courage and ability to overcome life's obstacles, a successful struggle against the odds and a reminder that human suffering is part of life.

Chapter 14

A Narrative Account of Skye

Sean Lessard

Prologue

Sometimes stories sit with me for a long time. I am not certain how to begin them. I don't always know the right way to share them or how to take care of them in an honorable way. I am learning. Hearing stories holds great responsibility and, as I write about the experiences of youth, I try to remember the voices of those who shared their stories with me. I am cautious when I write the stories of our Aboriginal youth. I am aware that stories can be read in more than one way. I try to think of a respectful way to write and share. I sit down often with the older ones in the community, and the Elders, and ask them to help me in this way. I often think of history and my own community and the stories that come from this place. I try to form an image in my mind as I write, thinking about how life might have been for our Elders, and the sacrifices they made to help us on our current journeys. The stories of the past help me, as I try to write about our youth and the challenges they face in their school stories. I am writing these stories with many thoughts on my mind. I am writing this particular story to help me to begin to remember again.

For the past 7 years I have taught at a large urban high school in central Alberta. In my previous role as a teacher in this setting, I often worked with youth who had difficulty finding their way and maintaining their school story. Many of my students of the past came from an Aboriginal place; some of the students embraced this story, others were in a state of development, and there were those who flatly rejected this script. I personally remember all those stories. I remember, as I write this, the difficulty in feeling comfortable and negotiating my feelings of uncertainty. I do remember denying who I was and trying to move away from knowing my cultural past and the roots that will always exist within. I remember the feelings that many of my students have and I write this story from a different lens and a stronger spirit than in times past.

I chose to write this particular story because it is what lies at the base of Skye's song, her story of school as I recall it. I wrote this specific story for Skye and her family and the wisdom that they continue to provide for me in the form of cultural teachings. As I share this story now, I ask those that choose to read it, to think deeply with the heart and the mind, and imagine the beat of many drums playing in the background ... as each of you begin to hear the sacred songs ... you will start to understand her story in a different way ... I would like to call it a "dance me home Skye song."

Bus Station Stories (First Meeting)

I was thinking about the many interesting people I had seen at the bus station as I waited for the arrival of a family that I had known in the past. I was wondering what our meeting was going to be like. It had been a long time since I last seen this family, and I wondered how they had been keeping.

I looked around the bus station and saw many people pacing, sitting, and talking as they waited for their bus to arrive. Each person had a different story, a unique history. I wondered what their stories were and what brought them to the bus station on this day. I sat in the bus station for over 3 hours waiting to connect with this family and to see their daughter, a student I once knew.

The nice thing about time is that it allows me to think and, as I waited, I conjured up memories from the past and jotted them down in my worn-out notebook. I wrote down many ideas about the times I had spent with this student and her family. I waited impatiently, fidgeting, hoping that they would come around the corner at any moment.

The family I knew, and was waiting for, adhered strongly to their cultural belief systems and relied on the Nakota traditions to keep them balanced in a challenging world. I met this family years ago. I was a teacher at the local high school. I was introduced to their daughter by a colleague. She thought that we would get along well because we both shared a common cultural heritage. I never did tell her that I was Cree and that this student I met was Nakota but that is another story for another day.

Sliding Backward in Time ...

As I sat in the bus station with my many thoughts, I remembered a particular day when I was introduced to a quiet young girl who excelled in sports and was from a nearby First Nation. The student I met had a unique and special name that stuck with me; it had meaning behind it. Her name was Skye. This young girl would barely look at me during our initial greeting, this was something which I had come to know and expect.

However, sitting in the bus station, I recalled that when I began to share my story with her, the space shifted and she slowly began to tell me about herself. I started the conversation by asking about her community and where her family was from. I always tried to help students to feel comfortable in that big school place. I wanted her and other students to know that they had a person that could assist them if needed. I often started conversations by asking about home and the community to find a common ground; to find a beginning. I recognized long ago that this school was a place where students could get easily lost. It was different.

Later in the week I had my next meeting with Skye but in a different place. I entered the gym to begin evaluations for the volleyball teams. I had at one time in life played college volleyball and assisted the school teams with their practices. On the far court I noticed Skye. I watched with interest, a quiet girl come to life on the volleyball court.

Skye was amazing to watch. As a player she was fast and fluid. She was more verbal than I had expected, often calling out plays and shouting out instructions. She was naturally talented and played at a very high level. I found it rewarding to watch her play this sport so freely. We had unexpectedly found another common thread. I was quietly proud of what I was seeing on this day. Skye was creating a different story for all of us.

I had the privilege to watch and informally coach this student athlete for the next 2 years. She came to me for help with training and skill development, always separate from her team. During these times we had many great conversations about life. She wanted to learn and always strived to become better. I appreciated these teaching moments.

Through time and the many games that were played I was eventually introduced to her family who never missed an opportunity to support their daughter. Her father, Arnie, was small in stature but projected a feeling of strength and commitment to his cultural path. We had many good conversations. They started off small and formal and developed over time, much like any good friendship. I often talked to Skye's mother and she always greeted me with a hug and kindness. Her mother was also a traditional woman, kind and dedicated to the values of her people. I enjoyed my conversations with Daphne and still see her gentle smile in my mind; it impressed on me the importance of family and happiness.

This is the family that I came to know during the school years and conversations that took place. I remembered that, when I watched a game, I always looked for them in the crowd. I often went and sat with them as they sat by themselves, alone and away from the rest of the parents; it is here where we visited. I have always loved sports and I could understand Skye's feeling for the game. It was her real reason for coming to school, not that much different than mine when I was young. Her family strongly supported all things that contribute to a healthy lifestyle.

An Invitation to Stand in a Different Relation

One of the memories I recalled as I jotted down thoughts in my notebook was being asked by Skye's father to represent the Nakota Nation in a hockey tournament. Her father had found out that I played in First Nation's tournaments competitively and they asked me to join them in a memorial tournament for a relative.

The invitation and the meaning behind the tournament still remains a highlight of my time with this family. I remember one afternoon, hearing a knock on my classroom door. I walked to the door and peered around the corner. There was Skye, her father, and her brother all waiting for me to reply to the invitation, and asking me if I could leave school early to make the first game. I chuckled to myself and told them that it would not be that good of an idea for me to leave my class in the middle of the afternoon to play hockey. However, I would most definitely be at all the other games. These stories of family stayed with me long after they took place. The hockey game was just a game. The gesture to walk alongside this family and play in the memorial tournament for a relative and their First Nation meant a great deal to me.

The moment I walked into the dressing room to play for their community felt different than other teams I had played on in the past. I met many family members from this Nation and, before we started the game, the coach, Skye's father, prayed. I recall the prayer specifically because we did not ask to win but to play safe and honorably and respect the other team and our First Nations in all we do. I remember the prayer because it was in two languages, and powerful in its message. These words stayed with me long past the event because we played for something different on this day. Stories of experience like this shifted my views and provided me an opportunity for learning by observing what was going on around me. This was a teaching.

The buses continued to arrive and depart. As I sat and waited in the bus station, many new faces appeared but I searched for just one as I scanned the crowd. To understand Skye, I need to understand her family. Skye is nested in the midst of family stories and family stories are cultural stories. Family is what Skye talked about often; it is what came first in her life. It was different than what I have ever experienced.

I had arranged that initial bus station meeting because I wanted to get her parents' thoughts on a project I was involved in at the university. I wanted to tell their daughter's story of school. I needed to see the family and ask permission to talk to their daughter about a subject that had been difficult for everyone. I wondered what their reaction might be to my request. I wondered if it was too sudden or if time had allowed healing for this story.

The Arrival ...

I sat in the local bus station restaurant sipping on old coffee and anticipating that I could see this family at any moment. It was going to be great to reconnect for the first time in many years. I had waited far too long. I wondered what Skye even looked like now. Would I recognize her? I wondered how she was doing in life. What type of job did she have?

As hours passed, I began to realize that I might have missed Skye or perhaps I hadn't quite understood the departure times. Even though I felt like going home after waiting for so long I decided that I would sit and wait. There was one last bus that was leaving in an hour. There was a chance to still see them and I was determined to follow through and see this out.

As the clock crept closer to the last bus leaving for her destination her family suddenly appeared at the sliding doors. The wait was worth it! I immediately packed up my belongings and made my way to the greet them. I was so happy to see them and we gave hugs all around, first to Arnie and then to Daphne. We laughed about our mix up in times and we laughed harder when I told them how many cups of coffee I drank while I was waiting. After several minutes of laughter and reconnection Skye made her way through the sliding doors. It was great to see her on this day. I went up to her and gave her a big hug. I had so many questions but they would be for another time.

I recognized her but I also worried about her when I saw her. She had lost quite a bit of weight and looked somewhat tired. We both laughed when we greeted each other and, in our own way, we sent messages through our jokes. I told her mom and dad that she needed to eat more, and that she needed bannock and soup to help her get strong. And, in her response, she told me that I needed to eat less bannock and soup because I had been getting too big. We laughed. This is the way it used to be and it was like old times in this moment.

We took a seat and talked, all of us together, sharing as much as we could in the limited time that we had. I told them about my work at the university and that I wanted to talk to Skye about her school story. She reassured me that it would be no problem and that she would be happy to participate. The only concern was that we didn't know when the next opportunity to talk would arrive. Skye's parents helped us with this next part. Arnie and Daphne proceeded to tell me that they were hosting a round dance in honor of Daphne's father. They explained that it was the fourth and final round dance for this important family member. I remember hearing them say "Come out and visit. You will learn all the kids' stories. We invite you." With these simple but powerful words I knew what had to be done. I sat with Skye's parents as she boarded her bus, making her way down the road to her new adult life. It was so good to see her family on this day. I am glad I waited. I wonder how the story would have changed if I had left.

Taking Me Home – Helping Me to Remember

A month later I found myself making preparations for the memorial round dance. I was still trying to find the perfect gift to bring to the ceremony. I looked at many places but always came back to a quilt that I spotted at the local mall. The quilt was crafted with fine details and it had a picture of a bear and a fish at the center, creating a picture in my mind worthy of this special event. I looked at this quilt and thought this would be an appropriate gift to honor the Elders. It felt right. It had been many years since I had made my way to a round dance. I went through scenarios in my mind trying to recall the proper protocol and how the event takes place. I was ashamed that I could not recall all the details; how could I have forgotten?

As I drove out of the city, I was thinking about the event and the significance. I was trying to imagine what this day was all about. I knew the invitation was special as this was the fourth and final round dance to celebrate the life of Skye's grandfather, Joseph Paul. The round dance started at 4 p.m. and was to finish at 4 a.m. with specific events to commemorate the day. I knew I needed to be there on this Friday night. The family had invited me to walk with them in their world, to share their stories and become part of something bigger. I knew that, in their own way, this kind family was teaching me, showing me a different way in life, one that I was forgetting.

I arrived at the dimly lit community hall and many cars lined the parking lot. From the outside the building looked somewhat run down, in need of some paint and repair. I knew what people saw when they looked from the outside. But I had been in these spaces before and knew what to expect. As I walked through the doors I was greeted with the familiar welcoming scent of sweetgrass. It always leaves a gentle haze in the air and invites me to relax and open my mind to the sharing story that was taking place all around me.

I entered this place and listened for the sound of the drum. I looked at the center of the hall and watched the stickman pass the drum sticks to a lead drummer. The drummer started with his family song, with many other men young and old joining around the table, to celebrate through the beats and voices of communities tied. I was beginning to remember. I continued to make my way to the middle of the hall where the drummers played. I watched as 15–20 drummers played a song together and sang in unison. People gathered around the drummers and held hands and started to move to the music, shuffling to the beat of the drum, in a circle, always a circle. I was here at a different place, a good place.

Many feelings came back to me as I heard that initial song played; the drums and voices are still on my mind. Seeing our people dance together makes me proud. The beauty of family and sharing was all around me and I could feel it. Now, as I write, I still remember it. As I listened to the song I looked for the patriarch of the family. I needed to find Arnie. I had protocol and the gift of the quilt that I needed to present to him, to honor this day. I did start to remember.

I found him at the back of the hall and walked toward him with the quilt tucked under my arm. We greeted each other and I presented him with the gift and protocol. He thanked me for coming and told me that he would find a special older one to pass my gift on to. I had never been with Arnie at an event like this. It was special to see. I can see him as I write this, and I can recall the events of the evening very clearly; they stay with me. He is a traditional man and he believes strongly in family.

As Arnie showed me around the hall, he introduced me to many of his family members. He invited me to sit with his family at the front of the hall and to help out when called upon. This was an honor that I proudly accepted. All five children were in attendance and his grandkids often tugged on his pant leg wanting to get up in his arms and be carried. Throughout the evening I had many moments to myself where I reflected with the sound of the drum in my ear. Somehow, the stories of school became more alive as I shared in this evening of remembrance.

As the night progressed, Arnie took me to the front of the hall and showed me two framed pictures. They were of the man I was here to honor, Joseph Paul, his father-in-law. Arnie spoke with great reverence as he told me stories of the past and explained the kind of man he had come to know. He told the stories as he showed me a picture of Joseph Paul in his traditional regalia. He talked of his father-in-law's great respect for culture and his role as a leader of his people. I saw in this picture a man that has many stories. The picture is a portrait from the side, and is filled with colors from the outfit that was designed for him. A cigarette gently rests on his lips.

The second photograph is an old black and white. In the picture, passed down to remember, a little baby rests in the arms of a family of three sitting in the grass with a tepee proudly raised in the background. The mother holds the baby in a tightly wrapped leather bundle. The family sits crosslegged. No one smiles in the picture. I wonder who took this picture on this day and what the people were talking about. Arnie tells me that this was Joseph when he was young and that this is how life was back then. These photographs helped me understand a little more about what this day was all about.

I was here to reconnect with this family and to honor their request to attend this event before I began conversations with their daughter about her school stories. The protocol was different than what is typical, and far different than the way I have heard other school stories. However, I knew that I must follow the lead and do what Arnie asked me; it was the right way. As I think about the many stories that Skye and I shared while we were in school, I see now that we never reached the deeper layered stories during our time together. I am only now realizing that I did not see all her gifts.

On this Friday night I watched Skye show me many layers, those that were not visible within the larger high school setting. I wonder why she was unable to present this side of her story. I wonder if I was truly listening. I watched Skye differently this evening as she took her nieces and nephews by the hand and showed them how to dance, the real way, the right way, always hand in hand.

What it Means to Dance ... Moving Away and Then Coming Back Home

As I sat with her family on this special evening, we shared thoughts and stories of the past. Skye spoke of the different ways in a big city. She said that it was different than where she came from. She talked about reserves that are close to the city and how they can change people. She shared a story about some boys from the nearby reserve who also attended the same high school as she had.

She talked of the past and changed her expression as she spoke. She said that these boys would make fun of her for holding hands during a round dance and for participating in cultural ceremonies. She told me this story for the first time on this evening. She said they laughed about this and said it was stupid. As time went on, she told me, she quit talking about it, and eventually quit doing it. She put her outfits away.

Her story amazed me. She said to me, "life changes you in the city" and that she should have "never quit dancing ... but Lessard I will get back to it. I am getting a new outfit made." When I think of the time spent and all the conversations with her that I have had, I think of this story and how she held onto it. I wondered why she waited until now to tell me. I wondered what other stories I didn't get to know.

As the night continued, I often sat alone thinking about how this occasion was beautiful. It was powerful to see families coming together and sharing in the dances and the song. I thought this must be the way the Creator meant for things to be where families shared together. It was real and intimate. At this dance there were no alternative substances to help me or anyone else feel good and to mask our emotions. The drums kept beating and the voices kept changing as new singers entered the circle. The songs were played for many different reasons. The songs were played to honor Joseph Paul. Singers came from many Nations and traveled great distances to sing a song for this man. During this evening there was no competition, just people coming together to remember.

I listened closely to the many honor songs, and I helped throughout the evening by bringing the drummers water and by serving the lunch to the Elders. Later in the evening, Skye and her mom took me by the hand and told me, "Come on, Lessard, come and dance with us." I reluctantly, and nervously, entered the circle and followed their lead as they helped me to remember.

I danced many times throughout that evening and listened up close with Skye as she provided the backup vocals for her father's honor song. I remember it this way. As we gathered around the circle I watched and the family joined Arnie as he sang, holding his grandson in one arm and beating the drum with the other. He never missed a beat; he was leading for his family in a real good way.

Three Sisters

I had arranged to meet with Skye in her new city which required a road trip. The drive was a peaceful 3-hour journey that helped me to focus my thoughts on the conversational relationship. I had never really come to know Skye's early school stories, and I was eager to learn more about the past. I wondered how our previous relationship would impact the way the conversation would flow. I wondered if I would be able to use the tape recorder to help record the stories or would this fit into the way we talked.

These are the questions that continued to cross my mind as I made my way down the highway, anticipating our future conversation.

I had many thoughts about her high school stories based on how I was situated within them as a teacher. However, the high school stories were only a small part of her stories. I needed to find out about the Skye that I didn't know. I needed to have conversations that looked at her life differently than the way that I knew. I had to reimagine what life was like for her in a different place than the one that I had come to know.

I met Skye at a local shopping mall. Her new job involved working the night shift so she came to our meeting place with no sleep. The interesting part of Skye, as I am getting to know her in a different way, is that very few things are done individually. A conversation sometimes means a conversation with the people she chooses to bring along. I had anticipated meeting Skye for roughly an hour and I assumed wrongly that it would be a simple exercise of visiting, catching up on the past and talking about school as we shared. The picture in my mind that I had was much different than the picture we created. Skye's two sisters also wanted to visit and with them came her little nephew who was also a part of this family conversation. At first I was nervous because it was not how I thought it would be but as we moved forward with the conversation, the sisters created a story for me that helped me understand.

The setting was a busy food court and it initially felt like I was in a job interview as I looked across the table and the oldest sister, Skye, and her youngest sister prepared to answer my questions about school. I started off with questions about school places. To me it felt like a panel with the three sisters answering questions and debating times, facts, and locations. The girls would often help each other remembering the schools of the past and the stories that took place within them.

Skye told her story of school as involving movement between her reserve and an urban center. Her story of school started with a city school in kindergarten and then back to the reserve for Grade 1. Her memories of school and place are vague. She did not remember specific school names, or places. She could only tell me whether or not she was at the reserve or in the city. Her story of early elementary school involved moving between the city and the reserve until Grade 3. From Grade 3 until Grade 7 she spent time at the reserve school. The family relocated to a different reserve school for Grades 8 and 9. The story of school and movement resonated with me. We carefully charted a timeline that the sisters helped me to develop. The school names or the names of teachers were not looked at as important details to consider. The girls could not remember specific names; they only remembered the stories that took place during these times. The story of school involved change and adaptability based on job opportunities for the family, reserve housing lists, and personal tragedy.

The stories of school began to appear and, with them, some of the sadness that rests with them. The girls' stories of school and their recollections of school are varied. Despite the great diversity and vantage points shared, the sisters all remembered their lack of photographs and the few school book memories that they had. The story the sisters shared with me is about a Christmas that they missed when their house burned down. The family lost everything on Christmas Eve and they remembered the dates and memories of it. The girls told me that they remember it at every Christmas and that there was something wrong with the furnace causing a fire. Their lives were interrupted and the evidence of the past became lost. The photographs and cultural reminders were destroyed leading the family to another new location and another new school. The past has many stories that I did not know. The importance of photographs in their current lives becomes more evident to me. The photographs of their grandfather are invaluable reminders of the past. I was beginning to understand more as I listened.

Teachings from Our Parents

The stories of school shifted back and forth from sports to the classroom and to the in-betweens. The story of place and learning from parents was evident in many of the stories shared that afternoon. The girls talked about learning differently and sticking up for each other in school. They talked about opportunities and how sports helped them out. They spoke of having next to nothing growing up and practicing golf on the dirt fields at the reserve, far removed from the places where I learned. The stories helped me to understand a part of their personal journeys.

The girls recalled times in the past when their mom and dad taught them sports, dancing, and culture. They laughed when they told stories and corrected each other along the way, sometimes disagreeing on the small details. As they told their stories, they moved backward in time to the intergenerational connections they shared with their cultural roots. They told me they had been practicing and learning about culture and traditional dancing since they were babies. I now know by walking alongside them that their cultural roots come from a place. The passing down of knowledge through the act of participation is a thread that weaves throughout their lives. The cultural stories and knowledge started before them, and before their parents as they told me stories about their grandfather who was a gifted man. He was a song maker and singer. He was a very spiritual person with special gifts. The girls spoke proudly of their grandmothers and grandfathers and how culture had always existed in their family.

"I Am the Luckiest Kid in the World"

For me, the words "I am the luckiest kid in the world" defined our conversation on this day. Skye and her sisters talked about times when things were not so good at school. A story that Skye told me takes her back to Grade seven at the reserve school where her dad was the school patrol officer. He found her smoking behind the school with some other girls. The sisters laughed as they shared this story with me. They told me that their mom at this time was a smoker but after that day she quit. She not only quit; she went into the school the next day and started an anti-tobacco group for the youth. Skye became the lead student. The girls laughed hard about this story and as they did, Skye interjected "I am the luckiest kid in the world! My parents care. A lot of people's parents weren't around, our parents were always around." The sisters all agreed.

I asked Skye what brought her to the high school where I met her. She told me that her parents wanted a better opportunity for her, and that the conditions in the community school were challenging. The decision to move to the city and start at a new high school was hard, because it was so different than what she had become used to at the reserve.

I now asked Skye about her experience at the high school and her first days in class. I asked her if she could remember. She told me that there were a lot of nice teachers. The work was difficult. It was different than what she had seen before. She said it was hard to do things by herself in a new city. She was used to having her parents around. During her time in the city she lived with her older brother and she had to learn to become responsible for her own school routine.

She also told me about some of her feelings coming from a new place and how she often felt low as a student. She explained to me an experience she had during one of the first days in class. The class went to a local driving range to play golf. She told me she was excited to attend because this was her favorite sport. However, she missed the school bus because she was not familiar with public transportation in this new city. She arrived late to the driving range but she still managed to walk there by herself. When she arrived, the teacher stopped the class and told everybody to "look at who is late." He then asked her where she was. She replied, "I am not a city person, I got lost." He laughed and said, "Are you sure about that? Are you sure you didn't get lost at the mall?" She told me, "And then, with everyone looking at me, they started to laugh."

Skye did not remember many stories from high school but this story stayed with her long after. She said, "I felt like quitting right there and going home. But then he would have been right about me." She said that day when she was at the driving range, "I felt like he thought I was just another dumb Indian. But he changed his mind when he saw that I could golf." She said,

"I felt this way many times especially being a female native golfer. It is different, Lessard, because it's not what people expect, they judge you before they see you play. If you are good you are all right. They don't expect you to be good." This was a story that I could relate to.

Her story of golf while in high school is one that she largely plays down. Skye became the first female Aboriginal golfer in the past 10 years to make the local school team. Skye changed the way golf was viewed and how she was viewed by those who worked with her. She became a two-time provincial medalist in golf and won many individual trophies for her performances in the province. Skye gained many positive accolades for her success in sports. However, as the sports coaches moved in and out of her life, between the seasons her academic performance began to slide. Many times in her Grade 10 year I personally advocated a shift in programming to encourage tracking of her performance and consistency in the teachers she worked with. I was told that programs cannot be adjusted after the school year has started, and that if we do this for one student then we have to do it for others. I could see from the outside what was happening. I felt that the Grade 10 core courses were critical points in her schooling and suggested strategies to provide a better chance at successful completion. I feared what could happen if she was removed from her peer group, and the few connections she was starting to develop.

The Grade 10 school year went by and Skye did not pass many of her core classes which required an adapted timetable in her Grade 11 year. The size of the school and the individual stories of students are difficult to locate on the school landscape. Schools are filled with many students' stories that are similar to Skye's. Skye began her Grade 11 school year in classes with many Grade 10 students and, as she did the previous year, she started the school year off positively, attending regularly and completing her assigned work.

It seems when I write this that each of Skye's school years had a rhythm. She started off the school year playing volleyball and staying connected to students and staff through the sports that she played, and the success she had within them. As the volleyball season ended, the first semester also came to an end, and she was on track in her courses. During the second semester, the year-long classes often dragged and while no sports were being played, she struggled to maintain and would grow somewhat distant. The connections and relationships to people are what sustained Skye and other areas fit into them and around them based on the strength of the connection.

Skye worked hard through her Grade 11 year and managed to successfully complete many credits. Skye described her schooling the following way, "I didn't always understand my work and I am too shy to ask for help, I felt dumb." She told me often during our conversations that she struggled with the school work and it was different than what she had learned on the reserve; the pace was too fast. She told me, "Do you know that I am actually smart, Lessard? I was the class valedictorian in my Grade 9 class at the reserve." I replied by simply saying, "I know you are."

The Grade 12 school year started and Skye was not in attendance for the start of volleyball tryouts. Her Grade 12 year was a big year. Many of the girls asked each other where she was, or if they had heard from her over the summer. As far as I knew she should have been there. After the first week of school, and long after volleyball tryouts, I recalled seeing Skye walk into the gym to tell me she was back. I walked over to greet her and her parents and I talked to them about their summer. I could sense that there was some uncertainty as to whether or not she would be coming to school in the city. I wondered what had changed over the summer. I wondered why the shift in their feelings. I knew by talking to her parents that they were concerned about their daughter and wondered if it was a good decision to return to the city for this school year.

The start to the school year did not go as I expected. The one area that Skye remained devoted to was always her sports. She started off the season a step slower and less confident in her abilities on the court. The performance in sports was the most insignificant part that I cared about, but it did tell me that life was shifting for her. I knew when watching her that something was different. I also knew that things were changing because she came late to practice and missed games, without any communication. In the two previous years she had never missed a game. She even played when she had minor injuries. She loved sports and never missed them. Skye had fallen off her path. She was attending class irregularly but my biggest concern was her distance. I knew her and I knew how she responded to embarrassment. She pulled away, went inside herself, and did not want to confront the difficulties that were taking place. I knew this was not what she wanted to do, or who she wanted to be but I could not reach her. I had lost her. She became silent and unwilling to have a conversation. She was hurting.

I remember the last time I saw her in the school setting. The volleyball team had a tournament and she missed the first game without telling anyone. The coach decided that he had to make a statement and he benched her for the next two games. I remember looking at her as she sat with her hands on her knees, staring at the floor. She did not talk to anyone that day. She was the best player on the team, one of the leaders, and I wondered where she had been. I wondered what happened to her. I remember talking to her parents after the game, and telling them that I was concerned. I told them I was worried about a number of things. I told them all that I could and that I didn't know how to help her at this moment.

I can still see them walking out of the gym with their little girl. This was the last time I saw her in my role as a teacher. This was the last moment that we shared before she moved to another city and eventually left her school story. I am happy that she moved, and that she went home with her family, to find herself again. I think at times we all need to go home to find out who we are and where we are going. Sometimes we need help. I believe that Skye and I helped each other out often throughout our time together. I know that she helped me to get back to a way that is good for me, a cultural way. She helped me to remember who I was and what I was forgetting. I think I am just starting to help her now, by continuing to believe in her and her school story. I believe that she will go back someday and follow the dreams that she has. I think in some ways she has already started. I look forward to sitting down with her and reading her this story. I wonder what she will think. I wonder what she will change. I wonder when she and her family will help teach me the next steps in my "Dance Me Home" song. I am hoping that when I hear the drum and the voices singing in the background that I will continue to dance. I am hoping that I will be holding my little girl's hand teaching her the right way to dance, always in a circle, only in a circle.

Chapter 15

Exploring Transitions within Lives

D. Jean Clandinin, Vera Caine and Pam Steeves

In this chapter, we shift our attention from the complexities of each youth's life to look across the narrative accounts to discern our understandings about transitions. As we worked alongside the youth over the months of conversations, writing and negotiating the narrative accounts, our attention was often drawn to the word *transition*. The youth told stories of transitions. They also told of how transitions were storied in their lives by others. As we attended to their stories, we realized the word transition frequently has a negative subtext when used to describe youth who do not graduate. High school completion is seen as a step in a successful transition to the next stage: post secondary education, apprenticeship, internship, work, and so on. Often successful completion of high school is seen as necessary to the transition to adulthood. Transition, used to describe the youth with whom we worked, signifies that youth fail to successfully move on in their lives, and that the changes they experience are not seen as constructive. The youth we came alongside were often seen as unsuccessful, not poised for that next step.

We also heard some of the youth described as highly *transient*,[1] with a sense that their high level of transience was a factor in their failure to successfully transition out of high school. This factor was usually linked to a sense of blame, for how could youth be expected to graduate, and

---

1. The word *transient* can be understood in multiple ways. Most often in the context of schooling it refers to students' attendance at any one school as brief and short lived. There is an underlying sense of a lack of commitment on the part of the student or parents to schooling.

Composing Lives in Transition: A Narrative Inquiry into the Experiences of Early School Leavers
Copyright © 2013 by Emerald Group Publishing Limited
All rights of reproduction in any form reserved
ISBN: 978-1-78052-974-5

successfully transition, if they were so transient. While we appreciate that transient means "quickly passing away," and "fleeting" and "non permanent" (*Concise Oxford Dictionary*, 1976, p. 1232), it is often linked to transition, which is defined as "passage or change from one place or state or act or circumstances to another" (*Concise Oxford Dictionary*, 1976, p. 1232), often abruptly. These two words, transient and transition, when used in relation to youth who do not graduate from high school, and when understood from within the dominant narrative of high school completion, directs our attention to a deficit or "less than" view of youth. As we attended to the youths' stories of their lives, we did not see their lives as non-permanent or fleeting. We saw them as grounded in complex contexts, contexts which called them to respond, to improvise, to reimagine who they were, are, and what to do next.

As we explore the narrative accounts of the 11 youth, we hope to offer a richer, more complex, concept of transition and to show that the lives of the youth are only fleeting when viewed from within the dominant school plotline of success and stability. While we are troubled by the common use of the word transition, we also know that it has relevance and meaning if we can offer a more complex understanding of it. As noted in Chapter 3, looking across the 11 narrative accounts focused on what we might come to know about transitions when understood narratively from the vantage points of the youths' lives as they told their stories to us. As we described in more detail in Chapter 3, we asked the authors of the narrative accounts to reread the narrative accounts they had negotiated with each youth, and to attend carefully where youth told stories of encountering times, and places, of tension and uncertainty. We then compiled the sections that were identified, always mindful not to fragment the lives of the youth with whom we worked. We (Pam, Jean, and Vera) then looked across the identified sections for resonant threads that helped us understand how we might understand transitions from within narrative understandings of the lives of the youth. We identified five resonant threads. In what follows we outline the five threads and then turn our attention to developing a narrative conceptualization of the youths' experiences of transition with attention to five qualities.

Thread 1: Composing Transitions with Attention to What is "Normal"

Kevlar began at the beginning, a beginning he sees situated in his early childhood stories (Figure 1).

In Kevlar's timeline we see how he carefully showed one telling of his life, a telling threaded around, and over, time, situated in places, and in relation

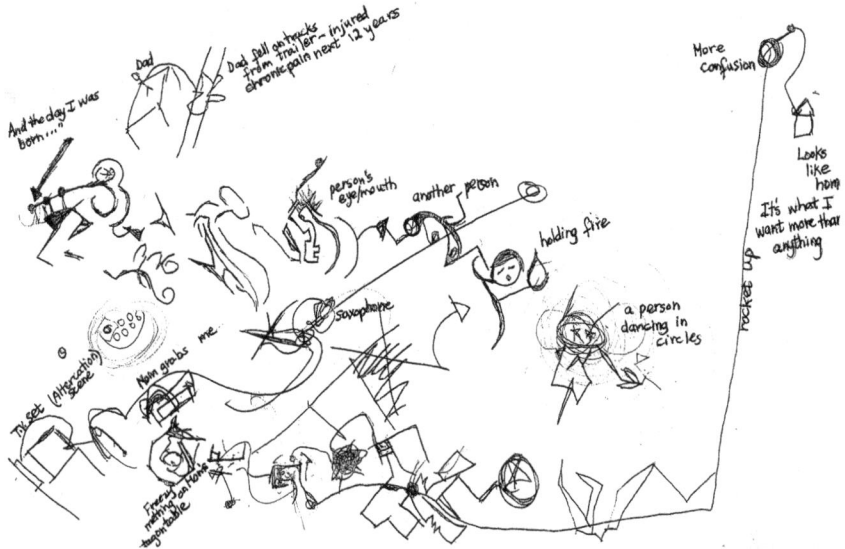

Figure 1: Kevlar's annal.

with people and events. Perhaps he sensed that he should start at the beginning of his life with his birth for he sketched a stick figure of himself as a baby in the hospital. He then showed he left that place, taken by his grandmother and his dad. With those words Kevlar told us who the characters that initially shaped his life are: a mother left without her newborn, a paternal grandmother, a father, and a baby. There was a kind of silence in the drawing as the next mark on his annal (Clandinin & Connelly, 2000) is several years later and showed a stick figure representing his father involved in an accident. We were drawn into the complex stories Kevlar told, but we were also attuned to the silences he created.

As Kevlar sketched, his emotional responses, the depth of his feelings, became evident by the intensity of the marks he made, as well as by the intensity of what he wanted to convey. The pictured story of the altercation with his mother, the "freezy" melting on the tiny octagonal table, the TV set, his mother grabbing him, are all clearly identified. His life began to fall apart after the events he marked around the altercation with his mother. Only a saxophone was visible as something that spoke to his school experience. After this, the marks on the annal became more obscure, graffiti-like. There seemed a lack of coherence and linearity as the marks gave way to scribbles. There was a change as Kevlar came to the present moment, a line drawn from the bottom of the page "rockets up" to more confusion and a drawing of a little house. This, according to Kevlar, represented "what I want more than anything." It was his imagined forward-looking story, a story of what he desired, a story of success. Kevlar composed his story of success in relation to the dominant narrative of successful transition — of moving out of your parent's house, of owning your own place, of having stable employment, and of showing commitment to ownership and work.

What Kevlar made clear in his sketch, and in his conversations with Pam, was that he has been engaged in composing his life over time, in multiple places, and in multiple relationships. As Kevlar told his stories of living through, and in, multiple tensions, he, too, was caught within the plotlines of the dominant narratives in the sense that these plotlines of what counts as "normal" were outside his experiences. He storied his life as "different" when he held it against what he imagined as "normal." Being able to compose his life as "normal" was important to Kevlar.

It is significant to note that Kevlar wanted to tell his stories to Pam. He made the initial contact and he stayed in touch over several months. At one point, almost a year after the time of the narrative inquiry, Kevlar emailed Pam to say he had "such good news" of a job in graphics/media and a little place he shared with another person in the new city in which he was now living. He told Pam "I'm sure you of all people would appreciate it." The stories he told Pam were important for him to tell. Perhaps they were an affirmation that he was trying to compose a life with narrative coherence, even if he was not able to live a *normal* life for much of his life. In the ways he told his stories, both in the annal and in the conversations, he made it clear that his was not a story of leaving school, but a story of how his "screwed up" upbringing made completing high school impossible. The focus on what was normal was threaded through his telling: being taken away at birth from his mother by his father and grandmother was not normal; living in a motel was not normal; being homeless was not normal; being kicked out of his house by his mother was not normal, and so on. In Kevlar's story it was his desire to live a normal life that kept him in school, kept him trying to find places to live, and, in the end, shaped his forward-looking story of life in an imagined house, and working at an imagined job.

We saw something similar in Ben's stories. He, too, told his stories as threaded around plotlines of searching to belong in the Canadian context, and of knowing what it meant to be seen as fitting in. Fitting in, blending into the Canadian diversity, being grateful, and making commitments to this new place, are part of the dominant social and cultural narrative of immigration to Canada; it comes with expectations.

While the dominant institutional narrative is one of the Canadian multicultural mosaic, there is a competing narrative that shapes immigrant lives so that they fit into the stories of school after an initial time of adaptation and accommodation. School programs are designed in accordance with this narrative, that is, special programs for a relatively short period of time for adaptation, and then integration into regular programming. Ben resisted any labels that identified him as separate, as newcomer, as immigrant from Burma, and, in any way, marked him as other. We saw that he knew the normal narrative for immigrant and refugee youth in schools as he resisted having his teacher share his stories in ways that showed that he was "other." Ben helped us understand adaptation in more complex ways. Adaptation does not mean giving up your heart and soul, which, for Ben, was tied closely and intimately to his home place of Burma, and to the intergenerational stories carried forward by his parents.

Christian, too, told his stories with a strong awareness of what was seen as normal. Christian knew his irregular school attendance and his body markings, including his haircut, fell outside what he knew was normal within the dominant school narrative. Knowing what was normal, and what was expected of youth, he tried, for a time, to fit in through regular attendance, and getting his hair cut. He awakened to how he was living a cover story as he tried to conform to the dominant narratives out of which normal was defined, and stopped after he felt he had proven that he could fit within the normal. While Christian knew what was normal and chose to fit in, or not, Kevlar desired what was normal and was often unable to fit in because of life contexts.

Normal, for Andrew, was congruent with the ways he wanted to compose his life, and gave him a way to fit into the dominant school narrative. He loved playing basketball and excelled at it. That allowed him to fit into what was normal by being part of the elite basketball team. While he knew he could live out the dominant school narrative, he kept secret his religious beliefs that are frequently seen as marginal to *normal* Christian beliefs. He experienced being not normal within the dominant school narrative when he became a sports star who was shamed by being kicked off the basketball team. However, unlike Christian who tried to live a cover story, Andrew accepted that he was not normal within the dominant school narrative as an expelled basketball player who experienced shame and alienation within the school.

When Jasmine came to Canada she was labeled an English as a Second Language (ESL) student at school. She accepted this positioning and did well in her first year of junior high school where flexible programming and an understanding teacher helped her learn English. However, when the special ESL programming ended, she was not accepted into the regular academic stream but was seen as requiring a modified program for less academic students. When she tried in later years to get into the "normal" academic course work, she was continually denied. She was judged by the way she spoke, told that her English was not *good enough*, perhaps not *normal* enough, to take regular academic programming.

Skye, too, had a sense of the normal stereotypes, knowing that she could be storied as "a dumb Indian" was she to resist her teacher's words when he questioned her late arrival at the golf course. She made a decision not to respond, preferring a cover story of silence that allowed her a space to know she was being labeled as "less than" but that let her hold on to her strong story of herself as a youth proud of her Aboriginal heritage, a good student, and an excellent golfer. Her silence created a space to hold on to her stories of who she was, at least in that moment.

What we sensed in the stories of the youth is that they were composing their lives, and telling their stories, with attentiveness to what was normal in the dominant institutional narratives in which their lives were situated. This sense of what counted as normal figured into the ways they were composing their lives. They located themselves in relation to the normal, sometimes trying to shape their own lives to fit with what they saw as narratively coherent with the normal, sometimes actively resisting the normal, and sometimes disregarding it, as they struggled to make sense of their ongoing life compositions. Normal may not have been the ways they chose to compose their lives but there was always the presence of normal as they negotiated their lives. This sense of knowing the plotlines of the dominant narratives, that is, what they saw as normal, provided a way of composing a life with divided attention, one imagined as normal, and one which was responsive to the lives they were composing over time and in different places.

Thread 2: Composing Transitions while Situated in Webs of Relationships

What Kevlar made visible in his annal was that, while he was nested in a complex web of relationships, the relationships were frequently provisional and seemingly destructive. His graffiti-like images that followed his rendering of the relational trauma with his immediate family showed the uncertainty and confusion with which he lived. In telling his stories to Pam, he spoke of growing up without the influence of his mother and father, without the stability of a family. However, he storied himself lucky to have been without their influence. Kevlar told his story as learning to count on himself, and of learning not to count on others. This separation from the web of relationships, at least at the time he was talking with Pam, allowed him to focus on trying to compose a life that included school, and that allowed him to continue to imagine moving ahead, and living a normal life.

However, other youth were more tightly caught in relationship webs. Ben, for example, was deeply embedded in the family web that included his parents, his sister, and his brother. It was a deep sense of family obligation and responsibilities that shaped his ways of living in the world. We saw that he was willing to not be in school, for now, in order to provide food and shelter for his siblings while they attended school. For him, composing a life that included school was something that would come later, when, perhaps, his siblings could support him as he was now supporting them. For Ben, his life composing was always in relation to this web of relationships in which he was embedded. His story was a communal family story where everyone would be allowed to attend school at some time. This family story was not one of children and youth attending from their early years (age 5 or 6) to graduation (age 18) in a linear sequence that shapes the dominant narratives.

Truong was also embedded in a family web of relationships, a web in which he was the strong male presence in the family. For many years Truong was the protector of his mother and his siblings, and of other children who were somehow identified as weaker, as needing help or protection. He composed his life, in part, as one of sacrifice as he found he was no longer able to attend school but was committed to providing financial, physical, and emotional support to his brother and sister so they could graduate from school. For Truong and Ben, high school completion was something to be attained, but it could not be attained without regard for the relational family web. They improvised forward-looking stories attentive not only to themselves but to the complex web of relationships within which they are embedded.

Andrew, too, was embedded in a web of family relationships shaped, in part, by the church. He was also, for a time, part of an elite school sports team. When he lost his place on the team, he rejected his team membership when he realized that he could not count on the team members, including the coaches. He continued to count on the support, and sense of belonging, created by his family web of relationships. He knew it was up to him to compose a life that allowed him to live out his imagined story of gaining a post secondary education and playing basketball, but knew his family relationships would continue to support him. It was the web of family relationships that enabled him to feel safe enough to continue to compose and live out a future story.

Jasmine's life was also deeply connected and shaped in relationships with her family and friends. Jasmine's family and friends valued a good education and shaped her move to "better schools" when she moved to another country in Africa. Jasmine was willing to spend all her time in study groups with her friends in order to do well in school. Even though she was an outsider in the new African country, where she "heard many horror stories about how her people working in the local houses as house maids were killed or abused," she was able to carry on with her story of excelling at school because of the relationship with friends and family who supported her. However, several years into attending school in Canada, she was overcome, crushed by a "glass ceiling" she felt was imposed on her because she was labeled an ESL (English as a Second Language) student. This time it was her stories to live by, who she was and was becoming, and not her physical body that appeared under threat. When she experienced these events, she was alone, unable to share her stories with her uncle, and with her supportive community group. She shared with Yi Li a dream of being blocked, of not being able to go forward. Eventually a new friend and her aunt encouraged her to take business courses at a college. With another web of relationships formed by her friend, her aunt, and the reappearance of her uncle, she improvised a new forward-looking story, one of saving her money to return to business college with the dream of owning a salon in Africa.

Robert's schooling experiences were interwoven within the relational web of family stories. The stories his brothers told of all three schools Robert attended eased his movement into them. As well intergenerational stories of working with his hands like his grandfather, a story Robert yearned for at school, bumped up against school stories where academic programming was privileged over courses in the trades. As school became less and less relevant to Robert, as more and more classes were skipped in junior high school and later in high school, Robert composed new stories outside of school where he worked with a family friend renovating houses and working on farm equipment. These webs of relationship shifted him out of school.

Skye, too, eventually left school. When her family felt that what she was experiencing in school was making her unhealthy and sick, her family moved her out of school, a move that allowed her to compose a further life in which she was not at school but was more closely held within the web of family relationships. For Billie Bob, it was when she lost her web of relationships at her junior high school that she was cut adrift and could no longer sustain herself in school. The web of relationships that seemed to matter most to Billie Bob were those she felt when in the school.

Relational webs were present in the stories that the youth told. Sometimes the webs were family webs of relationships, sometimes webs of friends and communities, and sometimes webs of school relationships. Sometimes all, or some, of the relational webs were at play in the youths' life composing.

Thread 3: Conflicting Responsibilities in Composing Transitions

As we attended to the stories of the youth we learned that in order to attend to their experiences of transition we needed to attend to the relational contexts in which the youth were composing their lives. Family obligations and responsibilities that may have been shaped in childhood were highlighted as the youth composed their lives. Many youth were composing lives in which they struggled to balance conflicting responsibilities that emerged from living within the institutional, cultural, and familial narratives, and which shaped their experiences as they composed their lives.

Truong struggled to compose his own life as he took on responsibility for his mother, his siblings, and more recently his young daughter. He worked part time from a young age in the same restaurant where his mother worked. His stories of leaving school were interwoven with his stories of needing to provide for, and protect, his family. Christian also struggled amidst conflicting responsibilities. His responsibility to attend to, and care for, his mother meant that he was less able to attend to school responsibilities. Even after he left school and found employment he continued to work to support his mother in multiple ways.

Lynn, too, lived out a strong story of family responsibilities. When her grandmother became ill, she focused her attention on caring for her grandmother, a responsibility that conflicted with her participation in school. Even though her grandmother wanted Lynn to complete school, Lynn was caught between caring for her grandmother and fulfilling her grandmother's dream of completing high school.

Being nested within the family web created comfort but also conflict for Robert. Robert told of being bullied at his elementary and junior high school. While Robert lived with family stories of not fighting and being a Good Samaritan, he also desired to stand up to bullies and to fight back when bullied. For fighting back in school, he was frequently put into detention. Living within the family web was frequently tension-filled for him around his experiences in school, as these actions in response to being bullied were not supported at home.

There is another way to think about relational contexts in transitions as the youth composed their lives within, and without, the institutionally structured world of school. Many of the youth initially told stories that fit with "normal" stories of school; stories such as being on the elite basketball team, stories of academic progress, stories of excellent attendance, and stories of leadership. Yet these stories of "success" in the story of school began to crumble as, for example, Truong, Christian, and Lynn bumped up against family responsibilities that were more pressing.

Thread 4: Composing Forward-Looking Stories Amidst Transitions

Kevlar continued to keep at his life composing; he found ways to do homework when he was homeless; he played on the computer while he lived in a motel room where it was not possible to invite friends to play; he found friends to stay with when he was kicked out. These particularities show, over time and multiple places, Kevlar's determination to compose a life that made sense, a life with narrative coherence. Faced with no certain way forward, he improvised ways to make sense in each situation. He continued to cling to the story of going to school, the story he told himself was most important.

In Ben's story he refused the taken-for-granted scripts offered to immigrant and refugee youth. He refused to accept the stories others told of him by rejecting their imposed compositions that would fix him in place. However, faced with rejecting the scripts given to him, he awakened to the lack of spaces where he could make up stories to live by. Through remembering and imagining, he composed a life, ways to keep going. For Ben, his desire was to continue on his routes of migration, knowing he was still on his way, in his way, and not fixed by others in place.

Christian was frequently stopped, frozen in his obligations, and responsibilities, to his family. His night shift job as a security guard was, in part, shaped by his responsibilities to care for his mother. His artwork and his tattoos were the ways he continued to move forward in composing his life. His artwork was the outward expression of how he was composing his forward-looking stories. He dreamt of working in a tattoo parlor as a place where he could engage in his art making. Andrew, too, kept trying to compose his life in ways that would allow him to play basketball. He kept at his dream of playing basketball and winning a scholarship to study and to play ball.

Jasmine composed her life in the face of tension and interruption. She was continually denied the opportunity in high school to move forward in academic course work that would lead to post secondary education and her dream of becoming a doctor or a pharmacist or work for the UN. Nevertheless she tried to continue her forward-looking story. For example, she improvised a "round about" way to take academic courses by going to summer school. She requested a different advisor in Grade 12, one that did not discourage her in seeking to undertake regular academic course work. When she was not given the help she asked for in grade 12, she left school rather than be continually "marked" as ESL and as not capable of doing academic course work. In conversation with her aunt and a friend she composed a new forward-looking story of attending business school with the dream of owning a hair salon in her African home country.

Robert, too, composed his life with attention to who he wanted to be and become. In elementary school he chose not to tell his teachers about the bullying but told his parents instead. In junior high school he decided to tell the teachers and principal but again that did not help him find ways to live easily in school. In high school he seemed to take matters into his own hands, deciding to ride his bike, and explore the neighborhood during physical education class, rather than be victim to bullies, or to the decisions of school administrators he did not respect. In high school he composed a way of attending school where he did well in classes when the teachers cared about him, and did not attend other classes. Eventually there were no classes that were relevant to his dream to learn a trade. He left school. He continued to compose his life in relation to his own dreams and in relation to his family, becoming an apprentice mechanic.

The youth, in the stories they told us, resisted having their lives fixed or frozen in places when they encountered tensions and interruptions to their stories to live by. They told their stories in ways that allowed us to see them making their way as best they could in the contexts within which they found themselves. For them their stories were not of being dropouts, but as people who were "not in school for now" and as people composing forward-looking stories.

Thread 5: Intertwining Transitions and Identities

Christian's tattoo, written in Chinese characters, means "family friends forever" when translated into English. These are the stories he lived by. By drawing forward his memories of past experiences, his father, and his relationships, he was able to not only construct, but also to disrupt, a story of family and relationships. He continued to live out these stories with his strong commitment to his mother and his sister. While we came to understand much about Christian's stories to live by, we did not gain a sense of what experiences enabled him to compose those stories to live by. He talked about his artwork with koi fish that could transform into dragons as the plot line of his imagined future story. He said, "it is impossible to swim over a waterfall and perhaps it is symbolic of my life. It represents my life a lot." Magic might be possible if many things aligned. It was, for him, an emplotted narrative, an imagined story of possibility.

Truong's memories and imagination were interwoven but, for him, they had not yet come together to allow him to compose what might be a good life for him. He spoke of wanting a peaceful life and of finding moments of peace with his young daughter. However, he remembered the need for violence in some situations and continued to know that if something came to him that required a violent response, he needed to be ready for it. He held only fragments of memories of what might be possible to compose what he saw as a good life. His experiences in Hamilton Elementary and Junior High School were times when he composed a life in school that allowed him to imagine future possibilities in school. But just outside the school yard there was uncertainty. Violence was always present. Memories of those who were loyal to him, and to whom he was loyal, shaped his stories to live by, and his imagined forward-looking stories. "You can't save the world but I can save myself, and my friends, my kid and my family."

Andrew's memories shaped in church settings about how to live with others deeply shaped what he felt he had to do when school events around the basketball team created interruptions in his stories to live by. He drew on memories of what he learned in church, from his family, as well as from what he learned from music lyrics to compose stories that helped him imagine ways to move forward. He spoke of his code of ethics that provided him with a sense of a plot line to shape his life into the future.

We see in the youth that life composing and imagination are inextricably linked. Transitions and identities intertwined as the youths' embodied imaginings composed new ways to shape a life allowing their stories to live by to continue. It is imagination that shapes the storied lives we live and tell. It is imagination that allows us to travel backward and forward yet simultaneously be attentive to the situations we are living. Memory provides threads to pull forward into present and future contexts, real and imagined. We saw the youth responding in improvisatory ways to the contexts in which they were living as they found they could no longer live by stories congruent with the dominant stories of school success, which included graduating from high school. Christian pulled from his art and his stories of physicality to imagine a new forward-looking story, one of being a tattoo artist. Kevlar drew from his memories of being alone with his computer, and making it on his own, to improvise ways forward with schooling that included attending an on-line program to finish high school and eventually to attend a design college. Andrew picked up threads of his love for playing basketball, his involvement with church and family, and his looking after foster children, as he improvised a forward-looking story that made sense, a story that allowed him to play basketball outside of school, and to improve his skills so he could win a basketball scholarship to attend postsecondary education and study social work.

Ben drew from a cultural narrative that shaped his story of looking after family. Although his dream of going to school was deferred, he improvised a new forward-looking story by pulling on the cultural and familial threads that allowed him to support his siblings' schooling with the hope that they would support him to attend school at some point in the future. When the dream of being a famous volleyball player was interrupted for Truong, he continued to live out his story of protector of those who are weaker, the story he had lived by since childhood. Even though he no longer attended school, he ensured that his siblings had an opportunity for schooling. His new forward-looking story, composed around memories and imagination, appealed to him because he saw it as continuing the story of sacrifice, which his parents lived for him.

Narrative Understandings of Transitions

We began this chapter drawing attention to the dictionary meaning of transition, as "passage from one form, state, style, or place to another" (*Concise Oxford Dictionary*, 1976, p. 1232). We showed how, in the dominant narrative, this too often implied an abruptness and certainty of change with a focus on the two ends of the process, the endpoint of one state and the onset of the next. We tend to see this reading of the word transition as a kind of technicist reading, a sense of fixed positioning, as one state is replaced by another. As we attended closely to the lives of the youth, we showed how we could understand transitions differently, that is, we could understand transitions narratively. In what follows we draw forward five qualities of transitions that we discerned in our work with the youth.

Qualities of a Narrative Understanding of Transitions

Quality 1: Shifting over time and place Thinking narratively about lives in the making we sensed much more gradual shifts as stories were carried forward, reshaped as new stories were gradually composed. For example, we did not see the youth in fixed positions, changing "overnight" from "student" to "dropout." The youth did not tell their stories in those ways. The youth were given the label "dropout" from within the institutional story of school. We wondered if labels are more easily assigned when the stories youth are living bump up against institutional narratives. We realized how easily the youth could be labeled: a student from another country became suddenly the ESL student; a student new to the school carried the label newcomer; a student who leaves school early is marked as dropout; and so on. These labels were imposed by those within the story of school and reflected a sense of who was authoring their stories. It was not the ways that the youth told their stories of their life composing. From the vantage point of the institutional narrative, the labels appeared to separate who was "normal" from who was considered "other." While the imposed labels were applied quickly to the youth, what became apparent was that each youth was composing a life, moment to moment, over time.

As we wonder about the institutional narratives *we* live within, we wonder too about the word transition. It would be dangerous to assume that we can label transitions. The youth did not use the term transition, we did. We wonder how youth themselves would see what are called transitions in their lives, particularly when they attend to what are called transitions over time. How would Kevlar, from a vantage point of now see what those in schools labeled as transitions? How would Ben restory his time in Canada long after his arrival? We wonder about how deeply the dominant institutional narrative of school has shaped their lives. Has their leaving, and their bumping up against the dominant narratives, forever shaped them? The discourse around youth, particularly around the lives of youth who left school without graduating, is filled with concepts such as resilience, risk factors, and transition. They all appear to be directed to a person assumed to be in a fixed position, living out the labeled script.

Yet, in our study, the youth resisted the label of dropout. They told their stories as not fixed but ever moving with the diverse situations in which they found themselves. We saw how their embodied sense of knowing from past experiences became part of new stories to live by and their forward-looking stories. We saw them making their way.

Quality 2: Composing lives as a process of change Our narrative inquiry drew on a narrative understanding of experience, that is, that we understand life making as a process; composed over time, in places, and in different relationships. As we experience, we change. We are in continual movement. Neither we, nor our relationships with the world itself, stay the same. Change is relentless, constant, and demanding as is life making. Understanding experience narratively opens the possibility that transitions speak to lives unfolding. Thinking narratively we puzzle through the whole of the youths' lives, their stories from the past, and their hopes and dreams into the future. Leaving school was not a single event. It happened in the midst of ongoing lives, ongoing stories, it did not define their lives. We were struck by the complexity of stories we were hearing when whole lives over time are considered. For example, listening closely to Truong and Andrew's stories we discerned a gradual waning of interest in school as their "belonging on sports teams" was denied. As these worlds closed, a tapering off began, more and more classes were missed, and eventually they left school. Yet, at the same time as the school stories of belonging on sports teams fade, we see that new forward-looking stories are emerging to sustain their life composing. Andrew continues basketball with his adult friends outside of school. Truong tells himself a story of being a protector to ensure his younger siblings are not hurt on their way to school. Ben must leave school in order to provide for his family but he improvises a new story to live by as his "going to school" story unravels.

We saw the youth continuing to compose their lives as the landscapes they were living within continually changed. We saw that leaving school was a change among multiple changes, the flux of daily living. Being assigned a label of dropout did not leave them fixed in place by a script to live within, a script with no way forward. We recognized agency in their stories as narrative threads of being and becoming continued to emerge. Listening to the youth's stories over time we discerned fluidity and movement as imagined, and remembered, storied moments recombined in ways that made sense when other stories were no longer working to move their lives forward, to continue to become.

Quality 3: Transitions as liminal spaces As we consider moments that might change our lives, times that in hindsight (Freeman, 2010) we might name as transitions, we turn to Heilbrun (1999) and her writing around liminality to help us consider what she calls living "in between destinies" (p. 102). Mindful of the work of Victor Turner (Driver, 1997) who attended the experiences of people as they pass over the threshold from one stage of life to another, Heilbrun considered the "in between" state created in transition. She describes the state as a liminal one, an indeterminate stage where we are neither here nor there. Because there is no prescribed story to live out in a state of liminality, Heilbrun writes of the possibilities that such spaces offer where we might write our own lines, compose our own plays and stories.

As we heard the youths' stories of leaving school, we saw how they began to gradually draw away, or, in some stories, be gradually pushed away, from approved institutional plotlines of going to school, going to post secondary, getting a job and so on. As scripted plotlines ended, other pulls became more pressing. Eventually, as they abandoned scripts written by others, we wondered if they saw that their lives were "in between destinies" (p. 102) and have seen a space, an opportunity, to write their own lives.

Heilbrun (1999) noted that "the most salient sign of liminality is it's unsteadiness, it's lack of clarity about exactly where one belongs and what one should be doing" (p. 3). Thinking about the stories the youth told us and considering Heibrun's notion of liminal spaces we wonder at the freedom the youth might feel in realizing they are writing their own lives now. Yet we imagine too the "uncertain ground" (p. 3) beneath their feet as they move from one world constructed within one institutional narrative with its particular rules and regulations to a world shaped by other narratives and, perhaps, by their choice of narratives to live out in relation to who, and what, matters in their lives. When there is no longer a prescribed story to fit into would having someone alongside, to reflect and wonder with them over time, have opened more possibilities for the youth?

Quality 4: Improvisation as part of transition Making up lives, improvising new "unheard of" stories in transition, is a way to provide narrative coherence (Carr, 1986). We are drawn to Carr who writes about our need for narrative coherence to make sense of our lives.

> Our lives admit of sometimes more, sometimes less coherence; they hang together reasonably well but they occasionally tend to fall apart. Coherence seems to be a need imposed on us

> whether we seek it or not. Things need to make sense. We feel the lack of sense when it goes missing. The unity of self, not as an underlying identity but as a life that hangs together is not a pre given condition but an achievement. Some of us succeed it seems better than others. None of us succeed totally. We keep at it. What we are doing is telling and retelling to ourselves and to others, the story of what we are about and what we are. (p. 97)

For example, Andrew and Truong can no longer make sense of their lives in school after their stories of being on elite sports teams at school are interrupted. They begin to imagine and compose different stories. Attendance at school was interwoven with being part of school sports teams so that when they were no longer part of these, going to school started to make no sense. New stories needed to be composed in order that they could live in ways that made sense to them, in order to create narrative coherence. As we struggle for narrative coherence in situations that do not match expectations such as the ones in which Andrew and Truong found themselves, Carr (1986) writes that "practical imagination" (p. 91) is involved. Practical imagination is a matter of coping with reality, "not of providing alternatives to it" (p. 91).

We see a link between practical imagination and improvisation. The *Oxford Advanced Learning Dictionary* online states the meaning of improvise is "to invent" without preparation and "to make or do something using whatever is available when you don't have what you really need." It is a way of coping with reality, rather than providing an alternative to it. We saw in the youths' stories, as their complex lives unfolded, how they began to improvise different stories they could live by when attending school was no longer making sense. Improvising a new story when the conventional story is no longer possible demands, according to Bateson (1994), living with peripheral vision such that, in embodied ways, remembered and imagined images, recombine to create new stories to live by. Bateson gives us a way to think about what the youth were doing as they left school. She writes that as people encounter new situations, as the youth described in multiple moments across their lives, "human beings make do with partial understandings, inventing themselves as they go along" (p. 9). Bateson's words suggest moment-to-moment embodied ways of improvisation as a way to compose lives across transitions.

Feature 5: Imagination and relationship as part of transitions Living in transition, on the cusp of another way of being, creating other worlds and improvising new stories to live by, requires imagination. In embodied ways experiences are remembered, and dreams are imagined, to reconfigure stories to live by. But what experiences are remembered and what experiences are dreamed? When imagination and memory are intertwined with relationships, we see the importance of attending to who we are, and are becoming, as responsible to, and for, our relationships. We are reminded of conflicting responsibilities for Ben, Lynn, Christian, Truong, and others. Familial, cultural, and institutional narratives in which they were embedded shaped their experiences and stories to live by. They struggled to live in relation to all of these. Perhaps they became adept at living in different worlds. Perhaps they developed peripheral vision through shifting between and across multiple responsibilities. They learned to live with uncertainty, never sure of what would happen next as prescribed roles and plotlines began to unravel. Relationships ignite imagination even as imagination ignites relationship. Relationships provide grounding from which to feel at ease, to make up other worlds, other ways of being. Relationships also provide opportunities to see things differently; broadening imagination of what could be when prescribed plotlines are no longer available. It is in relationships with friends and family such as Robert and his grandfather, of Andrew and his pastor, of Jasmine and her aunt and uncle, that we saw how the youth could continue to imagine new stories to live by after they left school. Being grounded in relationships allowed them to imagine new ways to compose their lives across transitions.

Summary

The youth we came to know are deeply committed to school, to composing their lives in meaningful and relational ways over time. Some of them have come to trouble the notion of normal, good, and successful, while others strive to live up to, or live out, these storied plotlines shaped by dominant plotlines. We see how their lives were not brought to a standstill as they bumped against institutional narratives of school, or when the label of "dropout" was affixed by others. Instead we saw movement. When their lives no longer fit within narrow plotlines defined in the story of school, they continued to invent themselves anew in a process of continual transition. We saw them improvising new stories to live by, drawn from multiple entangled narratives, in moments both lived and imagined.

We return to the words of transition and transient. They remain important to us, but we do not want to let a more technical interpretation draw our attention away from life composing in transition. What remains most significant, as we try to understand the lives of the youth with whom we worked, is a more complex understanding of how these terms are taken up by the youth, by us, and by others. Does commitment of schools, educators, other professionals, parents, and policy makers to efficient transitions within narrow institutional narratives of schooling trump commitment to the lives of youth in transition? Might schools and policy makers live with divided attention as the youth we met have done? Perhaps these questions deserve to be examined with attention to complexities, to shifts over time and place, to allow room to improvise and to imagine otherwise.

Chapter 16

Stories to Live By: Composing Identities

Pam Steeves, D. Jean Clandinin and Vera Caine

> Identity is a storied life composition,
> a story to live by.
> Stories to live by
> are shaped in places and lived in places.
> They live in actions,
> in relationships with others,
> in language, including silences,
> in gaps and vacancies,
> incontinuities and discontinuities (Clandinin & Huber, 2002,
>   pp. 161–162)

We begin with this narrative understanding of identity, which provides our conceptual lens into making sense of the stories the youth told of their lived experiences. We understand stories to live by as fluid, as evolving over time, as relational, as both personal and social, and as grounded in places. Identity, in our understanding, is situated within the three-dimensional narrative inquiry space.

> All stories are embedded within
> social, cultural, institutional, and family narratives
> that shape, and are shaped by,
> individuals' stories to live by (Clandinin, 2010)

We saw how these narratives that thread together the complex landscapes within which the youth lived, also shaped, and continue to shape, their diverse unfolding lives and were important as the youth composed who they are and are becoming. As part of a process of composing and living

---

Composing Lives in Transition: A Narrative Inquiry into the Experiences of Early School Leavers
Copyright © 2013 by Emerald Group Publishing Limited
All rights of reproduction in any form reserved
ISBN: 978-1-78052-974-5

their identities, we saw how important it was for the youth to engage in relational ways in the telling, living, retelling, and reliving of their experiences both in and outside of schools.

Lives Shaped by Landscapes Threaded by Multiple Narratives

> To see things or people small, one chooses to see from a detached point of view, to watch behaviours from the perspective of a system, to be concerned with trends and tendencies rather than the intentionality and concreteness of everyday life. To see things or people big, one must resist viewing other human beings as mere objects or chess pieces and view them in their integrity and particularity instead. One must see from the point of view of the participant in the midst of what is happening if one is to be privy to the plans people make, the initiatives they take, the uncertainties they face. When applied to schooling, the vision that sees things big brings us in close contact with details and with particularities that cannot be reduced to statistics or even to the measurable. (Greene, 1995, p. 10)

Living within, and in relation to, complex multi-storied contexts over time both shaped the youths' and their families' lives, as well as shaped the ways the youth began to understand their lives. Attending to what Greene refers to as seeing the details, and particularities, of seeing people big, was important to us in understanding the mundane, the everyday lived stories, as well as the sacred and cover stories (Clandinin & Connelly, 1995) the youth made visible to us. The stories the youth told highlighted, for us, the complexities of their lives but also made us aware of how they made sense of the ways the different kinds of narratives shaped their landscapes.

In the sections that follow, we attempt to attend to the multiple kinds of narratives that threaded through the landscapes of the youth. We realize that it is impossible to separate one kind of narrative, be it a social, cultural, geographic, familial, or institutional, from another so interwoven are they in the fabric of the youths' landscapes. However, we try to do this in order to show the multiple narrative threads that were important in shaping the youths' lives.

> By the end of the first day I had created my own new circle of friends
> Top tier.
> I'm feeling good
> designer clothes
> looking good

Life is good.
   But
I'm still insecure
it's just a different kind
of insecure
the kind
you don't talk about.

We all have cover stories
and
one of the ways
to be popular
is to not talk about
your insecurities.
You make yourself look
like you don't have
any.

> Once I came out of the closet
> my whole life was different
> by identifying myself as what I was
> it grows you stronger
> sometimes you get reactions
> people who are supportive
> sometimes
> people are indifferent and don't really care
> and then
> sometimes
> they say   oh
> you're a faggot
> that's gross
> i always knew my life would be harder.

Scott's stories speak to his understandings of his landscapes, the realities of discrimination, indifference, as well as to his inability to always fit in. Scott storied himself as shaped by the narrative threads of discrimination that were woven through social, cultural, and institutional narratives that shaped his multiple landscapes over time. Would it have mattered which school he went? Were his stories of leaving predictable? Could he or his family have anticipated these? We puzzled about such matters as we attended to Scott's stories about the complex interplay of these multiple narratives that threaded across his landscapes.

By Grade 7, Scott already had a sense there was a hierarchy among peers. His experiences made him feel that he was "better than some" students, but not as good as others. It wasn't long before he felt as if he didn't fit within the class system in his particular junior high school, and he began searching for a belonging place. Scott remembered his first day of junior high as a crucial day for him. Feeling self-conscious, he worried that others were judging him, much as he was beginning to judge others. He understood that "what I wore was important, and what I said, and how I looked, and those things were important." Scott acquired a sense of agency when he started both to speak out, and stand out, through what he said, and what he wore: "The more powerful I appear — people are going to want to hear what I have to say." He named himself as courageous. As he grew stronger, he no longer wanted to live a cover story (Clandinin & Connelly, 1995) by pretending to be someone he wasn't.

Lives Shaped by Landscapes Threaded with Familial Narratives

Familial narratives threaded the youths' landscapes in different ways. Sometimes the youths' families were present in visible ways, such as being present in homes and schools. Sometimes the youths' families were less visibly present. The youths' complex life stories show a sense of them composing their own lives, sometimes in conversation with others, including family members, sometimes alone. Kevlar chose to "get off the streets" himself and to live in a group home. "I just decided to change things 'cause I was going to die if I didn't." He chose to "accept it for what it was." For Kevlar, his family was not present in visible ways and, often, Kevlar figured out on his own who he should be, and become. Andrew also acted alone as he gradually drifted away from school. When asked if his mother had visited the school around the time he was kicked off the basketball team, Andrew said he did not think she could help. He had not asked her to come. He chose to accept the coach's actions. For him, doing what seemed the "right thing" was up to him. Lynn also acted alone. Disappointed in herself for selling drugs, she did so because she felt she had no other option to take care of her family. Other choices Lynn made were ones for which she was proud, for example, her choice to "grow," and get her dad and her brother "back" after the family disintegrated with the death of her grandmother. As Lynn composed a forward-looking story, she weighed her commitment to graduate from a postsecondary program in health care with her need to earn money to support her future life and her wish to parent a child. Lynn said, "I am not speaking to anyone. I rely on myself." Lynn struggled with who she knew she was, and what her life situations had shaped for her to become. In order to take care of her family, she composed her life in particular ways. Because she sold drugs as a way to financially support her family, she named herself "a hypocrite" because she regretted her actions. "I know I'm hurting people's families. I know I'm doing all that but I need to take care of mine. I need to support my family. I was taking care of my family. That's the only reason why I did it. I know it was a negative decision." Lynn is now on her own, although her family, particularly her grandparents who have now passed on, remain strong in the stories she is now trying to live out within a different context.

For some participants, staying in school did not fit with their forward-looking stories, and to stay meant conforming to stories others wanted them to live by. Robert lived by a strong family story given to him by his grandfather's story of "working with your hands," even though teachers and administrators supported a more academic route for him. Choosing a story more coherent (Carr, 1986) with what he had learned from his grandfather, Robert left high school and, after a short period of time, began apprenticing as a mechanic.

Many participants lived their lives threaded around plotlines of responsibility to, and for, family. They struggled to compose their own lives but did so in ways that allowed them to stay connected with one or more parent and siblings. Sometimes these responsibilities were financial. Truong lived out a story of being responsible in relation to his younger siblings and to his mother, and now to his young daughter. Truong began to live out this familial narrative early in life, getting a job in the same restaurant his mother worked in before he was of legal working age. He later contributed money to support the family and often provided physical protection for his mother and his younger siblings. In Lynn's story, too, we see her managing multiple responsibilities as she attended to household duties and cared for her grandmother. Christian was also composing his life attentive to a home life with a mother who had mental health issues and who struggled to find social support. Christian, with an absent father, in many ways needed to support his family financially and, like Truong, began to live a story of oldest male in the family. Like Truong, he positioned himself in a place where he could support and encourage his sister to stay in school. The stories of Lynn, Truong, and Christian were nested within familial narratives of family responsibilities. Attending to family responsibilities lived at the heart of composing their lives outside of school, and often made it challenging for them to negotiate attending to responsibilities they knew were important to composing a life in school.

Family stories, which are often formed intergenerationally, shaped the youths' responses, and responsibility, in relation to school. In other words, the youths embodied the stories taught to them by generations of family members. Robert, in particular, made this intergenerational dimension visible when he explored his work ethic. Explaining stories he lived by,

Robert said, "I have a strong work ethic installed in me." Tracing the story of this work ethic back to what he saw as its foundation, Robert highlighted how his mother's father had taught her to have a strong work ethic, knowledge she then passed on to Robert.

Reading across the narrative accounts, stories of several youth were shaped by family stories supporting the importance of high school. Lynn storied how her grandmother encouraged her to complete high school and tried to support her in doing so. Jasmine's and Billie Bob's stories also spoke of family stories that valued education. Jasmine's uncle provided both emotional and financial support after Jasmine moved to Canada. He encouraged Jasmine to do well at school and spent time helping her with schoolwork. Billie Bob's father provided financial support through two college programs, and a strong commitment to education was part of her stories to live by. As a youngster she loved school and did well. Later, with continual interruptions to her high school experiences, she chose to successfully complete assignments even when not attending school. When we spoke with her, she was still one credit short of high school completion but focused on obtaining her high school diploma so she can pass on the story of the importance of education to her daughter.

Lives Shaped by Landscapes Threaded by Cultural Narratives

Lynn reminded us that cultural narratives live in our skins and personal lives. "Anyone can see that I'm Native." Working to shift her stories to live by, Lynn was exploring her heritage, and had visited, and reconnected with, many of her extended family. "I'm Native. I'm full Cree. I'm just not Treaty. It [heritage] has already played a big part in my life." Lynn was living by her cultural narrative when she was expected to stay home and care for family members when her grandmother was sick. Lynn knew her cultural narrative in her body. For Skye, too, cultural narratives were powerful. She knew her intergenerational narratives were ones of knowing and being proud of one's culture. She knew dancing, singing, and song writing were part of the stories threaded back through her grandparents. Cultural narratives are not only embedded in the geographic places we are born into, or in the color of skin, but they come alive in the tensions on school landscapes that are diverse, and in contradiction with the youths' stories to live by. We saw this vividly in the story that Skye told of her teacher questioning where she had been when she was late for the physical education class. The color of her skin evoked multiple stories of who she was in the stereotypical story of being "Indian."

With each of his drawings Christian explained the connections to his Asian heritage that he visibly represented. In order to learn more about his

Asian heritage, he searched for information through schools, teachers, and the Internet. He had to compose his own cultural threads. His father was Asian. Christian does not recall his father ever living with his family. The last time he saw his father, his father did not recognize him and passed him by on the street just minutes away from Christian's family home. Christian was drawn to his Asian heritage: he chose to learn the language in school; he was familiar with Asian cartoon animation; and familiar with legends. In the absence of his father to help him make sense of this, he was trying to find ways to live who he was. Christian has no connections to the larger Chinese community. He taught himself a cultural narrative rather than learning from his familial stories, and spent many hours trying to figure out what being Asian could mean for him. In his early school years, his teachers seemed to recognize his interest and longing to find out more. His teachers in his later school years did not recognize this, and focused on the economic and violent implications associated with youth of Asian origin. In these moments his cultural narratives also become interwoven with the places he was living: the inner city, an area with high prostitution rates, with gangs, violence, and high rates of poverty.

Lives Shaped by Landscapes Threaded by Institutional Narratives

In the youths' stories, we saw schools as narrowly defined places for students to gain prescribed knowledge, skills, and attitudes. In their stories, we heard them speak of leaving their multiplicity, the wholeness of who they are, and the stories they are in the midst of living, at the door of the school.

> One of the rules was
> you had to take off your shoes
> when you come in for recess
> or change your shoes
> when you go outside
>
> I hated that.
>
> So
> instead of changing my shoes
> I would go and hug the teachers.
> I would tell them
> how pretty they were
> or
> how well I did
> or
> what I was learning.

> And the shoes?
> A non-issue.
> teachers didn't have to do it
> why should I?

Scott always seemed to question the school structures, as well as the stories of what schools were supposed to do. He, too, tried to shift the stories of school by his resistance to living up to the institutional narratives. He was not afraid to make these inconsistencies and bumping up places visible.

When Jasmine wanted to study subjects she knew would help her achieve her life goals and become who she wanted to be, she was told that her English was not good enough to attain those goals. She was forced to take courses that would not allow her to enter the postsecondary program of her choice. Within the institutional landscape, claiming an identity can be more challenging than passively accepting one. Many youth recalled labels that branded them as "less than," lazy, and not committed. We wondered about Truong who was seen as the "Asian" kid and was stereotyped, or Christian with his spiked haircut, or Ben who came from places we know little about. How did these institutional narratives play out in some of the stories of how fast a particular youth was expelled or dismissed? What happens when children and youth do not fit easily into the story of a "good" student? Christian had tattoos and a different hairstyle; he always felt he was easily judged, the story of him shaped by the place he lived, the "inner city," with the underlying social narratives of gangs, drugs, etc., that became inextricably linked with institutional narratives.

Some youth experienced the profound shaping of stories of school. Jasmine stated she had a strong academic background in Arabic, but when her only option for taking academic courses in the English language were outside of regular school days, her interest in school began to wane. Scott stated that he did not want to be placed in classes at a lower grade level because not only did he believe that he had the competence for the higher-level classes, he "didn't want to look like a fool. I didn't want people to think I was stupid."

There were also stories of shaming that were created as stories to live by composed by the youth bumped against stories composed by others within stories of school. The crumbling image of Ben lives so vividly in Vera's mind, the sense of him sinking into a pit, where others can't see, can't ask, can't dwell on the difference of others. We did not hear him tell stories of inquiry, of questioning, no sign of a more critical ontological stance in his life. We sensed a kind of emotional defeat that grew out of both Ben's and Scott's stories, stories that neither could shake, but which they refused to live by. We sensed feelings of disgrace that lived far beyond the moments of initial shaming. The shaming was not easily erased, and, for Ben, shaped how he could interact. Ben's only agency, much like Scott's, remained in looking away. At the same time both wanted to be heard and have their stories told. Skye, while the teacher attempted to shame her, resisted becoming the character the teacher attempted to cast her into.

Shame also came from a sense of class-consciousness, something Kevlar was acutely aware of. Kevlar said his high school was an "amazing school 'cause it's in Shaftsbury. Everything is. The people are a lot cleaner. They're from a higher grade, like they're just more upscale I guess. And there's just not all the bullshit ghetto drama like the city has." Kevlar often could not reveal the places he lived when he went to school. He did not want to evoke feelings in others that he was "less than." That was not as easily done for others. For Ben, the color of his skin and his lack of ability to speak English well became instant outward identifiers. He was unable to negotiate power differentials and felt obliged to answer his teachers' questions. He felt powerless when his stories were told, without his consent, to others, both in and out of classrooms.

Christian was sensitive to his notion of belonging and responsibilities toward school, a notion fostered in his elementary school years in a school he described as providing him with a place he belonged and a place where he developed a strong understanding of friendship. His early school experiences seemed to reinforce his value of education and he cared about his schooling. When he was asked to attend the public attendance board in high school, he cut his spiky, colored hair, hair that expressed who he was and expressed his sense of belonging to a group of friends. He hoped that by cutting his hair he would break free of the negative storylines created for him by the school. His hair remains short and well combed now, in an effort to retain employment. However, at no point in his stories did Christian mention that the change in haircut shifted the response of others.

Lives Shaped by Landscapes Threaded by Linguistic Narratives

Ben's stories to live by also bumped up against the stories of school of immigrant students. Ben talked about how he felt that others saw him as less able because he did not speak English as well. Like Ben, Jasmine also moved to Canada from another country. An academically strong student, Jasmine had dreams of becoming a doctor or a pharmacist or of working for the United Nations. She saw Canada as a place of hope and possibilities. Labeled as an ESL student, she was not allowed to take the academic courses she needed to go to university. Although she managed to find her way around the system, taking a couple of courses during the summer and passing them, Jasmine finally lost heart and left school early. Growing up in a family that valued education, Jasmine knew that she would return to school one day, but only on her own terms. For Jasmine, becoming an adult amidst a new language and culture was not an easy process as she struggled to compose an identity in Canada.

Lives Shaped by Landscapes Threaded by Geographic Narratives

Christian tried to reconcile his story of himself as of Asian heritage with his story of being Canadian, and his story of where he lived. It seemed that the efforts of reconciling these tensions with the stories told of him in school made it impossible to engage in schooling in ways that Christian found meaningful.

In Ben's stories, we saw how his life was embedded within a cultural narrative, shaped over time and by geography. He saw himself as Burmese, yet he was uncomfortable being named so by others in public. One could not so easily follow the patterns of assimilation and multiculturalism, and Ben was often reminded of this by being placed in an ESL class, and by the stories teachers told about him: that he was different, that he was less able. Ben's routes of migration geographically, and through different school systems and cultural experiences have greatly influenced his stories to live by. In Skye's stories there is another geographic narrative at work as she moved from the nearby reservation to the urban high school; she, too, followed routes of migration as she moved from the reservation setting to the urban setting and back again. These moves also shaped her stories to live by.

Experiencing Landscapes as Filled with Competing and Conflicting Plotlines

Attempting to make meaning of the stories youth told us meant we stayed close to the contexts of their lives and to their stories to live by. As we attended to the cultural, social, familial, linguistic, and institutional narratives within which the youths composed their lives, we noted competing and conflicting plotlines that shaped their stories to live by. The youths' stories spoke of, and to, contradictions between cultural narratives, familial narratives, and stories of school. Many of the youths were caught in these contradictions. At times it seemed as though they were trying to compose lives that allowed them to shift between, and across, multiple conflicting plotlines. Youth were trying hard to tell, and live, stories of who they were.

We saw moments in which family stories and school stories bumped against each other. We saw family stories and school stories in contradiction as Robert storied his grandfather telling him that high school students were supported either for going to university or trade school. Robert soon learned his desires to enter a trade were neither acknowledged nor supported in the stories foregrounded in the high school he attended.

Complex, multilayered, and continuous tensions resonated through many of the youths' stories. Lynn's stories portrayed the contradictions between her life in home and family and her life in school. After the death of her grandmother, Lynn storied how difficult it was to continue to live out her grandmother's desire that she finish school. She was caught amidst multiple plotlines of family responsibilities, family conflict, the need for money, her desire to be a mother, and living out her grandmother's desire for her.

Ben lived all his life within competing cultural and familial narratives of family responsibility. For a time he tried to compose a new story of himself through his love of art work after school where he spent so much of his time. But when the course was taken away he gradually left school, "there was no point in going." Entwined in stories of obligation, Ben lived out an acceptable competing story of working in order to help his younger sister to live out her dream of going to university. In a kind of "taking turns" manner consistent with the cultural and family narratives he lived within, Ben expected that his sister would provide funds for him to carry on his education at a future date.

Resisting the Shaping of Storied Landscapes

Like others we wonder about the importance of "resistance as part of the tension created as storied lives met on storied landscapes" (Huber, Huber, & Clandinin, 2004, p. 187).

> *I didn't care*
> *because I always knew*
> *that I didn't need a high school diploma to define myself.*

Early on and persistently in our work, we noticed many participants, including Scott, resisted the story of being labeled as dropouts or school leavers. Scott reminded us that his stories to live by are far more complex than the story of school and schooling. For other youth, being positioned as an early school leaver gave them little chance to "drop" back in, something a few participants were now contemplating. Tensions arose when participants spoke of others referring to them as dropouts, and how not accepting that label supported them to express who they were and were becoming. Thinking hard about what they were telling us, and realizing many of them felt there was no place for their voices in school, we wondered if by resisting the story imposed on them — that is, of being high school dropouts — they were reclaiming their voices. Scott described it in the following way: "I still don't identify myself as a high school dropout ... I tell people I completed 3 years of high school ... and it put me in a position where at 20 years old I have a professional job ... when I think of high school dropout I think of the guy who works at 7–11 and can't afford his rent ... and that's not who I am. I'm not a high school dropout. I'm, I'm somebody ... who recognizes the unimportance of high school ... I just chose ... not to finish high school." Scott made visible that the label ascribed to him by others did not, and does not, resonate with who he understands himself to be, or who he sees himself becoming. Scott's story of a high school dropout, that is, someone who struggles financially and is not able to make ends meet, is a fairly common stereotype. This is not the story Scott is living, nor is he willing to be defined, or confined, by the label.

Indeed, as Jasmine resisted the "glass ceiling" that she felt was imposed on her during high school, she seemed to be protecting her stories to live by in deciding to leave school early. Even after leaving school she refused to accept the courses that were provided for her to improve her English in a local college. She resisted the accompanying story of her English as "not being good enough" and, instead, showed agency, working and saving enough money to take courses of her own choosing, courses that would help her attain her newly configured dream, that of owning a salon back in Africa, part of the forward-looking stories she wanted to compose. Neither did non-achievement of a high school diploma shape Scott's understandings of who he was, or who he could become. He showed us it did not shape the stories he is living, in his current and past work places. Since leaving high school, Scott has been engaged working with youths who have been victims of bullying or, to use Scott's words, "abused ... by peers." Scott speaks of his current work site as a place, and space, where his voice is heard and reverberates into the lives of youths who are, perhaps, in danger of leaving school early.

Robert resisted allowing teachers to define who he should be and should become. He resisted teachers who didn't care about, or respect, him in the way his family taught him. He resisted curriculum (the D.A.R.E. program) when only one point of view was allowed. Eventually he resisted going to school altogether when he found few opportunities to learn the trades because it was a curriculum thought to be "less than" in his school. Robert felt he had to leave school in order to continue learning. He did so in his out of school life eventually leading to his apprenticeship as a mechanic. The last words in his narrative account are telling, "I do enjoy learning."

We heard them struggle to develop and sustain a sense of agency embodied in their lives as they unfolded over time. Participating in the study itself was, for many, an act of choice that shaped a sense of authoring/authority in their lives.

Gray (2009) draws on Mishler (1999) to speak of resistance as providing a way to explore the impact of social influences on the personal narratives of people in marginalized social positions. We attended closely to the positioning of youth and were attentive that the youth were composing their identities on elementary, junior high, and senior high school landscapes as well as on complex home and community landscapes.

Representing Their Stories to Live By

Christian's drawings represent in many ways his stories to live by (Figure 1). Characters in the drawing are his friends and he represents himself as a youth of Asian heritage. His friends and his link to his cultural background are important to Christian; both matter deeply to him.

Figure 1: Christian's drawings 6.

Even so in Christian's drawings there are some apparent outward representations of who he is. He takes up each representation in turn in order to rebut or confirm those that could define him. He has learned early that the stories that express who he is are also stories that bump up against the notion of a good student, citizen, or youth. Christian speaks of norms and expectations, not as black or white or as boxes that one did, or did not, fit in, but as ways to make and impose judgment and exclude. He talks about his feelings of being judged in schools, that his Asian heritage combined with his hairstyle carried the story of him as a gang member — and this association also carried other stories. As we looked across his texts we knew it must have been difficult for Christian to find a place that acknowledges who he was, without also wanting to define him at the same time.

We saw other ways the youth expressed their stories to live by in both visible and invisible ways. Kevlar and Truong's tattoos, Scott's dress, and distinctive haircuts, were some of the visible ways. Less visible ways could be seen in Billie Bob's attempts to work with vulnerable people and to shift the stories of her community.

Shifting Their Stories to Live By

Through Christian's drawings he talks about the process of transformation. Merging multiple images of people and animals and masks into one image is a reminder that fish and dragon and lives transform and live in close relationship. It is a complex, layered, and interwoven sense of identity; it has always been this way, as far back as Christian shared his stories to live by. Vera was drawn to him because of this complex sense of identity; in many ways a commitment to who he is, and is becoming, was visible early on. Christian's stories to live by are strongly shaped by a notion of loyalty and commitment, stories that help us understand why he might have left school. Being the primary care giver to his mother, who struggled with depression; the absence of his friends at his new school; the death of his grandmother; and the increasing family responsibilities he took on in his father's continuous absence were plotlines of the stories that shaped his departure from school.

We were drawn into Christian's stories to live by through his sense of authenticity and also his sense of change. Shared transformations across waterfalls where the merging symbolizes a shift, as a koi fish is being changed into a dragon were possible if the koi fish can move over the waterfall. The drawings of the koi fish, the transformations and clear markers of authenticity in Christian's images and tattoos can be read as one kind of representation of his stories to live by. The drawings become central, storied as tattoos they take on a different life. Living on the skin allows the images to be moving and breathing on the body and in the body. Christian both comes, and stays, alive in this way, his story of leaving is one of the moving, breathing on the body, and in the body, and finally leaving to attend to multiple responsibilities and stories to live by of his own and that of his mother and sister. We saw these shifts in many of the youths' stories to live by. They were very much in the midst, always becoming.

Conclusion

Looking at stories of early school leaving over time opened possibilities for a deeper understanding of the youths' lives. As we attended to the cultural, social, linguistic, geographic, and institutional narratives within which the youth composed their lives, we noted competing and contradictory plotlines that shaped their stories to live by. We too were aware that we needed to note "the moments when possibilities for new stories bubble up. Moments when it might be possible to shift the course of a story" (Clandinin & Connelly, 1998, p. 161).

Chapter 17

A Reflective Turn: Looking Backward, Looking Forward

Vera Caine, Sean Lessard, Pam Steeves and D. Jean Clandinin

As we take a reflective turn on our years of work alongside the youth, we revisit the personal, practical, and social/theoretical justifications of our narrative inquiry. In Chapter 1, Pam, Vera, and Jean represented fragments of their autobiographical narrative retellings in order to come to an understanding of who they were in relation to the experiences of those who leave school early, that is, youth who left school before graduating. Now, as we revisit those opening pages, we realize how much we have been shaped by the experiences of participating in this inquiry alongside the youth. Who we are now, and who we are becoming, that is, our stories to live by, have shifted. As well we have shifted what we now recognize about the experiences of leaving school early in terms of theorizing identity and of conceptualizing transitions. In what follows we make explicit some of these shifts.

Shifting Personal Justifications

As Pam inquired into her early experiences of school and of living with Matthew, she made visible her experiences of moving between multiple schools, several provinces, and different countries. As she engaged in her autobiographical narrative retellings she realized she could well have been seen as a *transient* child by those in schools. Her family too might have come into question as to their commitment to school. Her stories to live by were profoundly shaped by the different places she lived and attended school but also by the constancy of her relationships, particularly her relationship with her sister. Her stories were threaded with comfort to explore and to imagine otherwise while living through multiple and continually changing school landscapes. But these stories shifted as she became a mother to Matthew, a child with disabilities. As a young mother, her moves from one place to another were more intentional, less fuelled by imagining otherwise, more fuelled by a search for a place where Matthew could be viewed in respectful, educative ways. The struggle to find places of acceptance for Matthew as a unique and whole child awakened Pam to understanding, in new ways, the importance of composing a life in relationship. For Pam and Matthew it was important to work with someone who could come alongside, someone like Megan, a speech therapist, or the yellow school bus driver who understood that children compose their stories to live by both in and out of schools.

As Pam inquired into the lives of the youth in the study, she began to attend more closely to who comes alongside. She wondered what it means to come alongside youth, whose lives, like all lives, are always in the making, always on the way. She also attended more closely to the multiple scripts that are at work, scripts that label and define, and that hold the potential to become autobiographical prisons. The scripts that followed Matthew created limitations and separation for him and for her as his mother, and she too saw this reflected in the scripts given to the youth in our study. Such scripts had not followed her as a child moving from place to place. The stories she learned to hear, as she heard the stories of the youth, shifted Pam's sense of the importance of helping youth attend to, notice, but also resist the scripts that are assigned from within institutional narratives, as well as from within cultural narratives. As she came alongside Kevlar, both his imagination and hers were ignited. Kevlar, as they talked together about his story of leaving school said, "reflecting on it with someone is different than reflecting on it yourself." Spending sustained time with youth, allowing them the possibilities to name places of bumping up, resisting, as well as becoming, supported Pam to see new possibilities for researchers to attend to participants over time, to recognize and acknowledge people's lives in diverse social contexts and places.

As Vera inquired into her experiences of attending school and of leaving school early, she made visible how school was, for her, a narrowly defined place. She knew school as a place where rules silenced lives, where following the prescribed plotlines that flowed from institutional narratives was what mattered most. She knew early in her life what happens to those who did not follow these prescribed expectations, which formed plotlines to live out or to live up to as Carr (1986) would say. She learned how school was a difficult place when living out, and making visible, a strong sense of relational responsibility. Early on, she began to question schools as good and educative spaces for youth. Eventually she learned to live within the story of school, by living a cover story, choosing to live the story well enough that she could eventually graduate.

At the outset of the work with the youth, Vera knew coming alongside the youth would call her to revisit her early school experiences that came with tears, questions, and hard life stories. What she awakened to as she came alongside the youth was the complexity of interwoven narratives, times and places when cultural, familial, and institutional narratives bumped up against each other. She learned how difficult it was to not be able to renegotiate spaces of re-entry through living cover stories, to not be able to imagine the possibility of engaging in negotiations with those within institutional narratives. She learned that institutional plotlines were similar across diverse social contexts; the similarities were expressed in achievement of individual grades, through competition between peers, and through compliance. Vera's stories to live by shifted once again to see the importance of finding adults who were able to come alongside to help open spaces of resistance, as well as to open possibilities in what seemed to be closed familial, institutional, and cultural plotlines. For Vera questions were also raised around what counts as schooling, and what counts as education. She wondered through the study if there is a place that schooling and education interweave.

As Jean inquired into her experiences, she made visible her knowing of two worlds, the world of school and the world of home. Moving between these two worlds, Jean showed how the world of school is a place of dis/ease for those who do not fit in, do not easily belong in schools where the plotlines are differentiated not only by grades and achievement but also by access to clothing, food, and material goods. Living in two such different worlds made the tensions and contradictions visible to Jean from early on in her life. The school world was not, however, privileged in Jean's familial narratives. High school completion was a choice, not an expectation. Jean's stories to live by were composed between worlds, valuing both the home and school worlds, choosing to teach, but always knowing that children and families lived in both worlds, that the worlds each person inhabited could be shaped by radically different plot lines.

Coming alongside the youth in this study shifted Jean's stories to live by as she came to see how constrained the narratives are for some youth, and how difficult it is for those who live easily within the dominant stories of school to even see, or imagine, the complexities of the youth's lives, and worlds they live within. How the gaze from within the stories of school makes invisible the lives of youth and families whose stories do not fit those dominant plotlines and how important it is to recognize and attend to the youth who struggle to be recognized, to be seen.

In these brief retellings, Pam, Vera, and Jean attempt to show how profound their experiences alongside the youth have been, and continue to be, as the stories of the youth live in us, and call us to attend to our ongoing lives in new ways. These shifts have altered our personal vantage points, have shifted who we are in our relationships as teachers, parents, friends, colleagues, family members. We have, as Maxine Greene (1995) would have it, become otherwise once again.

In our work we were joined by others, who lived alongside youth and whose lives were also changed in profound ways. As we write this book we are reminded by Sean of the importance of shifting schools to become more welcoming, more innovative, and more belonging places. In the next section we revisit the practical justifications of the study as Sean makes visible the shifted ways he works with youth in schools. As Sean recounts how his work in schools has changed, we are reminded how this change was possible through coming alongside the youth in the study, and the shift this relationship has had on his stories to live by, on our stories to live by.

Shifting Practical Justifications

We begin with a piece Sean wrote as he described a summer teaching program and how he came to co-compose such a program with the youth in the high school where he worked. As Sean returned to work in schools at the completion of the study, his stories to live by too had shifted, and with those shifts, came new ways to live in schools, new ways to restory institutional narratives.

Red Worn Runners[1]

Sometimes 5, sometimes 18, one time 30 but every day through August the Red Worn Runners have been inspiring me as we shuffle, sprint, and navigate our way down the dusty roads of Enoch Cree Nation[2], always wearing red–red t-shirts that is. It is a beautiful thing to experience and we always start at the local school in the town site, stretching, slowly getting ready for a run. Sometimes I love this daily ritual, other times I loathe it; it depends how my body is feeling. But we stick together through this, one day at a time. Girls,

---

1. A name the youth came up with for our daily running group during the summer months.
2. Enoch Cree Nation is a reserve in Treaty 6 territory located west of the city of Edmonton. It is a community that Sean has worked with for the past 10 years in education and sport.

boys, young people, and older people like myself make this trek daily throughout August. Sometimes we run 4 kilometres in a day, and we always make sure to jog by the community health centre and the Band office.

It is interesting because now people wave at us when we jog. They used to look at us with mistrust. There was doubt in their glances. They quietly shook their heads as they saw youth move in a different way. I like visiting with the youth about the run and how it feels. They say they love it and now I am starting to believe it, as they log their kilometres and look towards the poster[3] *to see how far they are going, to see how far they have been. Did I tell you ... man you should see these kids run. It is beautiful — no training, no fancy gyms — just the town site; bumpy dirt roads with truck imprints embedded in the earth ... then the sandy gravel of the back roads towards the potato plantation, our target turnaround.*

Wheat fields and canola fields are on each side. They seem to be our only fans some days and they seem to wave us on. No judgments there. We run and the youth tell me they have never done this before, never seen the fields as I describe them, never seen the beauty in them like I do. I am hoping and thinking they see it now. I am hoping they see something different within themselves.

We are all in a line, a long red line, staying as close together as possible. And when the Red Worn Runners take off into the distance, it is magical. It takes me home every time we run; home to the gravel roads and the farms of my youth, to the wheat fields and barley fields, and the beautiful sounds and smells that I cannot imagine in the city. The reserve is a beautiful place when I let myself see it this way, shifting what I see by running through it. I think the kids felt it this past week as an Elder's van pulled us over on kilometre 3 on that sandy dirt road and an older woman shook all the kids' hands out the window. We thought we were going to get scolded, but no ... she told them to keep it up, to keep running. They were smiling like local celebrities. We all smiled, the closest to fame we will probably ever get ... it's that internal fame that we should be celebrating anyways.

I also think the kids felt it when guest runners from the city started to join us on the run and when we ran past Elder Bob's house and a little red fox was watching us on the driveway ... watching the Red Worn Runners snake through the sandy obstacle course. We talk about treaties, families, relationships, and the beauty of creation on the morning jogs. We are simply moving knowledge (Basso, 1996). *This is the living curriculum* (Clandinin & Connelly, 1992) *they talk about, the familial curriculum* (Huber et al., 2011) *acknowledged. I did*

---

3. We tracked our kilometers each day on a poster that hung in the classroom. The distance ran, participants, dates, and individual goals were detailed on it.

not think that the kids would continue but it goes to show you how much I don't know. They showed up every day and even run on their own these days.

Now, as September rolls in, I heard that the other day on the reserve a couple of people were running. They told the boys it was because of seeing them. I guess they are local celebrities after all. They laughed when they told me. I love those kids. It is a beautiful thing to watch Joe with his braid and Michael ... they are running straight to the west, running at a pace that I can only consider in my mind. They glide. I wonder what they are thinking of when they run. The Red Worn Runners will continue to be on my mind as the leaves get ready to turn and the farmer swaths down the majesty to the left and the flowering yellow to the right. It is indeed a beautiful thing, one I won't soon forget. I hope we keep running. Sometimes 5, sometimes 18, one time 30, today just me. The Red Worn Runners inspired me to shuffle, sprint, and navigate my way down the dusty roads of Enoch Cree Nation, always wearing red–red t-shirts that is.

In the foregoing section, Sean makes visible some of his experiences in shifting the practices of one school, a very practical shift in both how the curriculum is lived, and how policies are lived out. The above description is part of this shifting set of practices working with youth throughout the summer months of July and August. Sean, with some of his colleagues, organized a series of summer school courses for youth within their high school. They decided to offer the courses in the home place of the youth; that is, in Enoch Cree Nation. Social Studies, Aboriginal Studies, Wellness, and Math were some subjects they taught on a daily basis in the home place of the youth. Sean credits the genesis of thinking about summer school in a different way to the ideas and the words of a friend of his who takes the traditions and history that live within her home community very seriously. One day in a university class, Alvine Mountain Horse[4] talked about ceremony, customs, language, and her traditions and how these are "just starting now" at home in the summer months, and how important it was to "go home," "to acknowledge" this time. Her thoughts and the way she described the urgency to get back home coupled with the experiences of working alongside the youth in the study shifted Sean.

This statement stayed with Sean as he wrote and re-wrote it in relation to how each summer, as a teacher, he moved in the opposite direction of the youth with whom he worked. He wound down. He slowed down. He stepped away from work with youth, the school came to a halt in a sense, it moved in a different rhythm (Clandinin et al., 2006), a different

---

4. A fellow student, colleague, and friend who continues to teach about the many traditions of the Blackfoot people.

direction, it closed down. Sean wondered about the possibilities that might emerge from imagining and paying attention to the lives of the youth more closely and acknowledging the experiences that they live during these summer months. Sean wondered what might happen at a Pow-Wow school or a Sun Dance seminar where the experiences of family and community weave their way throughout the learning process. What would have happened to Skye Song Maker, a participant in this study who Sean worked alongside? What would have happened to her family? To her community? Would her stories of school and education have shifted and allowed her to complete high school?

As Sean engaged in the events and writings that shaped the new program, he slipped back in time and thought of the seasonal rhythms that have defined much of his life, the summer months situated between the end and the beginning of school and where those times took him. Mostly they took him home to memories of growing up on a farm and the moments of silence and sunshine in a rural setting. Sean thought of the summer months and the engrained sense of freedom during this time. Sean believed it came from a place. The stories and what was important to him during this time shaped his understanding as he participated in the program and continued to make sense of "just starting now."

As part of his autobiographical work, he wrote a narrative about a special place on his family farm that he used to frequent growing up. It was an old fox den surrounded by Saskatoon berries. He described how he used to go sit and enjoy the quiet moments of summer, celebrating the peacefulness and simplicity when he was surrounded by nature during the pause of those summer months. He thought of the importance of place over time when he thought of the lives of the youth and how the summer months must be sacred in so many different ways for them. He thought of the community in which they lived and the importance of time and the coming together moments in ceremonies and cultural events. It is the "just starting now" moments that were important.

The traveling between places, the visiting between families, and, of course, the dancing and drumming comes alive every weekend during the summer months. As he thought about this, Sean traveled back once again to the fox den berries of his youth and how places over time are important to celebrate and think about — the moments of finding a place and connecting to it that continue to shape his experiences moving forward. The summer months were the times when the land came alive for him as it marked a period of time that would take him to different places. Even if it's on the family farm, it is what pulls him in the present when he thought of what matters most in relation to the stories of the youth, when he thought of the "just starting now."

In what follows he slides back once again and recalls ...

Fox Den Berries

A mystical time in the company of the trees. I always looked forward to the late days of summer and the early fall as the landscape continued to change. I would eventually be met by purple and red in the form of berries. Saskatoons surrounding ... wild raspberries calling, and now I can see more clearly why this was the chosen place. I could reach out from my sitting spot, my resting place ... thinking within, reaching in all four corners ... and in the directional spaces in between I could see the purple exhibition of growth. I could eat and wonder ... think in silence and enjoy the beauty of creation. I can now see the magic in these moments ... the freedom of place that is not often considered in the busier moments of adult life — the significance of place and paying attention to the surrounding sights and smells, the movements that fill the eyes, the stillness that creates reflection and meditation ... instilling lasting images are creative moments of youth that I must continue to remember.

Time and connectivity were linked to the experiences of place ... movements and freedoms. It was all about the fox den berries on sunny days in the summer moments of my youth. I recall and enjoy the experiences when thinking back. The trees would always change though. They start to change now in my mind as the winds begin to pick up ... yellow shades and orange hues starting ... not much green anymore as I looked up ... an umbrella of colors visible to the eyes. The sun continued to find a way to dart through and cast different shadows ... uneven shapes ... leaves were missing where they once provided covering. The leaves start to dance differently at this time ... they fall at different moments, coating my sitting spot ... gently sweeping over my imprints. Accompanied by a jacket now, still sitting and thinking ... I continue to go to place ... the trees move different ... the fox den berries start to fall ... shrivelled up over time, baked on the branches, reminders of what was once there ... it was a special time. Even the grass, the welcoming grass that protected that place, would dance back and forth. No longer green, now it became more brown and yellow. It sounded different. It made a crisp call ... a whispering sound. If I listened carefully I could hear it.

As I looked out through the trees in these moments I see the dust picking up ... blowing across the tops of the wheat fields to the south. Soon to be harvested for another year, the fields could be seen clearly now ... they still provided protection from the outside world ... a wall of yellow and gold protected the place.

Frost comes always ... now it is coating the trees, no longer easy to sit ... the sun doesn't feel the same way ... no longer sitting time ... no longer thinking time in the same place in the same way. Time changes the landscape.

The fox den berries are more difficult to find in the city ... not impossible, but difficult. The sightlines change as I get older. I need to continue to look inward and take the time to go back to place, to move around the earth mounds *based on the seasons, and let the sun rays cast their magic. To find the places and moments of reflection that are important to moving forward ... continued growth ... to free the expressions within ... let them come out in different ways. One never knows what might be tucked carefully in the in-between places ... as I look back and think of the compilation of trees that sat in the middle somewhere between the farmhouse to the north and the wheat fields to the south. The fox den berries in the pausing moments of summer take me home always.*

Pow-Wow[5] School

The stories of summer and the moments of going back home in his mind helped locate Sean in relation to the youth and helped him understand how he was beginning to hear the stories of the youth. As a teaching team, by going to Enoch Cree Nation and teaching within the place of Enoch, Sean and his colleagues shifted the way in which they participated and moved the experiences to ones of co-composing (Connelly & Clandinin, 1990), paying particular attention to the family and community stories (Huber et al., 2011) that were important to the youth. The youth allowed them to walk alongside (Clandinin & Connelly, 2000). They taught gently within their home place. It was important to pay attention to the silences and the gaps (Clandinin & Connelly, 2000) as the things left unsaid also taught Sean and his colleagues. The youth with whom Sean worked in the study with the early school leavers taught him to be open to new possibilities of teaching, to remember that youth could learn outside of school buildings in places that mattered to them and their families.

In the summer they started each day by meeting at the local school on the reserve early in the morning. At times, this meant traveling from house to house picking up those who were missing, reminding the youth there was work to do, but also showing the youth that they were committed as teachers to be there daily. To begin each day they all gathered around in a circle on the grass in front of the school and slowly stretched, talking about the daily plan, connecting and re-connecting through the shared process, and then they ran.

As a group they wanted to do something different, spend time together that was different, not always teaching school within the boundaries of a classroom and a building. They decided to start their days together by

---

5. "Pow-Wow" School was the name provided by the youth in their summer school experience. They called school this name affectionately because we started the class by meeting at their community Pow-Wow.

jogging but it really was mostly about the coming together and doing something collectively, learning about the places within the community by traveling to them. They logged their daily journeys and set goals, encouraging each other to participate, to show up for the run, even if their bodies didn't feel like it. The coming together always created a space for conversation (Clandinin et al., 2010)[6] where they talked and connected, where questions were often posed to imagine what life might have looked like within Enoch at times in the past.

As they jogged, the youth pointed out places they remembered or told stories of people who lived in certain houses within the town centre and rural back roads of the reserve. The youth had clear memories of where they had traveled in their younger years, running and playing when life seemed so much simpler. Sean asked many questions in the morning jogs and it became part of getting to know each other in such a different way than what they were used to. It was so much more than the hallway passing-by conversations they engaged in at the public school during the hours of school time. Each day Sean traveled down the road to the reserve from his suburban home. He made his way entering into a new place with a different way of being in relation (Connelly & Clandinin, 1990). It changed the relationship significantly as Sean was asked to travel to the youths' world, to their home places and community place. As Sean traveled each day, and started to learn alongside them, he began to teach alongside them — to learn from the youth who showed him parts of their worlds (Lugones, 1987).

Throughout the summer Sean and the youth traveled often to each other's worlds (Lugones, 1987), to different places over time. It was a constant negotiation, a lesson in moving in and "out of ease" (Lugones, 1987, p. 168). The transition and negotiation as Sean traveled back and forth often took him home, in his mind, to his reserve, to his farm, to the moments of being at ease and comfort. He thought of the multiplicity (Greene, 1995) between places and how the youth were in a place of comfort being within their community. Sean thought of how he negotiated spaces in his life and how, in each world, he moved differently. He participated differently. He wondered if the youth felt the same way when they left their homes early each morning and went to an urban school place and found themselves in constant negotiation, out of ease, perhaps uncomfortable as the school stories changed and shifted.

---

6. A resonant thread found in the research project entitled, Composing Lives: A Narrative Inquiry into the Experiences of Youth who Left School Early. Conversational spaces: a resonant thread that marked a space in schools to share, to open the dialogue in the relationship; the youth spoke of "having no safe places to talk or share when life became difficult."

A Reflective Turn: Looking Backward, Looking Forward 251

As Sean traveled back to the details and the moments of developing something different with the youth, an educational experience that could shift their stories is what he hoped to achieve. The thoughts of school and working within the community interested him as he looked over each student's school profile.[7] Through the conversations with the youth about plans beyond high school and how Sean could support their efforts, he recognized a need to try something different. During the regular school year he often took the youth to post-secondary institutions or community events to provide opportunities to imagine what life might look like beyond Grade 12. As he looked at the numbers and listened to the stories of many of the youth, he found that much work was needed to assist in this process of high school completion and post-secondary planning. Many youth were missing required courses that would make it impossible to graduate.

The youth pointed out long ago, and repeatedly, that graduating is very important to them and that they do have dreams that are very real which involve attending school beyond Grade 12. Many youth expressed a desire to go to college, university, and prepare for the future by getting a "good job." It was evident many youth had never attended a summer school program in their 2 years of high school and Sean was puzzled by why this might be. He started to look back and found this to be consistent over the previous 5 years. Seldom had First Nations' students enrolled and/or attended a summer school session, adding to the complexity of a disproportionate dropout rate (Gillmore, 2011). School, in its current summer model, often provides an excellent opportunity to learn and study in shorter summer sessions in the month of July. Many youth in the public school system attend summer school to alleviate their regular school schedule or prepare themselves in the summer session for post-secondary entrance, as the classes are often smaller and more compact.

Thinking about Layers ...

The information Sean gathered showed that rarely did students from First Nations take summer school courses within school settings. He started to ask more questions, mostly to himself, as to why this might be. It came down to lack of transportation from the reserve in the summer, and the need

---

7. School profile refers to the student information system, demographics, and credit count. Note that specific courses are required for graduation/100 credits in total according to the Alberta standards.

to work and be employed by the reserve as a summer work student. This is a two-to-four week summer employment opportunity, which provides some spending money, but also important school money for the following year. It made perfect sense to Sean as he had conversations with the youth and they told him how important $200 to $400 could be. School money bought them school clothes, a phone, or a laptop, and this school money was needed. Lugones (1987) writes of "being at ease in the world" and the attributes that might make this possible (p. 68). The school money is an important consideration of "being a fluent speaker" within the urban school setting, or of being "happy," and how this may lead to ease within the world of school. Technology such as laptops and cell phones are the norm, and in some ways markers of belonging, identifiers within the school place. Sean remembered his school experiences, he thought of school clothes and how each year he prepared for school by going shopping. He could not imagine how it would feel to be without school money and how the youth continued to remind him of what is important in their lives.

The layers are complex and are not often considered, or are simply missed in the process. It is not that school is not important or that graduating is not a priority, but it became evident that Sean needed to pay careful attention to the life and the stories that exist within the community. The difference between 3 and 5 credits in a school sense may be the difference between graduating and not graduating, going to college or not going to college. It is not as easily understood by what the numbers might tell him (Greene, 1995). Bateson (1994) reminded him in a different way when she wrote,

> concentration is too precious to belittle. I know that if I look very narrowly and hard at anything I am likely to see something new-like the life between the grass stems that only becomes visible after moments of staring. Softening that concentration is also important-I've heard that the best way to catch the movements of falling stars is at the edge of vision. (pp. 103–104)

Sean thought about these words and how they connected to what he might be missing in only looking at life from a school perspective, trying to figure out what fits, how to sort, and why things are not working within the current system. As those of us who worked with the youth who left school early learned, school and life are interwoven and cannot be separated (Bateson, 1994). Sean attended to the back and forth between worlds, paying closer attention to the negotiation of spaces, the attributes connected to being at ease in a world. He was listening more carefully to what the youth and the families shared. Their words and their silences were powerful.

Going Back to Place

Sean thought of how important it was to do something different within education to shift the story that has existed for the youth in Enoch by making it possible to attend summer sessions, and still receive opportunities for the school money that makes their lives easier. By providing an opportunity to take summer school to meet graduation requirements, but to also do school in a very different way, Sean and his colleagues quickly found 45 youth who were interested. Instrumental to the process and setup of these classes was the ability to work and identify teachers who were willing to try teaching beyond the 4-hour sessions, 5 days a week, in a traditional summer school setting.[8] Flexibility and relationship, borne out in a willingness to try, created a space for imagining different ways of doing things attentive to the youths' complex lives. Classes and information-sharing networks were quickly created through email and text messaging. Simple reminders and spaces for conversation between the teachers and students were established. In many ways students drove the process of how school needed to look for them to be successful. Sean and his colleagues learned a great deal along the way about what was important to the youth, what interested them, and how they looked at learning and school. Mini-retreats were a part of the plan for schooling where students sometimes engaged in full-day sessions within the community. Through experiences, students learned how math or social or art could be thought of differently.

It became easier to write and think about some concepts that were prevalent in text books by going to places and writing about them, thinking about them, and having conversations that so often are pushed out of the regular school lessons because of time constraints. Sean learned by going to places physically, that by moving the experience to a place of comfort where the youth became his teachers within the reserve, within their community, they became one of the sources of knowledge. They showed what was important to them and how their lives looked in this place. Sean learned life was very different for each youth and each family. He learned who they wanted to invite in to help make sense of the history of Enoch — sometimes grandmothers, uncles, traditional language speakers, and Elders. It varied depending on what they were learning and who they were in relation to the person. Being out there with them their relationships shifted dramatically

---

8. Summer school traditionally is held in the month of July, 5 days a week in 4-hour time slots. The informal policy states that if students miss two classes, they are ineligible to pass and are removed because they will not meet curricular outcomes or time requirements.

and shaped the way they worked together within the formal curriculum. The most significant shift occurred between teacher and student.

So often in education the word relationship is discounted as being soft or less rigorous. The summer months and the commitment of the youth showed otherwise. The work did not seem like work when the terms of the relationship shifted and Sean and the other teachers came alongside. Sean had to just let go, let the youth show him what counted for knowledge. Sean bought each student a journal and asked them to jot down reflective notes during the days, or images so they could remember what was happening regarding some of the events that occurred over the summer. Their family stories often emerged through the pages of the journals written in daily. As Sean read the stories and saw the images that the youth recorded, he found out so much more about how they connected to the experiences and how often a forward-looking story (Lindemann Nelson, 1995) of life beyond high school was emerging through the tattered pages of the journals.

The more Sean came to know, the more differences he saw between the youth, their stories, and their stories of family and community that are not often considered in the dimly lit hallways of the public high school where teachers and students usually came to know each other; we too saw this in the stories we heard in the study with the early school leavers. The *Red Worn Runners* is a way of honoring the youth who joined him on this journey that was so rewarding yet exhausting. The *Red Worn Runners* were about coming together, moving slowly, attending carefully, and trying something different in education by following the youth and letting them show what was important to them within their home communities. Sean, the other teachers, and the youth moved many directions throughout the summer to many different places, on reserve, off reserve, to the conversations they had with many community members that enriched the mandated curriculum, shifting the focus to the living curriculum. Sean often said, "when you write the mandated final exams and diploma exams, you need to experience difference to be able to write to it." Many community members, relatives, and Elders from this place spoke to the youth. Most of the students had never visited with them in this way or asked questions about the community and the stories that live there.

The stories from community members of the past, and experiences through telling and re-telling stories (Clandinin, Davies, Hogan, & Kennard, 1993) were powerful to consider as Sean, the other teachers, and the youth thought about their words and experiences in relation to the textbook summaries. The words seemed to come alive when they heard stories about the Chiefs, Elders, and the formation of the community where the youth live and ride a bus to the public school. They talked about history and learning from the past to understand who they are in the present (Clandinin & Connelly, 2000) and being proud of the differences. They traveled back and forth and in between places throughout the summer. They co-created a different space for thinking by traveling to each other's worlds through the relational. A liminal space (Heilbrun, 1999) was created.

Sean noted the need to continue to pay closer attention to community and the familial curriculum (Huber et al., 2011) by going to place and paying attention as a group to what is possible because some of the stories are so present. As they sat together through the summer, they discovered that many of the greatest resources were grandmothers, grandfathers, cousins, and parents. By asking them to help them understand some of the history they were co-creating, something totally different and special was emerging and continuing to grow, something that the youth and the teachers involved could now speak to, and about, through their relationships. The *Red Worn Runners* helped them to think about this as they ran to places that summer that none of them imagined quite possible before they started. The *Red Worn Runners* and the process of starting the day differently through exercise, conversation, and embedded in the relational-taught Sean this. They all started seeing education and what it could be differently, even if it started by running down a sandy road and sharing memories through the movement.

As Sean recalled the sharing of the interim and final research texts and the narratives co-composed with the youth who left school early, he thought of Skye Song Maker. He wrote and re-wrote and shared the negotiation of the stories along the way, paying attention to the family stories, their wishes that her name not be changed within the narrative, because her name comes from a place of ceremony. It was gifted to her when she was born. Sean learned in the process to stay awake to what is important and listen to what is important to a family, to the stories that he shared, recognizing that stories can be shared in many ways once they go out in the world (King, 2005). He remembered sitting and eating with Skye's family and starting to read what they had created together. As he shared they looked at him and her mother spoke, "This is a good story of our family Sean ... this is a real good story ... not a bad story and we thank you for that" (Personal communication, 2010). Skye Song Maker and her family continue to help him in the present to stay awake and not take for granted the experiences that are shared in the relational process of narrative inquiry. It is through their shared stories that they stay with him and continue to weave their way into who Sean is and is becoming alongside youth and families.

Shifting Social Justifications

In the preceding two sections of this chapter we returned to the personal and practical justifications of our work with the youth. In the first section we showed how our stories to live by shifted as we learned to live and tell new stories through engaging with each other and the youth in this study. In the second section we illustrated just one of the shifts in practice that Sean undertook as he lived and told new stories in his teaching. We could tell other stories of practice, of attending to children, youth, and families in other studies in new ways, of attending differently as we teach and practice in communities and schools.

However, in this section we want to draw attention to the new theoretical insights from our work. There is much talk about the need to pay attention to transitions. We were troubled by common views of transition and how these notions focus our attention in schools, in policies and procedures affecting youth. Focusing on the event of transition obscures our view of youth *living in and through* transitions. Narrative understandings of stories to live by as always in motion, open to shifting and changing, drew us to reconsider the life composing of youth who left school early, a transition out of school. Through attending carefully to the lives of the youth our understandings shifted in ways coherent with a narrative conceptualization of transition. We came to understand in more complex ways how stories to live by are shaped by, and are shaped in, embodied moments of transition. We were also awakened to the pedagogical possibilities (Huber, Caine, Huber, & Steeves, in press) in transitions.

We began this book with understandings of identities as stories to live by, a narrative way of linking personal practical knowledge and contexts. We began with an understanding of identities, stories to live by, as fluid, as embodied, as shaping and shaped by context, and as temporal compositions that are always open to shifts and changes. Identity making is a relational process that is also a process in the midst and on the way. These understandings did not shift in some ways but in other ways we came to deeper understandings of what we mean by stories to live by.

As we attended to the lives of the youth as they became visible in the youths' told stories, we attended both to what they knew, and to the contexts or knowledge landscapes within which they lived in schools and outside of schools. As the institutional knowledge landscapes offered them fewer and fewer possibilities for continuing to compose their life identities, their stories to live by, they did not freeze. They drew upon their embodied knowledge composed over years and in multiple other contexts and relationships to shift their stories to live by. Awakening to different plotlines that shaped their knowledge landscapes, they improvised ways to make sense of their lives. Sometimes they chose to move schools, or to leave schools for a short time, or to shift from some relationships to other relationships. They made these shifts attentive to always searching for ways to make sense of their stories to live by that linked their knowledge and their storied contexts. Bound within multiple storied landscapes, the youth showed us how they improvised something new that allowed them to move forward, to keep at life composing within schools, to keep trying to make school work for them until their only possible way to achieve narrative coherence was to leave school.

Seen at any one point in time or from within any one narrative vantage point, perhaps their stories to live by appeared incoherent and without purpose. Their life compositions, seen from within the institutional narrative of school, did not appear to have the normal single-track upward trajectory (Bateson, 1989) that stories of school seem to demand. Seen over time, and from within the stories the youth were telling, we noted the narrative coherence in their stories to live by that they were continually composing. They showed that they were composing lives that did have narrative coherence, which did make sense as they sustained their life composing even as they met situations that called forth discontinuities.

Identities, stories to live by, are powerful life forces that can be shifted to allow youth to continue with life composing despite the strength of the dominant institutional and social narratives that attempt to create non-sensical situations for them. The youth showed us how imaginative and creative they could be when faced with the force of the dominant narratives. Their identities, their stories to live by, could be shaped by the dominant narratives but the youth could also resist the shaping of the dominant narratives by their imaginative responses. As stories to live by bumped against scripted plotlines we awakened to transitional moments as times "when it might be possible to shift the course of a story" (Clandinin & Connelly 1998, p. 161).

Heilbrun (1999) would call these moments of transition liminal spaces, places we inhabit where we might begin to write our own stories. As their landscapes shifted, youth used their practical imagination (Carr, 1986) to "write" new forward-looking stories that spoke to who they were and who they were becoming. Imagined stories to live by are not planned in transition but rather they are improvised out of embodied knowledge and imagination. They live in the flow of a person's life as they live them.

Evolving Wonders

Engaging in this study has opened up new wonders. It has shifted our research agendas in significant ways as we wonder about the seeming inflexibility of stories of school, of how they bind and shape so many lives. We wonder about the pressing down of dominant stories of school where it makes sense for youth to leave school early rather than to continue to struggle within constraining spaces. The landscapes, threaded by institutional, social, cultural, linguistic, and familial narratives too often leave no spaces for fluidity, for shifting, or shaping new stories of education no matter how hard the youth try to make such spaces.

Since we ended our formal engagement with participants, Jean and Pam alongside others, have begun to listen to teachers who leave teaching after just a few years into a teaching position as well as teachers in their second and third years of teaching who are in the midst of beginning to teach. *Stories to live by* for some have become *stories to leave by* (Clandinin, Downey & Huber, 2009) as beginning teachers spoke of being unable to find places on school landscapes where they can live out the wholeness of who they are. The institutional stories of school are too narrow and prescribed to offer safe spaces for conversation, from which beginning teachers transitioning to new school landscapes might reconfigure their stories to live by in fluid improvisatory ways. Some beginning teachers had to leave school in order to continue to compose their stories to live by.

In another study, Jean, Vera, Sean, and others have come alongside Aboriginal youth in junior high schools (Grades 7–9 in Alberta) to inquire into their stories of school and education. We are also interested in their families' stories. We situated our study in a junior high school, as this is often a time of multiple transitions and a time when youth and their families begin to most visibly bump up against the institutional stories and expectations. In our study we work closely with Elders, community stakeholders, and policy makers; their experiences and insights help us better understand the institutional stories of school. We are building upon our wonders of the common places and borderlands between education and schooling from a narrative vantage point.

While these studies have remained close to the landscapes of schools, Vera alongside others continues to work closely with pregnant and early parenting women in precarious housing situations and how their early stories shape our understanding of the familial, cultural, and social stories of education and schools. In other work, Vera and her colleagues are working with youth and young adults who are homeless, street involved, experiencing mental health issues and who have few meaningful access points to care and schools. Many of the youth have left school early and have tried to negotiate alternative schooling arrangements, while also providing care to children, friends, and themselves. Access to meaningful and relevant mental health care is severely limited by the youths' experiences of stigma; stigma that is based in part on their social conditions of homelessness, as well as leaving school early.

Contemplating Old Wonders

In the next section we turn, with some longing, to our wonders about the youth now. We have heard from some of them. They do stay in touch when we can help them by writing reference letters for them, by affirming their sense making, and by continuing our conversations with them. There are moments when they connect simply to let us know they are okay, they have a new job, they have a home, or they dream of going to college next year.

When we concluded the study, we came to some understandings. What we share in these pages are considerations for now. But we continue to wonder. Where are these young people with whom we worked so closely? Young people who have so much to teach us about life composing in the face of adversity, in the face of a social story that marks early school leavers as uneducated, as dropouts, as underachievers, or as rebels and so on. We wonder how those who were already parents, like Truong and Lynn, are making sense of their children's experiences in school. How do their stories of early school leaving interweave with their dreams of schooling and education for their children? We wonder about the intergenerational stories, about their parents and grandparents, about what happens to their relationships over time. How will Christian or Ben's sisters recount their families' stories, of taking care of others, of creating opportunities for other family members to stay in school? We imagine that we will return to the participants to come alongside yet again, to hear how their stories continue to unfold and enfold them.

We also wonder about their teachers. Were their teachers shaped by the lives of their students? Does the principal of the school so many story as their belonging place, remember these youth? We think of Sean and how the stories of Skye, her sisters, her parents and her grandparents have shaped him. Do other teachers also remember? And we wonder if we can help teachers and nurses and social workers learn to notice and to attend to the lives of all of the youth they meet, including the ones who find themselves enmeshed in multiple competing and conflicting plot lines.

We wonder about those who engage with educational policies, with practices of school boards, of institutional stories, and measures of success. How do they make sense of the continuing trend of youth to leave school early? Will we only attend in ways that retell the story of school as a good and educative place for all youth? Are there ways to attend that compel our imaginations to create new possibilities for schools, such as the *Red Worn Runners*? Are others engaged in shifting the literal and metaphorical walls of schools, to make them places of communities where people can come to and, most of all, return to? We realize that for some, schooling is equivalent to education. We wonder if we were to consider this question in ways that included the stories of Skye Song Maker, of Ben, of Robert, of Jasmine, of the *Red Worn Runners*, and many youth we came to meet, would our answers and ways to move forward change, at least for now?

References

Abar, B., Abar, C., Lippold, M., Powers, C., & Manning, A. (2012). Associations between reasons to attend and late high school dropout. *Learning and Individual Differences, 22*(6), 856–861.
Alberta Education. (2008). *Accountability pillar results for Annual Education Results Report (AERR)*. Retrieved from http://www.education.alberta.ca/search.asp?%20q=852263
Alberta's Commission on Learning. (2003, October). *Every child learns, every child succeeds: Report and recommendations*. Retrieved from http://education.alberta.ca/media/413413/commissionreport.pdf
Alberta Education. (2012, April). *Alberta high school completion rates*. Edmonton, AB: Government of Alberta.
Anisef, P., Brown, R. S., Phythian, K., Sweet, R. E., & Walters, D. (2010). Early school leaving among immigrants in Toronto secondary schools. *Canadian Review of Sociology, 47*(2), 103–128.
Appleton, J. J., Christenson, S. L., & Furlong, M. J. (2008). Student engagement with school: Critical conceptual and methodological issues of the construct. *Psychology in the Schools, 45*, 369–386.
Archambault, I., Janosz, M., Fallu, J., & Pagani, L. (2009). Student engagement and its relationship with early high school drop out. *Journal of Adolescence, 32*, 651–670.
Archer, L., & Yamashita, H. (2003). "Knowing their limits"? Identities, inequalities and inner city school leavers' post-16 aspirations. *Journal of Educational Policy, 18*(1), 53–69.
Arcia, E. (2006). Achievement and enrollment status of suspended students: Outcomes in a large, multicultural school district. *Education and Urban Society, 38*(3), 359–369.
Ball, S. J., Maguire, M., & Macrae, S. (2000). *Choice, pathways and transitions post-16. New youth, new economies in the global city*. New York, NY: Routledge.
Basso, K. H. (1996). *Wisdom sits in places: Landscape and language among the Western Apache*. Albuquerque, NM: University of New Mexico Press.
Bateson, M. C. (1989). *Composing a life*. New York, NY: Plume.
Bateson, M. C. (1994). *Peripheral visions: Learning along the way*. New York, NY: HarperCollins.
Behnke, A., Gonzalez, L., & Cox, R. (2010). Latino students in new arrival states: Factors and services to prevent youth from dropping out. *Hispanic Journal of Behavioral Sciences, 32*(3), 385–409.
Bickerstaff, S. S. (2011). 'I felt untraditional': High school leavers negotiating dominant discourses on 'dropout'. *Journal of Education – Boston University School of Education, 190*(3), 37–46.

Boardman, J. D., Alexander, K. B., Miech, R. A., MacMillan, R., & Shanahan, M. J. (2012). The association between parent's health and the educational attainment of their children. *Social Science & Medicine, 75*(5), 932–939.

Bowditch, C. (1993). Getting rid of troublemakers: High school disciplinary procedures and the production of drop outs. *Social Problems, 40*(4), 493–509.

Bowers, A. J. (2010). Grades and graduation: A longitudinal risk perspective to identify student dropouts. *Journal of Educational Research, 103*(3), 191–207.

Bowlby, G. (2005). *Provincial dropout rates – Trends and consequences*. Ottawa, ON: Statistics Canada.

Bowlby, J. W., & McMullen, K. (2002). *At a crossroads: First results for the 18- to 20-year-old cohort of the Youth in Transition Survey*. Ottawa, ON: Human Resources Canada, Statistics Canada.

Bradley, C. L., & Renzulli, L. A. (2011). The complexity of non-completion: Being pushed or pulled to drop out of high school. *Social Forces, 90*(2), 521–545.

Bradshaw, C. P., O'Brennan, L. M., & McNeely, C. A. (2008). Core competencies to prevent problem behaviors and promote positive youth development. *New Directions for Child and Adolescent Development, 122*, 12–32.

Brown, T. M., & Rodriguez, L. F. (2009). School and the co-construction of dropout. *International Journal of Qualitative Studies in Education, 22*, 221–242.

Buber, M. (1947). *Between man and man* (R. G. Smith, Trans.). London: Kegan Paul.

Bushnik, T. (2003). *Learning, earning and leaving: The relationship between working while in high school and dropping out*. Ottawa, ON: Statistics Canada.

Bushnik, T., Barr-Telford, L., & Bussiere, P. (2004). *In and out of high school: First results from the second cycle of the Youth in Transition Survey, 2002*. Ottawa, ON: Statistics Canada.

Cabus, S. J., & Witte, K. D. (2011). Does school time matter? On the impact of compulsory education age on school dropout. *Economics of Education Review, 30*, 1384–1398.

Caine, V. (2010). Visualizing community: Understanding narrative inquiry as action research. *Educational Action Research, 18*(4), 481–496.

Caine, V., & Steeves, P. (2009). Imagination and playfulness in narrative inquiry. *International Journal of Education and the Arts, 10*(25), 1–14.

Canadian Council on Learning. (2009). *2009 composite learning index: Indicator fact sheet*. Ottawa, ON: Canadian Council on Learning.

Carr, D. (1986). *Time, narrative and history*. Bloomington, IN: Indiana University Press.

Cassidy, W., & Bates, A. (2005). "Drop-outs" and "Push-outs": Finding hope at a school that actualizes the ethic of care. *American Journal of Education, 112*(1), 66–102.

Choi, J. (2005). Inventing memories: Returnees' retrospective narratives of street experience. *The Urban Review, 37*(4), 303–327.

Cisneros, S. (2002). *Caramelo*. New York, NY: Vintage Contemporaries.

Clandinin, D. J. (1983). *A conceptualization of image as a component of teacher personal practical knowledge in primary school teachers' reading and language programs*. Unpublished doctoral dissertation. University of Toronto, Canada.

Clandinin, D. J. (2010). Narrative understandings of lives in and out of schools. *LEARNing Landscapes, 3*(2), 15–20.
Clandinin, D. J., & Cave, M. (2008). Creating pedagogical spaces for developing doctor professional identity. *Medical Education, 42*(8), 765–770.
Clandinin, D. J., Cave, M. T., & Cave, A. (2010). Narrative reflective practice in medical education for residents: Composing shifting identities. *Advances in Medical Education, 2*, 1–7.
Clandinin, D. J., Cave, M. T., & Cave, A. (2011). Narrative reflective practice in medical education for residents: Composing shifting identities. *Advances in Medical Education and Practice, 2*, 1–7.
Clandinin, D. J., & Connelly, F. M. (1986). Rhythms in teaching: The narrative study of teachers' personal practical knowledge of classrooms. *Teaching and Teacher Education, 2*(4), 377–387.
Clandinin, D. J., & Connelly, F. M. (1988). *Teachers as curriculum planners: Narratives of experience.* New York, NY: Teachers College Press.
Clandinin, D. J., & Connelly, F. M. (1992). Teacher as curriculum maker. In P. W. Jackson (Ed.), *Handbook of research on curriculum* (pp. 363–401). New York, NY: Macmillan.
Clandinin, D. J., & Connelly, F. M. (1995). *Teachers' professional knowledge landscapes.* New York, NY: Teachers College Press.
Clandinin, D. J., & Connelly, F. M. (1998). Stories to live by: Narrative understandings of school reform. *Curriculum Inquiry, 28*(2), 149–164.
Clandinin, D. J., & Connelly, F. M. (2000). *Narrative inquiry: Experience and story in qualitative research.* San Francisco, CA: Jossey-Bass.
Clandinin, D. J., Davies, A., Hogan, P., & Kennard, B. (1993). *Learning to teach, teaching to learn: Stories of collaboration in teacher education.* New York, NY: Teachers College Press.
Clandinin, D. J., Downey, C. A., & Huber, J. (2009). Attending to changing landscapes: Shaping the interwoven identities of teachers and teacher educators. *Asia-Pacific Journal of Teacher Education, 37*(2), 141–154.
Clandinin, D. J., & Huber, J. (2002). Narrative inquiry: Toward understanding life's artistry. *Curriculum Inquiry, 32*(2), 161–170.
Clandinin, D. J., Huber, J., Huber, M., Murphy, M. S., Murray Orr, A., Pearce, M., & Steeves, P. (2006). *Composing diverse identities: Narrative inquiries into the interwoven lives of children and teachers.* NewYork, NY: Routledge.
Connelly, F. M., & Clandinin, D. J. (1988). *Teachers as curriculum planners: Narratives of experience.* New York, NY: Teachers College Press.
Connelly, F. M., & Clandinin, D. J. (1990). *Shaping a professional identity: Stories of educational practice.* New York, NY: Teachers College Press.
Connelly, F. M., & Clandinin, D. J. (1999). *Shaping a professional identity: Stories of educational practice.* New York, NY: Teachers College Press.
Connelly, F. M., & Clandinin, D. J. (2006). Narrative inquiry. In J. Green, G. Camilli & P. Elmore (Eds.), *Handbook of complementary methods in education research* (3rd edn., pp. 477–487). Mahwah, NJ: Lawrence Erlbaum.
Craig, C. (in press). Teaching, teacher education, and the best-loved self. *Asia-Pacific Journal of Education.*

Davis, J. E. (2006). Research at the margin: Mapping masculinity and mobility of African-American high school drops outs. *International Journal of Qualitative Studies in Education, 19*(3), 289–304.

Davies, S. (1999). Subcultural explanations and interpretations of school deviance. *Aggression and Violent Behavior, 4*(2), 191–202.

Davison, C. (2003). *Modern pathways and evolving definitions: Reframing Aboriginal school drop-out' in a northern Canadian context*. Calgary, AB: Centre for Health and Policy Studies, University of Calgary.

Davison Aviles, R. M. (1999). Perceptions of Chicano/Latino students who have dropped out of school. *Journal of Counseling & Development, 77*(4), 465–474.

Dei, G., Mazzuca, J., McIsaac, E., & Zine, J. (1997). *Reconstructing "drop-out": A critical ethnography of the dynamics of Black students' disengagement from school*. Toronto, ON: University of Toronto Press.

Dekkers, H., & Claassen, A. (2001). Drop outs-disadvantaged by definition? A study of the perspective of very early school leavers. *Studies in Educational Evaluations, 27*, 341–354.

Dewey, J. (1938). *Experience and education*. New York, NY: Collier.

Drewry, J., Burge, P., & Driscoll, L. (2010). A tripartite perspective of social capital and its access by high school dropouts. *Education and Urban Society, 42*(5), 499–521.

Driver, T. (1997). *Liberating rites: Understanding the transformative power of ritual*. Boulder, CO: Westview.

European Commission. (2012). *Conference report: Reducing early school leaving: Efficient and effective policies in Europe*. Brussels, Belgium: European Commission Directorate-General for Education and Culture.

Fall, A., & Roberts, G. (2012). High school dropouts: Interactions between social context, self-perceptions, school engagement, and student dropout. *Journal of Adolescence, 35*(4), 787–798.

Fallis, R. K., & Opotow, S. (2003). Are students failing school or are schools failing students? Class cutting in high school. *Journal of Social Issues, 59*(1), 103–119.

Feinstein, L., & Peck, S. C. (2008). Unexpected pathways through education: Why do some students not succeed in school and what helps others beat the odds? *Journal of Social Issues, 64*, 1–20.

Fine, M., & Weis, L. (2003). *Silenced voices and extraordinary conversations. Re-imagining schools*. New York, NY: Teachers College Press.

Finn, J. D. (1989). Withdrawing from school. *Review of Educational Research, 59*, 117–142.

Finn, J. D., & Rock, D. A. (1997). Academic success among students at risk for school failure. *Journal of Applied Psychology, 82*, 221–234.

Freeman, M. (2010). *Hindsight: The promise and peril of looking backward*. New York, NY: Oxford University Press.

Gasper, J., DeLuca, S., & Estacion, A. (2012). Switching schools: Revisiting the relationship between school mobility and high school dropout. *American Educational Research Journal, 49*(3), 487–519.

Gillmore, J. (2011). *Trends in dropout rates and the labour market outcomes of young dropouts*. Ottawa, ON: Statistics Canada.

Gleason, P., & Dynarski, M. (2002). Do we know whom we serve? Issues in using risk factors to identify drop outs. *Journal of Education for Students Placed at Risk*, *7*(1), 25–41.

Gray, J. (2009). Staying at school: Reflective narratives of resistance and transition. *Reflective Practice*, *10*(5), 645–656.

Greene, M. (1994). Multiculturalism, community and the arts. In A. Dyson & C. Genishi (Eds.), *The need for story: Cultural diversity in classroom and community* (pp. 11–27). New York, NY: Teachers College Press.

Greene, M. (1995). *Releasing the imagination: Essays on education, the arts, and social change*. San Francisco, CA: Jossey-Bass.

Hallet, D., Want, S. C., Chandler, M. J., Koopman, L. L., Flores, J. P., & Gehrke, E. C. (2008). Identity in flux: Ethnic self-identification, and school attrition in Canadian Aboriginal youth. *Journal of Applied Developmental Psychology*, *29*, 62–75.

Hango, D., & de Broucker, P. (2007). *Education-to-labour market pathways of Canadian youth: Findings from the Youth in Transition Survey*. Ottawa, ON: Statistics Canada.

Hankivsky, O. (2008). *Cost estimates of dropping out of high school in Canada*. Ottawa: Canadian Council on Learning.

Hanna, W. J. (2003). Mobility and the children of Langley Park's immigrant families. *The Journal of Negro Education*, *72*(1), 63–78.

Hare, J., & Pidgeon, M. (2011). The way of the warrior: Indigenous youth navigating the challenges of schooling. *Canadian Journal of Education*, *34*(2), 93–111.

Harris, L. R. (2008). A phenomenographic investigation of teacher conceptions of student engagement in learning. *Australian Educational Researcher*, *35*(1), 57–79.

Hattam, R., & Smyth, J. (2003). "Not everyone has a perfect life": Becoming somebody without school. *Pedagogy Culture & Society*, *11*(3), 379–398.

Hay, C., Khalema, E., Haluza-Delay, R., van Bavel, J., Lake, B., & Bajwa, J. (2004). *Equity in Edmonton schools*. Edmonton, AB: NAARR.

Heilbrun, C. (1999). *Women's lives: The view from the threshold*. Toronto, ON: University of Toronto Press.

Henry, K., Knight, K., & Thornberry, T. (2012). School disengagement as a predictor of dropout, delinquency, and problem substance use during adolescence and early adulthood. *Journal of Youth & Adolescence*, *41*(2), 156–166.

Hickman, G. P., Bartholomew, M., Mathwig, J., & Heinrich, R. S. (2008). Differential developmental pathways of high school dropouts and graduates. *The Journal of Educational Research*, *102*, 3–14.

Hodgson, D. (2007). Towards a more telling way of understanding early school leaving. *Issues in Educational Research*, *17*(1), 40–61.

Huber, J., Caine, V., Huber, M., & Steeves, P. (in press). Narrative inquiry as pedagogy in education: The extraordinary potential of living, telling, retelling, and reliving stories of experience. In *Extraordinary pedagogy for working within school settings serving non dominant students* (Vol. 37). Review of Research in Education.

Huber, J., Murphy, M. S., & Clandinin, D. J. (2011). *Places of curriculum making: Narrative inquiries into children's lives in motion*. London: Emerald.

Huber, M. (2008). *Narrative curriculum making as identity making: Intersecting family, cultural and school landscapes*. Unpublished doctoral dissertation. University of Alberta, Canada.

Huber, M., Huber, J., & Clandinin, D. J. (2004). Moments of tension: Resistance as expressions of narrative coherence in stories to live by. *Reflective Practice, 5*(2), 181–198.

Improvise. (2012). *Oxford Advanced Learner's Dictionary*. Retrieved from http://oald8.oxfordlearnersdictionaries.com/dictionary/improvisation#improvise__8. Accessed on December 6, 2012.

Janosz, M., Archambault, I., Morizot, J., & Pagani, L. S. (2008). School engagement trajectories and their differential predictive relations to dropout. *Journal of Social Issues, 64*, 21–40.

Janosz, M., Bisset, S. L., Pagani, L. S., & Levin, B. (2011). Educational systems and school dropout in Canada. *School Dropout & Completion*, 295–320. doi:10.1007/978-90-481-9763-7_17

Janosz, M., LeBlanc, M., Boulerice, B., & Tremblay, R. E. (2000). Predicting different types of school drop outs: A typological approach with two longitudinal samples. *Journal of Educational Psychology, 92*(1), 171–190.

Jeffries, R., Nix, M., & Singer, C. (2002). Urban American Indians "dropping" out of traditional high schools: Barriers and bridges to success. *High School Journal, 85*(3), 38–47.

Jimerson, S. R., Anderson, G. E., & Whipple, A. D. (2002). Winning the battle and losing the war: Examining the relation between grade retention and drooping out of high school. *Psychology in the Schools, 39*(4), 441–457.

King, T. (2005). *The truth about stories: A native narrative*. Minneapolis, MN: University of Minnesota Press.

Knesting, K. (2008). Students at risk for school dropout: Supporting their persistence. *Preventing School Failure, 52*(4), 3–10.

Kronick, R. F., & Hargis, C. H. (1990). *Who drops out and why – And the recommended action*. Springfield, IL: Charles L. Thomas.

Lam, S. (2011). Pathways to school completion: An international comparison. In S. Lamb, E. Markussen, R. Teese, N. Sandberg & J. Polesel (Eds.), *School dropout and completion: International comparative* (Vol. 21). Studies in Theory and Policy. doi:10.1007/978-90-481-9763-7_2

Landis, R. N., & Reschly, A. L. (2011). An examination of compulsory school attendance ages and high school dropout and completion. *Educational Policy, 25*(5), 719–761.

Langhout, R. D., & Mitchell, C. A. (2008). Engaging contexts: Drawing the link between student and teacher experiences of the hidden curriculum. *Journal of Community & Applied Social Psychology, 18*(6), 593–614.

Lee, F. W., & Ip, F. M. (2003). Young school drop outs: Levels of influence of different systems. *Journal of Youth Studies, 6*(1), 89–110.

Lee, T., & Breen, L. (2007). Young people's perceptions and experiences of leaving high school early: An exploration. *Journal of Community & Applied Social Psychology, 17*(5), 329–346.

Lessard, A., Butler Kisber, L., Fortin, L., Marcotte, D., Potvin, P., & Royer, E. (2008). Shades of disengagement: High school dropouts speak out. *Social Psychology of Education, 11*(1), 25–42.

Lindemann Nelson, H. (1995). Resistance and insubordination. *Hypatia, 10*(2), 23–43.

Lugones, M. (1987). Playfulness, "world" – Travelling, and loving perception. *Hypatia, 2*(2), 3–37.

Mac Iver, M. (2011). The challenge of improving urban high school graduation outcomes: Findings from a randomized study of dropout prevention efforts. *Journal of Education for Students Placed at Risk, 16*(3), 167–184.

McCain, M. N., & Mustard, F. (1999). *Reversing the brain drain: Early study*. Final report, Ontario Children's Secretariat, Toronto, ON.

McGrath, B. (2009). School disengagement and 'structural options': Narrative illustrations on an analytical approach. *YOUNG: Nordic Journal of Youth Research, 17*(1), 81–101.

McGraw, A. (2011). Shoving our way into young people's lives. *Teacher Development, 15*(1), 105–116.

Mendelson, M. (2006). *Aboriginal peoples and post secondary education in Canada*. Ottawa, ON: The Caledon Institute of Social Policy.

Mishler, E. (1999). *Storylines: Craft artists' narratives of identity*. Cambridge, MA: Harvard University Press.

Murphy, M. S. (2004). *Understanding children's knowledge: A narrative inquiry into school experiences*. Unpublished doctoral dissertation. University of Alberta, Canada.

Munns, G., & McFadden, M. (2000). First chance, second chance or last chance? Resistance and response to education. *British Journal of Sociology of Education, 21*(1), 59–75.

Norris, C., Pignal, J., & Lipps, G. (2003). Measuring school engagement. *Educational Quarterly Review, 9*(2), 25–34.

Olafson, L. (2006). *It's just easier not to go to school. Adolescent girls and disengagement in middle school*. New York, NY: Peter Lang.

Olafson, L., & Field, J. C. (2003). A moral revisioning of resistance. *Educational Forum, 67*(2), 140–147.

Olson, M. R., & Craig, C. J. (2009). "Small" stories and meganarratives: Accountability in balance. *The Teachers College Record, 111*(2), 547–572.

Orfield, G. (Ed.) (2004). *Drop outs in America. Confronting the graduation rate crisis*. Cambridge, MA: Harvard Education Press.

Pearce, M. (2005). *Community as relationship: A narrative inquiry into the school experiences of two children*. Unpublished doctoral dissertation. University of Alberta, Canada.

Pharris-Ciurej, N., Hirschman, C., Willhoft, J., & McGrath, B. (2012). The 9th grade shock and the high school dropout crisis. *Social Science Research, 41*(3), 709–730.

Polyani, M. (1969). *Knowing and being*. Chicago, IL: University of Chicago Press.

Porche, M., Fortuna, L., Lin, J., & Alegria, M. (2011). Childhood trauma and psychiatric disorders as correlates of school dropout in a national sample of young adults. *Child Development, 82*(3), 982–998.

Porowski, A., & Passa, A. (2011). The effect of communities in schools on high school dropout and graduation rates: Results from a multiyear, school-level quasi-experimental study. *Journal of Education for Students Placed at Risk, 16*(1), 24–37.

Randolph, K. A., Rose, R. A., Fraser, M. W., & Orthner, D. K. (2004). Examining the impact of changes in maternal employment on high school completion among low-income youth. *Journal of Family and Economic Issues, 25*(3), 279–299.

Schwab, J. J. (1954/1978). Eros and education: A discussion of one aspect of discussion. In I. Westbury & N. Wilkof (Eds.), *Science, curriculum and liberal education: Selected essays* (pp. 105–132). Chicago, IL: University of Chicago Press.

Sefa Dei, G. J. (2008). Schooling as community: Race, schooling, and the education of African youth. *Journal of Black Studies, 38*, 346–366.

SickKids. (2005). *Early school leavers: Understanding the lived reality of student disengagement from secondary school*. Final report, Ontario Ministry for Education and Training, Toronto, ON.

Siggner, A. J., & Costa, R. (2005). *Aboriginal conditions in census metropolitan areas, 1981–2001. (Trends and Conditions in Census Metropolitan Areas, No. 2005008e)*. Ottawa, ON: Statistics Canada.

Smyth, J., Down, B., & McInerney, P. (2010). *'Hanging in with kids' in tough times. Engagement in contexts of education disadvantage in the relational school*. New York, NY: Oxford.

Smyth, J., & Fasoli, L. (2007). Climbing over the rocks in the road to student engagement and learning in a challenging high school in Australia. *Educational Research, 49*(3), 273–295.

Smyth, J., & Hattam, R. (2001). "Voiced" research as a sociology for understanding "dropping out" of school. *British Journal of Sociology of Education, 22*(3), 401–415.

Smyth, J., & Hattam, R. (2002). Early school leaving and the cultural geography of high schools. *British Educational Research Journal, 28*(3), 375–397.

Smyth, J., & Hattam, R. (2004). *"Dropping out," drifting off, being excluded: Becoming somebody without school*. New York, NY: Peter Lang Publishing Inc.

Smyth, J., & McInerney, P. (2007). "Living on the edge": A case of school reform working for disadvantaged adolescents. *Teachers College Record, 109*(5), 1123–1170.

Smyth, J., & McInerney, P. (2011). Whose side are you on? Advocacy ethnography: Some methodological aspects of narrative portraits of disadvantaged young people, in socially critical research. *International Journal of Qualitative Studies in Education*, 1–20. doi:10.1080/09518398.2011.604649

Smyth, J., & McInerney, P. (2012). *From silent witnesses to active agents: Student voice in re-engaging with learning*. New York, NY: Peter Lang Publishing Inc.

Statistics Canada. (2005). *The daily. Education matters: Trends in dropout rates among the provinces*. Retrieved from http://www.statcan.gc.ca.login.ezproxy.library.ualberta.ca/daily-quotidien/051216/dq051216c-eng.htm

Stearns, E., & Glennie, E. J. (2006). When and why drop outs leave high school. *Youth and Society, 38*(1), 29–57.

Steeves, P. (2000). *Crazy quilt: Continuity, identity and a storied school landscape in transition – A teacher's and a principal's works in progress*. Unpublished doctoral dissertation, University of Alberta, Edmonton, AB.

Tanner, J. (2001). *Teenage troubles: Youth and deviance in Canada*. Scarborough, ON: Nelson Thomson Learning.
Tanner, J., Krahn, H., & Hartnagel, T. F. (1995). *Fractured transitions from school to work. Revisiting the drop out problem*. Don Mills, ON: Oxford University Press.
Taylor, A. (2002). I honestly can't see the point: Youth negotiation of the ideology of school completion. *Journal of Education Policy, 17*(5), 511–529.
Terry, M. (2008). The effects that family members and peers have on students' decisions to drop out of school. *Educational Research Quarterly, 31*(3), 25–38.
Tilleczek, K. (2011). *Approaching youth studies: Being, becoming, and belonging*. New York, NY: Oxford University Press.
Tilleczek, K., Ferguson, B., Edney, D., Rummens, A., Boydell, K., & Mueller, M. (2011). A contemporary study with early school leavers: Pathways and social processes of leaving high school. *Canadian Journal of Family and Youth, 3*(1), 1–39.
Toohey, K. (2000). *Learning English at school: Identity, social relations and classroom practice*. Clarendon, UK: Multilingual Motto.
Transition. (1976). *Concise oxford dictionary* (p. 1232). Oxford University Press.
Tuck, E. (2011). Humiliating ironies and dangerous dignities: A dialectic of school pushout. *International Journal of Qualitative Studies in Education, 24*(7), 817–827.
Vaughn, M. G., Fu, Q., DeLisi, M., Beaver, K. M., Perron, B. E., & Howard, M. O. (2010). Psychiatric correlates of bullying in the United States: Findings from a national sample. *Journal of Personality Disorders, 24*(6), 709–720.
Vaughn, M. G., Wexler, J., Beaver, K., Perron, B., Roberts, G., & Fu, Q. (2011). Psychiatric correlates of behavioral indicators of school disengagement in the United States. *Psychiatric Quarterly, 82*, 191–206.
Weis, L., & Fine, M. (2005). *Beyond silenced voices: Class, race, and gender in United States schools* (Rev. edn.). New York, NY: State University of New York Press.
Willis, P. (1977). *Learning to labour*. Farnborough, UK: Saxon House.
Wishart, D. (2009). Dynamics of education policy and practice for urban aboriginal early school leavers. *Alberta Journal of Educational Research, 55*(4), 468–481.
Wotherspoon, T., & Schissel, B. (2001). The business of placing Canadian children and youth "at-risk". *Canadian Journal of Education, 26*(3), 321–339.
Zhao, G. (2007). *The power of stories: A narrative inquiry into immigrant children's and parents' intergenerational stories of school*. Unpublished doctoral dissertation. University of Alberta, Canada.

About the Authors

Claire Desrochers is currently an adjunct professor in the Centre for Research for Teacher Education and Development (CRTED) at the University of Alberta. Following a 13-year career as a French Immersion teacher in public schools, she worked as a curriculum consultant with the Ministry of Education and pre-service teacher educator at Campus Saint Jean of the University of Alberta. Her interest in shaping educative spaces for pre-service teachers to learn about themselves in relation with diversity is grounded in her narratives of experience as a mother, teacher and teacher educator. Her doctoral dissertation entitled 'Towards a New Borderland in Teacher Education for Diversity: A Narrative Inquiry into Pre-service Teachers' Shifting Identities Through Service Learning' received the Outstanding Teacher Education Doctoral Dissertation Award in 2008.

Marilyn Huber currently works in the Curriculum Branch at the Ministry of Education in Alberta. As a secondary teacher she worked with youth in junior and senior high schools, and their families, in rural and urban Alberta. She obtained her PhD in education from the University of Alberta in 2008. Her publications include the co-authored book *Composing diverse identities: Narrative inquiries into the interwoven lives of children and teachers*. Her research interests include narrative understandings of youths', family members' and teachers' identity making as their lives intersect on school landscapes.

Sean Lessard has lived somewhere between Montreal Lake Cree Nation, Treaty 6 territory and North Battleford, Saskatchewan. These places shape, and continue to shape, the prairie narratives of his youth. He has travelled between these places and the stories of experience that guide him in the present come from within these places he has 'lived'. These stories have also taken him to the Centre for Research for Teacher Education and Development in Edmonton, Alberta, and to the schools in the surrounding places. He has been a youth worker, teacher, teacher educator and consultant. Currently he is an assistant professor at the University of Regina, a place that takes him near to the landscapes of his youth again. His stories, situated in the personal, the social, place and temporality, create a space where he can move both backwards and forwards, inwards and outwards when thinking of lives. They shape who he is becoming.

Yi Li is assistant professor, Department of Curriculum, Teaching and Learning, University of Manitoba. A former university English teacher in Shanghai, China, she immigrated to Edmonton, Canada and obtained both her MEd (2001) and PhD (2006) from the University of Alberta. Her research program began with her master's thesis where she explored the experiences of transitions of international students from China. Her doctoral dissertation continued this exploration and interpretation of experiences of international students. It was a narrative inquiry into the experiences and meanings of home and homelessness among international students in Canadian universities. Her post-doctoral work in hope research also used narrative inquiry to understand international students' experiences of hope in Canadian high schools. Her research interests include teaching English as an additional language, teacher education and development, international education, narrative inquiry and hope.

Joy-Ruth Mickelson had a wide exposure to foster children in the United Kingdom, all of whom had complex family histories. These experiences continued, as she moved to Canada, as a social worker. During this time she had many positive relationships and understandings of mutual concerns with Aboriginal students and their families. In her later role as a school psychologist, children whose learning difficulties were paramount became a focus of interest. At the Centre for Research for Teacher Education and Development (CRTED) during her PhD work she learned about narrative inquiry. Its beliefs fitted with the 40 years of stories she had heard and she wrote papers about approaches to those inquiries with colleagues and presented at conferences. Her dissertation followed those beliefs. A fellow student introduced her to Lynn. She had shared, with Lynn's permission, some of her history. When Lynn started to tell her story Joy Ruth felt the waves of other students' lives and experiences echoing in her ears.

Marni Pearce is the Director of Cross-Ministry Services with Alberta Education in Edmonton, Alberta. Her work involves collaborating with government and community partners on a variety of initiatives to ensure that Alberta's vulnerable children, youth and families are safe, healthy and successful at learning. She has over 20 years of teaching experience – in elementary school settings and at the University level. Marni has also been a school counselor, a consultant and a community based researcher. In her research she has had a particular interest in children who live on the margins of schools. In her doctoral work she focused on listening closely to the unfolding stories of children as they composed identities while living in diverse communities. Marni emphasises the importance of cross disciplinary relationships in both her research and work. She has co-authored the book *Composing diverse identities: Narrative inquiries into the interwoven lives of children and teachers*.

About the Editors

Vera Caine joined the Faculty of Nursing at the University of Alberta in January 2009. She completed her MN and PhD (Educational Policy Studies) at the University of Alberta. Vera's clinical practice relates to community health nursing and nursing in remote northern communities, as well as vulnerable populations within the inner city. She has engaged in research alongside Aboriginal peoples and communities to explore the social determinants of health in relation to health disparities and inequities. Her SSHRC funded research focuses on the educational and schooling experiences of urban Aboriginal youths and their families. Her CIHR funded (Co-PI) research focuses on HIV and AIDS and the provision of care. This work builds on Vera's collaborative narrative inquiry research alongside Aboriginal women and families living with HIV. Vera is a member scholar of the International Institute for Qualitative Methodology, an affiliate member of the CRTED, as well as the chair of the Boyle McCauley Health Centre, an inner city Primary Health Care Centre.

D. Jean Clandinin is professor and director of the Centre for Research for Teacher Education and Development (CRTED) at the University of Alberta. A former teacher, counsellor and psychologist, she is author or co-author of many books. Four books and many chapters and articles were published with Michael Connelly. Their latest book, *Narrative inquiry*, was published in 2000. She also authored one book based on her doctoral research and another coauthored book was based on research from an experimental teacher education program. A 2006 book co-authored with seven former students, *Composing diverse identities: Narrative inquiries into the interwoven lives of children and teachers*, drew on several years of research with children and teachers in urban schools. This book has been awarded the 2006 Narrative Research Special Interest Group Outstanding Book Award and the 2007 AERA Division B Outstanding Book Award. She edited the *Handbook of narrative inquiry: Mapping a methodology* (Sage, 2007). Her most recent book entitled *Places of curriculum making*, published in 2011, was awarded the 2012 AERA Narrative Research Special Interest Group Outstanding Book Award. She is the current co-editor of Teaching and Teacher Education, a position she shares with Mary Lynn Hamilton.

Pam Steeves, PhD is an adjunct professor in the CRTED at the University of Alberta. She has over 25 years of diverse teaching experiences ranging from the primary classroom to graduate teacher education, where her teaching focus was on becoming a narrative inquirer. Pam's research has developed through her involvement with the CRTED, as Horowitz Scholar in teacher research, as research associate and currently as an adjunct professor. Pam has authored and co-authored numerous book chapters and publications related to narrative inquiry and to narrative inquiries with diverse children, teachers, principals and pre-service teachers. Among these, the co-authored book *Composing diverse identities: Narrative inquiries into the interwoven lives of teachers and children* was awarded the 2007 AERA Division B Curriculum Studies Outstanding Book Award. Most recently she engaged in research with newly graduated teachers as they began to compose their lives on school landscapes.

Index

Alongside, 1, 3–6, 9–10, 13, 57, 60, 66, 69, 112, 115, 189, 194, 201, 207, 221, 241–244, 246–247, 249–250, 254–255, 258–259

Composing, 1, 3–6, 8, 11, 15, 43, 50–51, 53, 73, 85, 103, 115, 129, 145, 153, 167, 177, 191, 207–208, 210, 212–220, 223, 225, 227–229, 231, 233, 235, 237, 239, 241–242, 249–250, 256–257, 259
Co-composing, 249
Commitment, 26, 115, 119, 125–126, 193, 207, 210, 217, 223–224, 228, 230, 238, 241, 254
Competing stories, 235
Conflicting stories, 90, 234
Conversation, 12, 48–49, 52–54, 56–57, 60, 62, 66–67, 85, 99–100, 105–106, 111–112, 115–116, 129–130, 143, 146–147, 153–154, 167, 174, 177–179, 186, 193, 199–200, 202, 204, 216, 228, 250, 253, 255, 258
Cultural narratives, 230–231, 234, 242

Drop outs, 18, 22–28, 35, 39

Early School Leaving, 1, 3–4, 15–19, 22, 25, 28–30, 32, 34, 36–41, 130, 146, 239, 259
Embodied, 3, 9, 51, 218, 220, 222, 229, 236, 256–257

Familial narratives, 215, 228–229, 234–235, 243, 257
Field texts, 43, 48, 50
Forward looking stories, 165, 177, 210, 213–218, 220, 228, 236, 254, 257

Identity, 18, 29, 34–37, 51–52, 58, 95, 222, 225, 232, 234, 238, 241, 256
Improvise, 6, 208, 218, 222, 224
In school landscapes, 4, 60, 203, 230, 237, 242, 258
Institutional narratives, 3, 45, 212, 219, 223–224, 227, 231–232, 234, 239, 242–244

Liminal, 221, 255, 257

Narrative beginnings, 6–7, 10–13
Narrative Inquiry, 1, 5–6, 15, 38, 43–45, 48–51, 53, 73, 85, 103, 115, 129, 145, 153, 167, 177, 191, 207, 210, 220, 225, 241, 250, 255

Negotiation of relationships, 49, 68

Out of school landscapes, 4

Parents, 8, 20, 23, 31, 40–41, 54, 58, 60, 63–66, 78, 124, 131, 141, 148, 150, 160, 194–196, 201–202, 204, 207, 211–212, 216, 218, 224, 244, 255, 259

Place, 5, 8, 12, 25, 33, 44–45, 48–49, 53, 55, 66–67, 69, 74, 86, 88, 96–97, 105–107, 115–118, 125–126, 131, 133, 135, 137, 140, 142–144, 146–147, 150, 152–153, 158–160, 168, 170, 172, 174, 178–179, 181, 185, 188, 191, 193–194, 196–197, 200–202, 204, 208–211, 213, 216, 219–220, 224, 228–229, 232–233, 235–236, 238, 242–243, 245–250, 252–255, 259

Plotlines, 10–12, 210, 212, 221, 223, 229, 234–235, 238–239, 242–243, 256–257

Push outs, 17–18

Recognition, 17

Relational ethics, 49

Relational responsibilities, 49, 52

Relationships over time, 259

Research puzzle, 12, 43

Research texts, 43, 50, 255

School stories, 6, 29, 150, 191, 198–200, 214, 220, 234, 250

Silence, 5, 11, 34, 209, 212, 247–248

Social narratives, 232, 257

Sociality, 44, 48

Stories of school, 5–6, 104, 108, 146, 197, 201, 210, 215, 218, 232–234, 243, 247, 257–258

Stories to live by, 3, 10–12, 51–52, 58, 110, 121, 214, 216–218, 220, 222–223, 225, 227, 229–239, 241–244, 255–258

Teachers, 3–6, 9–10, 17–19, 24, 30–34, 36, 38, 40–41, 55–60, 62–68, 70–71, 73–74, 79–83, 87, 89, 92–97, 101, 107, 109, 117–121, 131, 133, 147–148, 151–152, 155, 162, 169, 173, 183, 200, 202–203, 216–217, 229, 231–234, 236, 244, 249, 253–255, 258–259

Temporality, 44, 48, 174

Three dimensional narrative inquiry space, 44–45, 50, 225

Transience, 182, 207

Transition, 1, 4, 15, 17, 23, 28, 39, 43–44, 51–53, 73–74, 85, 91, 103, 115, 129, 145, 153, 167, 177, 191, 207–208, 210, 214, 219–225, 241, 250, 256–257